Martyrdom, Sacrificial Libation, and the Eucharist of Ignatius of Antioch

Martyrdom, Sacrificial Libation, and the Eucharist of Ignatius of Antioch

Frederick C. Klawiter

LEXINGTON BOOKS/FORTRESS ACADEMIC
Lanham • Boulder • New York • London

Published by Lexington Books/Fortress Academic
Lexington Books is an imprint of The Rowman & Littlefield Publishing Group, Inc.
4501 Forbes Boulevard, Suite 200, Lanham, Maryland 20706
www.rowman.com
86-90 Paul Street, London EC2A 4NE, United Kingdom

Copyright © 2022 by The Rowman & Littlefield Publishing Group, Inc.

All rights reserved. No part of this book may be reproduced in any form or by any electronic or mechanical means, including information storage and retrieval systems, without written permission from the publisher, except by a reviewer who may quote passages in a review.

British Library Cataloguing in Publication Information Available

Library of Congress Cataloging-in-Publication Data Available

ISBN 978-1-9787-1275-1 (cloth) | ISBN 978-1-9787-1277-5 (pbk)
 | ISBN 978-1-9787-1276-8 (ebook)

In loving memory—to my parents: Aleen, Wally, and Dolores; my sisters: Mary Armstrong and Sue Revell; my mother-in-law and father-in-law: Helga and Forrest Gottschalk; my grandparents: Mary and Gil Erickson, Clara and Frank Klawiter; my great aunt and uncle: Otha and Fred Klawiter; my paternal aunts and uncles: Betty and Frank Klawiter Jr., Vi and Clayton Lurvey, Ruth and Oscar Waller; my maternal aunts and uncle: Ruth Doolittle, Dorothy Schumacher, Iva and Francis Ginsbach; my sisters-in-law and brothers-in-law: Eunie and Oliver Gottschalk, Meva and Frosty Gottschalk, Ruth and Ben Hook, Bill Gottschalk; my cousin: Anne Ginsbach; my nieces: Sandy Panopolos, Marcy Reisetter, Maury Larson; my mentors, teachers and friends: Greta and Helge Christiansen, Kay and Howie Peckham, Ellen and Frank Gellerman, Mick and Ev Winnett, Maxine and Ev Little, Beth and Don Walker, Ruth and Harold Posey, Lawrence Loomis, Curly Eleeson, Nellie and Martin Bakke, Pearle Mallory, Florance Jordan, Margaret Wikle, Milt Simons, Tryg Eklund, Don Toft, John Townsend, Dick Bakke, Lee Hayden, Dick Ageton, Denny Luce, Jim Moe, Cherie and Rich Luerssen, Shirley and Ron Moon, Dick Ronken, Tom Robertson, Verna and Dick Hopewell, Joy Hamrin, Arnold Pfeiffer, Chester Hauge, Faye Frick, Barney Kremer, Charles Sidlo, Felix Schwartz, Ben Rossow, Ann and Bill Reinsmith, Ray Merritt, Bob Quintal, Guy March, Thomas Green, Clyde Harbison, Carl Grimm, John Willard, Betty Viste, Carl Grupp, Connie and Orvis Hansen, Herb Krause, Mary and Les Baylor, Gladys and Ralph Nelson, Roger Gobbel, Judy Warren, Paul Hasvold, Betty and Ken Scoones, Martha and Nelson Schultz, Bill Fleisher, Grace and Stanley Olsen, Fritz Rusch, Suzie Rusch, Don Sneen, Art Olsen, Duane Addison, Larry Sather, Jim Wagner, Ken Holum, Richard "Pete" Peterson, Jim Limburg, Fred Fritschel, Sheldon Tostengard, and Mark Jerstad—with profound gratitude for their joy of life, laughter, hospitality, generosity, kindness, affection, steadfast love, guilelessness, integrity, curiosity, wisdom, gentle sense of humor, patience, guidance, encouragement, grace, and dignity.

Thanks to the editors at Fortress Press—Gayla Freeman, Neil Elliott, and Jessica McCleary. Gayla had confidence in me and my proposal for a book about the Gospel of John, Ignatius, Polycarp, and the New Prophecy. Neil helped me focus on what should be central, and he put the first draft in acceptable computer form for publication. As editor, he went beyond the call of duty to edit and type in correct form what I had no ability or know-how for doing. I appreciate his patience and generosity. Jessica, likewise, showed admirable patience in working to produce a book without the stains of typesetting errors, my typos, and other mechanical mistakes.

For their computer skills and help, I thank the following: to Frank Jasper-Stump for installing the Greek font; to my dear granddaughter, Eleanor Sherline, for editing/typing chapter 2 and for assembling/typing the bibliography; to Lisa Fuller for typing/editing the index.

It is my good fortune to live five miles from Andrews University (Berrien Springs, MI). Without its superb library collection of primary and secondary sources in classical literature, Greco-Roman history, ancient Judaism, and early Christianity, the book would not exist. Many thanks to its staff for their kind assistance in helping me use the computer software in finding the primary and secondary sources essential to researching the essays in this book.

Contents

Abbreviations	ix
Chapter 1: Introduction	1
Chapter 2: Ignatius and the Issue of Sacramental Realism	9
Chapter 3: John 6:53—The Scandal of a Crucified Messiah as Divine Wisdom, and Martyrdom as "Eating His Flesh and Drinking His Blood"	33
Chapter 4: Martyrdom, Sacrificial Libation, and the Eucharist/Agape of Ignatius	57
Chapter 5: John 19:34—The Death of Jesus as a Sacrificial Libation and "Living Water"	87
Chapter 6: The Tomb of Polycarp: Sacrificial Libation and a *Refrigerium*	99
Chapter 7: Conclusion	135
Appendix: The Dating of Ignatius	149
Bibliography	169
Index	177
About the Author	181

Abbreviations

ANRW	Aufstieg und Niedergang der römischen Welt
CCSL	Corpus Christianorum: series Latina
CH	Church History
CSEL	Corpus scriptorum ecclesiasticorum Latinorum
EC	Early Christianity
HTR	Harvard Theological Review
JBL	Journal of Biblical Literature
JCLW	Jewish and Christian Liturgy and Worship
JECS	Journal of Early Christian Studies
JTC	Journal of Theology and Church
JTS	Journal of Theological Studies
M	Mishnah
NTS	New Testament Studies
RAC	Rivista di archeologia Cristiana
SL	Studia Liturgica
SP	Studia Patristica
T	Tosefta
VC	Vigiliae Christianae
ZNW	Zeitschrift für die neutestamentliche Wissenschaft

Chapter 1

Introduction

1. BIOGRAPHICAL CONTEXT

Scholarship is both individual and communal. The scholar stands on the shoulders of those who have gone before. Scholarship often answers the questions of the previous generation.

My parents were Lutheran, as were their parents. My formal education in early church history was at Luther Theological Seminary (St. Paul, MN), where through the teaching of Carl Braaten and Gerhard Forde I was introduced to the study of the evolution of Christological dogma; and through Tom Kraabel's instruction I learned Koine Greek and Ecclesiastical Latin. In Kent Knutson's course in the doctrine of the church, my eyes were opened to see that St. Paul's understanding of the eucharist in 1 Corinthians does not express sacramental realism, that is, the belief that in receiving the consecrated bread and wine, one is receiving the body and blood of the crucified, risen Jesus Christ. I am very grateful to those four persons for their enlightening and invaluable instruction.

A course in Luther and the Reformation left me wondering about the meaning of sacrificial offering in the eucharist. In his *Babylonian Captivity of the Church*, Luther had rejected any conception of sacrifice that implied that Jesus' body and blood could be offered to the Divine by the priest. For Luther, the forgiving presence of the crucified, risen Jesus Christ was a gift to be received "in, with, and under" the bread and wine by the communicant rather than an appeasing sacrifice to be offered to the Divine by the priest. Later, in my career as a historian of the ancient church and a member of the religion, philosophy, and classics department at Augustana University (Sioux Falls, SD), my question became—how did one speak and think of the Christological dimension of sacrifice in the eucharist in that period of church history before the appearance of sacramental realism? This book attempts to answer that historical question.

Although about 80 percent of this book was researched and written in the last seventeen years (after I had retired), it presupposes twenty years of teaching at Augustana University. It was there that I matured as a church historian and thrived in a department where meetings and social gatherings with spouses were alive with joy, laughter, humor, kindness, and theological/philosophical dialogue with a creative give and take.

With regard to understanding Ignatius, I am especially indebted to four persons: Paul Hasvold, whose chapel sermon at Luther Seminary communicated the power of Ignatius' gospel; Robert Grant, whose commentary showed that Ignatius had almost memorized 1 Corinthians; Maxwell Johnson who helped me see how Ignatius' gospel is expressed in his understanding of the eucharist; and Jan Heilmann, whose careful, thorough, and learned peer review of an earlier draft of chapter 4, has made that argument much more persuasive in its published form here.

During the last seventeen years, monthly meal fellowship conversations with Maxwell Johnson have provided me with encouragement and insight, enabling me to answer the question about the sacrificial aspect of the eucharist. Maxwell possesses a masterful grasp of primary sources concerned with baptism and eucharist, and his knowledge of secondary literature is almost encyclopedic. Without his insights and bibliographic guidance, this book would not exist. He has read earlier drafts of every chapter and given invaluable feedback. I am deeply grateful for his scholarly input and friendship. In a few places, I have chosen not to follow his suggestions; so if there are mistakes in the book, they are probably mine and not his.

2. PREPARING THE GROUND

The purpose of this book is to demonstrate that sacrificial libation—in addition to being a significant metaphor for understanding the redemptive power of Jesus' crucifixion and the faithful acts of his disciples who offered their lives in martyrdom—was a ritual act in the celebration of the eucharist in Syria and Anatolia in the early second century. Thus, chapter 4—"Martyrdom, Sacrificial Libation, and the Eucharist/Agape of Ignatius"—is the centerpiece of this book because Ignatius is the best evidence for the thesis that a ritual of sacrificial libation (the pouring of wine into a dish or bowl that rested on the altar) was a component of a eucharist/agape in the early second century.

However, since the consensus of scholarship in the twentieth century was that Ignatius was a sacramental realist (someone who believes that the consecrated elements of bread and wine, per se, are in reality the flesh and blood of Jesus Christ), it is necessary to show in chapter 2 that Ignatius was not a sacramental realist. Moreover, since scholars have used Ignatius' alleged sacramental realism to argue that *John* 6:51b-58 also expresses an early form of sacramental realism, it is necessary in chapter 3 to show that *John* 6:51b-58 does not express sacramental realism. In addition, *John* 6:51b-58 should not be employed in order to argue that Ignatius was a sacramental realist. Thus, chapters 2 and 3 clear the way for a fresh view of Ignatius' understanding of the eucharist/agape—viewing him without using the lens of sacramental realism.

In chapter 3, I argue that in *John* 6:51b-58, the "eating and drinking of Jesus' flesh and blood," is a metaphor for internalizing/digesting his life and violent death, in the belief that in his life and violent death, Divine Wisdom is revealed. The "scandal" (6:60–61; 16:1–2) of the Johannine gospel is that of believing in Jesus as the Messiah whose crucifixion is a revelation of Divine Wisdom and the consequent risk that discipleship could mean martyrdom. "Eating the flesh and drinking the blood of the Son of Man" (6:53) expresses with eucharistic images the scandal of the Johannine gospel and the scandal of martyrdom—that a disciple may be required to appropriate/ingest the life and death of the crucified-risen Messiah Jesus by her/his own sacrificial death (martyrdom).

If this interpretation is accurate, it corresponds to the way in which Ignatius' expresses his desire for martyrdom—for "the bread of the Divine which is the flesh of Jesus Messiah . . . for drink, his blood which is imperishable agape" (*Rom. 7.3*). Ignatius' desire to appropriate the reality of the crucified-risen Jesus through his own sacrificial death is clearly expressed in the cultic language of the eucharist/agape. And significantly, in the same letter, Ignatius also employs another cultic image in order to express the meaning of his sacrificial death: it will be a sacrificial libation.

3. DEVELOPMENT OF THE ARGUMENT

Chapter 4 focuses on the cultic image of sacrificial libation. Ignatius tells the Roman Christians that when he faces the wild animals in the Colosseum, they will become "instruments of his sacrifice" (4.2). He will be "poured out as a sacrificial libation to God (σπονδισθῆναι θεῷ) while the [Roman Christian] altar is still prepared" (2.2).

Sacrificial wine libations were a common feature of Greco-Roman culture and were offered in situations where wine was drunk—whether at a family meal, a gathering of members of a club, a festive celebration of a birth, a rite of initiation, a marriage, or a visit to a cemetery in order to remember a loved one and offer her/him a wine libation.

The invocation of a Deity with prayer and supplication is an essential component of a wine libation. A cup/bowl is filled with wine, and the supplicant pours some of the wine into a dish on the table where members are eating or on the hearth of the home or on the altar of a temple while invoking/praying to the Deity. At a cemetery, the wine libation is poured into a pipe which goes down to the ashes or corpse of the loved one. In a peace agreement between two parties, a wine libation is a component of the cultic ritual which seals the covenant/agreement of peace.

In the ritual of animal sacrifice, a libation completes the sacrifice when wine is poured on the flame of the altar where the flesh of the animal is being burned. In Hellenistic Judaism, a wine libation was a significant feature of the Tamid temple service: the twice daily (at sunrise and sunset) congregational worship in which there was a whole burnt offering of a lamb and a grain offering together with the blood of the lamb and a wine libation poured on the altar. The wine libation was called "the blood of the grape" (*Sirach* 50:15).

Chapter 4 argues that in Ignatius, "sacrificial libation" refers to a ritual act that was part of eucharist/agape practice in his day. As a remembrance of Jesus' redemptive death, it symbolizes the pouring out of his blood as an act of sacrificial agape—the act of laying down his life for his disciples. The drinking/pouring of wine from the eucharistic cup is a symbol of both receiving the "imperishable agape" (*Rom.* 7.3) of Jesus Messiah and expressing it in a life that ends in martyrdom—a pouring out of blood as a libation of agape to the Divine for the sake of the unity of the church and for the sake of witnessing to the Divine Truth revealed in the life, suffering, death and resurrection of Jesus Christ.

By examining the depiction of the stoning of the first Christian martyr, Stephen (*Acts* 7:59–8:1; 22:20) and passages in St. Paul (*Phil.* 2:17), the Apocalypse of John (5:6; 6:9–10; 16:5–7; 17:4–6), and the Synoptic Gospels (*Mark* 14:24; *Matt.* 26:28; *Luke* 22:20), I will show that sacrificial libation is the metaphor utilized in order to describe the martyrdom of Stephen and Paul; and in Revelation the deaths of the martyrs are sacrificial libations poured onto a heavenly altar. In Mark and Matthew sacrificial libation is an image depicting the blood of Jesus poured out in his death; and in Luke, the eucharistic "cup is the new covenant in my blood, that is, the cup poured out [ἐκχυννόμενον] as a sacrificial libation in behalf of you" (22:20). Here, a sacrificial libation seals the new covenant of peace (cf. *Jeremiah* 31 [38 LXX]:31–34) between Jesus and his disciples: the wine being poured from a cup (a libation) is the analog for Jesus' redemptive death establishing "a new covenant in my blood."

When the Jerusalem temple and altar were destroyed in 70 CE, martyr-altar shrines probably evolved in the cemeteries of the seven churches of Revelation; and altar-tables probably evolved in house churches. It seems quite plausible that Ignatius' "desire to be poured out as a sacrificial libation while the [Roman] altar is still prepared" (*Rom.* 2.2) expresses his hope that his martyrdom as a sacrificial libation would be synchronized with the Roman Christian eucharist in which a libation was poured on a dish resting on an altar-table. The assumption seems to be that Ignatius hopes his own martyrdom as a sacrificial libation will coincide with the moment in which Roman Christians are enacting a sacrificial libation in their eucharist. A similar link between martyrdom as a sacrificial libation and eucharist is evident in Ignatius' letter to the Philadelphians in which he encourages unity in their eucharistic assembly—"for there is one flesh of our Lord Jesus Messiah [cf. Pauline *Eph.* 5:31–32] and one cup for unity of his blood [cf. *1 Cor.* 10:16], one altar. . . . My brethren, I am overflowing with agape for you, like a sacrificial libation . . ." (4.1–5.1).

It seems, quite probable, that the cluster of "eucharistic assembly—cup—altar—sacrificial libation" are held together in Ignatius' imagination because at Antioch, the character of a eucharist/agape contained the ritual of pouring wine from a cup into a dish on an altar-table as a memorial of the redemptive, sacrificial death of Jesus Messiah. This conclusion makes sense of Ignatius' desire to be poured out as a libation in the Colosseum "while a [Roman Christian] altar is still prepared," and it is consistent with the Synoptic Gospels' depiction of the last supper where Jesus' death is imagined as a drinking of his cup and a sacrificial libation that seals his covenant with his disciples.

4. SACRIFICIAL LIBATION AND THE *REFRIGERIUM*

In Ignatius' eucharist/agape, a sacrificial libation was poured: wine being poured from a eucharistic cup (a libation) was the analog for the blood of Jesus shed/poured out in his sacrificial death—a death that establishes and seals "a new covenant in my blood" (*Luke* 22:20) with his disciples. This is a covenant of peace and forgiveness (cf. *John* 20:19–23).

Even though my case for a sacrificial libation in the eucharist of Ignatius will be completed by the end of chapter 4, the body of the book contains two more chapters. These chapters will show that both Ignatius and Polycarp, bishop of Smyrna and friend of Ignatius, accepted and participated in the funerary practice of *refrigerium*, that is, a gathering of family and friends at the tomb of a loved one in order to remember and give thanks for that person by sharing a meal of food/drink. The singing of songs and the offering of prayers were components of a *refrigerium*. Common belief among both Greeks and Romans was that a deceased one was nourished and "refreshed" by the sacrificial libation. Hence, this funerary custom is referred to as a *refrigerium*.

This custom existed in both the eastern and western part of the Roman Empire and entailed visits to the grave, five times within the first forty days following the burial and thereafter—probably four visits per year, including the birthday of the deceased one. By demonstrating the high probability of both Ignatius and Polycarp supporting and participating in the funerary custom of *refrigerium*, the anomalous character of a sacrificial libation in Ignatius' eucharistic practice is removed since—if sacrificial wine libation was part of his funerary practice at Antioch, the existence of a sacrificial libation in his eucharist is not unique or anomalous.

In order to demonstrate the likely existence of Polycarp's funerary practice of *refrigerium*, in chapter 6 I analyze the *Martyrdom of Perpetua and Felicitas*, a document reflecting the viewpoint of the *New Prophecy* at Carthage, North Africa, ca 204 CE. Since the *New Prophecy* originated in Phrygia, Anatolia, about ten years after Polycarp's martyrdom, I assume that the views of the *New Prophecy* at Carthage concerning a *refrigerium* were held also by Polycarp's community at Smyrna.

Chapter 5 will prepare the ground for chapter 6 by showing that the Fourth Gospel—which was the favorite gospel of the *New Prophecy* and the community of Polycarp—expresses the belief that the death of Jesus is an eschatological fulfillment of the hopes associated with the festivals of Tabernacles, Passover, Hanukkah, and daily worship (Tamid) at the temple. I will argue that when the Evangelist underscores the testimony of blood and water issuing from the body of the crucified Jesus (when the soldier thrusts his spear into the side of Jesus, 19:34) he expresses a correlation with the water and wine libations that flow onto the temple altar during the festival of Tabernacles (water libation) in conjunction with the offering of Tamid (wine libation). This testimony expresses the Johannine gospel: in Jesus' sacrificial death—a blood libation—the power of death is overcome and the life of the Divine Spirit ("living water" issuing forth from Jesus' body, which is the temple of the Divine; cf. *John* 2:18–22; 7:38–39) is present for anyone who believes in Jesus. The Johannine depiction of Jesus' death as a sacrificial libation illuminates Polycarp's martyrdom and Perpetua's martyrdom as deaths which, conceived of as sacrificial libations, possessed redemptive power.

When Polycarp was martyred by being burned at the stake, his body could not be consumed by the blazing fire, and he had to be stabbed. Blood and a dove came forth from his side (*Mart. Poly.* 16.1). The libation of blood put out the blazing fire, thus ending the persecution at Smyrna (1.1; 16.1) and releasing into the arena the Divine Spirit (the dove).

Chapter 6 probes also the function of a sacrificial libation in remembering the martyrdom of a Christian. *The Martyrdom of Polycarp* describes the gathering of Christians at St. Polycarp's tomb, singing hymns, offering prayers with joy and gladness, and seeking "to commune" (17.1; 18.2–3) with him. This description looks similar to the Greco-Roman pagan funerary custom of *refrigerium*, that is, a picnic at the tomb of a loved one in which food and wine were shared among family members and friends, songs and prayers were offered. There is evidence to suggest that a eucharist at the tomb of St. Polycarp looks like a *refrigerium* in which Christians poured libations into his tomb as a way of communing with him and remembering the sacrificial libation he had offered in behalf of them in his martyrdom.

I increase this probability by examining the visions of Perpetua and Saturus. Those visions reveal the customs and beliefs of a Christian *refrigerium* that, quite probably, reflect the practice and belief of Christians of Asia Minor. They reveal that when a confessor gives her/his witness unto death and attains paradise, s/he continues to share in meal fellowship, is capable of enjoying the scent and beauty of flowers, and is available to hear Christian prayers rising from the earthly church. All of this is offered in a *refrigerium* at the grave of a martyr—a refrigerium that gives refreshment to the martyr.

In addition, by examining the concept of "refreshment" in the letters of Ignatius, I will argue that he approved and supported the funerary practice of a *refrigerium* at the tomb of a martyr. Hence, the existence of a *refrigerium* in the *New Prophecy* together with Ignatius' probable support of that funerary practice supports the high probability of a *refrigerium* at the tomb of Polycarp.

5. SACRIFICIAL LIBATION IN THE EUCHARIST/ AGAPE AND IN THE *REFRIGERIUM*

In the concluding chapter, I will argue that the act of the sacrificial wine libation was, quite probably, part of a Christian's worship life (a eucharist/ agape libation) and part of a Christian way of remembering deceased loved ones—whether they be saints, martyrs, or dear friends and relatives. The sacrificial wine libation functioned in a significant way in Christian gatherings—to inspire, encourage, and maintain a fellowship of laughter, joy, love, affection and admiration between the crucified, risen Messiah, the members of his body on earth and the saints who had died. The sacrificial wine libation was both image and act in the one hundred year period of 70–170 CE for Christians in Anatolia and Syria.

Chapter 2

Ignatius and the Issue of Sacramental Realism

One of the central features of the gospel in the letters of St. Ignatius is the eucharist.[1] Three passages have been crucial for discerning his understanding of the eucharist. One, "the eucharist is the flesh of our savior, Jesus Christ, [the flesh] which suffered for our sins, which the Father raised by his goodness" (*Smyr.* 7.1). Two, "I desire the bread of God which is flesh of Jesus Christ, [the Messiah] of the seed of David, and for drink I desire his blood which is imperishable love" (*Rom.* 7.3). Three, his exhortation to the Ephesians—to be obedient to the clergy while "breaking one loaf which is the medicine of immortality" (20.2). These texts have been the basis of a consensus of scholars that Ignatius believed the elements of bread and wine, per se, were, in reality, Christ's flesh and blood. Commenting on *Smyr.* 7.1, William R. Schoedel says, "it is sufficiently impressive as to suggest that sacramental realism is taken for granted (and even emphasized) by Ignatius."[2] Regarding *Eph.* 20.2, Paul F. Bradshaw claims that Ignatius' letters "certainly attest" to the "conviction of the eucharistic presence of Christ . . . the bread is medicine of immortality . . . it is the flesh of Christ."[3]

---

1. For the letters of Ignatius, I am using the critical editions of Karl Bihlmeyer and Wilhelm Schneemelcher, *Die Apostolischen Väter*, vol. I (Tübingen: J.C.B. Mohr, 1956) and the *Loeb Classical Library of The Apostolic Fathers*, ET Kirsopp Lake, vol. I (Cambridge: Harvard University Press, 1959). All translations are mine. This chapter is a reworking of my essay, "The Eucharist and Sacramental Realism in the Thought of St. Ignatius of Antioch," *SL* 37.2 (2007), 129–63.
2. William R. Schoedel, *Ignatius of Antioch* (Philadelphia: Fortress Press, 1985), 21.
3. Paul F. Bradshaw, *Eucharistic Origins* (Oxford: Oxford University Press, 2004), 87.

In this chapter, I argue that these statements of Ignatius must be interpreted in the context of his refutation of a heterodox christology, his understanding of martyrdom, and the unity of the church. This essay examines the scholarly arguments for sacramental realism in Ignatius and concludes that they neglect the ecclesial dimension of his eucharist and make assumptions about the existence of sacramental realism that have no historical basis. A solid foundation for the judgment that Ignatius held the belief of sacramental realism does not exist in the letters of Ignatius.

1. EUCHARIST AND MARTYRDOM: THE LETTER TO THE ROMANS

While at Smyrna, on the western coast of Asia Minor, as one of the prisoners in the custody of ten Roman soldiers awaiting the departure to Troas (whence they would cross the Aegean for Neapolis, the port of Philippi, in route to Rome), Ignatius writes to the Roman church addressing it as "pre-eminent in agape" and expressing his fear that with a misguided love they might seek to effect his release (inscr.; 1.2; cf. 4.1; 6.2; 8.3): "Allow me to be an imitator of the suffering of my God. Whoever has him [Christ] in himself may imagine what I desire and sense my suffering while fathoming the thoughts that possess me" (6.3).[4] Insofar as his present suffering is congruent with Christ's suffering, Ignatius believes this to be Christ within him. Ignatius had known the prophetic indwelling of the Spirit (cf. *Phd.* 7.1–2), and a prophet can sense the thoughts of others (cf. *Matt.* 9:4; *1 Cor.* 2:11; 14:24–25). Anyone with the Spirit, Ignatius implies, should be able to understand his thoughts concerning martyrdom. In another letter, Ignatius links his suffering with Jesus Christ: "It is solely because of the name of Jesus Christ that I am enduring everything so that I may share my suffering with him (εἰς τὸ συμπαθεῖ αὐτῷ) while the perfect man himself (αὐτὸς ὁ τελείος ἄνθρωπος) is empowering me" (*Smyr.* 4.2).

Ignatius can endure the suffering by sharing it with the Christ within, who sustains him. Martyrdom is a fellowship with Jesus Christ in the midst of a suffering like his.[5] To the Romans, Ignatius likens his suffering to a woman giving birth—"the pain of childbearing (ὁ τοκετός) is upon me" (6.1). This suffering will end in new birth, for Ignatius will receive "pure light" and "shall become a man" (6.2). Images of birth pangs, childbearing, receiving the pure light, and becoming a man are suggestive of martyrdom as a second baptism. His love (ἔρως) for perishable things has been crucified and replaced

---

4. Thanks to Maxwell Johnson for his critical evaluation of an earlier draft of this section.
5. I agree with Karin Bommes (*Weizen Gottes. Untersuchungen zur Theologie des Martyrium bei Ignatius von Antiochien* [Cologne: Peter Hanstein, 1976], 94) that Ignatius "never says that Christ suffers in him."

by "the living water . . . speaking within him, 'Come to the Father' " (7.2).[6] This is the Spirit inviting him to approach God, receive the "pure light" and put on the "perfect man" (*Rom.* 6.2; cf. *Smyr.* 4.2).

The sequence of images suggests going from baptismal waters into the light, receiving the humanity of Christ, and then participating in a meal—for Ignatius responds: "I receive no pleasure in perishable food (τροφῇ φθορᾶς) nor the delights of this life. The bread of God, I desire, which is the flesh of Jesus Christ, [the Messiah] of the seed of David. And as drink, I desire his blood, which is imperishable agape (ἀγάπη ἄφθαρτος, 7.3)." This sequence of going from baptism and then participating in a eucharistic meal reflects the ritual pattern of early Christianity. And since martyrdom was understood as a second baptism, Ignatius' longing for a eucharistic meal is understandable.

Lothar Wehr[7] sees "imperishable agape" as a term for the eucharist. He understands the parallelism of the passage as "the bread of God [I desire] which is the flesh of Jesus Christ" and "as drink [I desire] his blood, which is imperishable agape." By making drink/blood a pair in parallel with bread/flesh, "imperishable agape" stands by itself as a description of the bread and drink. Even though it seems to me that the "which is" connects the pair of bread/flesh and blood/imperishable agape, I agree with Wehr that "imperishable agape" is a reference to the eucharist. This is an instance of Ignatius' delight in using a word or phrase to connote both a christological and an ecclesiological reality.

"Imperishable agape" refers to the agape revealed in Jesus' passion ("his blood") and the agape encountered in eucharist fellowship. In the *Rom* 7.3 passage, "imperishable agape" is not simply a christological reference (paired with "the blood of Jesus Christ"); it is also contrasted with the "perishable food" (τροφῇ φθορᾶς) of this life in which Ignatius finds no delight. "Imperishable agape" must also connote the nourishment provided by the agape fellowship of the eucharist meal.

In fact, it appears that in Ignatius' understanding, "agape" and "eucharist" are synonyms for the same liturgical event. At Smyrna where the heterodox were abstaining from Polycarp's eucharistic worship and in Ignatius' mind, were lacking "agape" because they had no concern for a widow or orphan, none for the prisoner or the hungry and thirsty (6.2)—Ignatius reminds them that "no valid eucharist" can be done without the bishop, without whom "it is not lawful . . . to baptize or do an agape" (ἀγάπην ποιεῖν, 8.1–2). I agree with Andrew McGowan who concludes from this passage that in Antioch and

---

6. In *John* 7:38–39, the "living water" is the Spirit which appears after Christ's death and resurrection.

7. Lothar Wehr, *Arznei der Unsterblichkeit. Die Eucharistie bei Ignatius von Antiochien und im Johannesevangelium* (Münster: Aschendorff, 1987), 133–40.

western Asia Minor of the second century, the "agape" meal and "eucharist" were synonyms for the same event.[8]

At first glance the passage of *Rom.* 7.3 seems to identify bread/wine with the flesh/blood of Jesus Christ. But in context, the images of bread and wine illuminate instead the reality of Ignatius' martyrdom. He uses these images to express the sacrificial meaning of his death. Requesting that Roman Christians not attain his release, he assures them that he desires to be "the food of wild animals" (4.1) so that he can "attain God": for "I am grain of God (σῖτός εἰμι θεοῦ) and through the teeth of wild animals I am ground in order that I may be found to be pure bread."[9] Roman Christians should "pray to the Messiah in behalf of me" that the wild animals become the instruments of "a sacrifice (θυσία)." They should entice the wild animals to make a complete meal of Ignatius so that nothing is left of him (4.2).

Ignatius has crucified his own desire for the food of perishable things and longs only for the food of the eschatological banquet of God. Viewing himself as food for the wild animals who will be instruments of his sacrificial death, Ignatius depicts his martyrdom in the symbol of grains being milled and turned into a loaf or piece of "pure bread." The image and thought are reminiscent of how grain and bread are understood symbolically in the eucharistic teaching of *The Didache*.

There, one piece of bread stands for the unity of the church. The one piece, made up of many grains that had been scattered on the hills, represents the many human beings scattered throughout the world who are gathered together and made into one—the many grains were gathered and the bread made up of these grains "became one." "Let your church be gathered together from the ends of the earth into your kingdom" (9.4). God is petitioned "to make it [the church] perfect in your agape" (10.5).

Likewise, Ignatius expresses a deep yearning for the unity of the church. His rock-like conviction is that the bishop represents that unity. A greeting from a bishop is a greeting from everyone in his church; in the one person of a bishop the many members of his church are represented.[10] Symbolically the one and the many are represented in the bishop. As a planting of God,

---

8. Andrew B. McGowan, "Naming the Feast: Agape and the Diversity of Early Christian Meals," *SP* 30 (1997), 314–18. Thanks to Maxwell Johnson for directing me to this article. Since the eucharist had a common meal of sharing in which the poor and hungry received food, the eucharist was an agape event. Cf. *Acts* 2:44–47.

9. *Rom.* 4.1: I agree with Schoedel (*Ignatius*, 175) that "pure bread"—the reading of Eusebius (*Hist. eccl.* 3.36.12) in citing Irenaeus' quotation of Ignatius—is the most probable reading. The Greek texts of the long recension ("pure bread of God") and of the codex of Ignatius' martyrdom which incorporated the Romans' letter of the middle recension ("pure bread of Christ") look like later scribal attempts to emphasize the sacramental character of the bread.

10. In receiving Onesimus, bishop of Ephesus, Ignatius saw the church of Onesimus. He says the same with regard to the visits of two other bishops, Damas and Polybius (see *Eph.* 1.3; *Mag.* 2.1; *Trall.* 1.1).

Ignatius sees himself as grain and his martyrdom as the process in which his grains will be ground and milled (by the teeth of the wild animals) so that he might be transformed into "pure bread." In offering himself as a sacrifice, Ignatius' love for God and members of the church will be perfected. Ignatius identifies himself with the bread, a symbol for the unity of the members of the church with the flesh of Jesus Christ who offered himself as a sacrifice of agape. In martyrdom, Ignatius will become completely one with Christ and his church. He will become "pure bread." This metaphor will appear again; for when Polycarp, bishop of Smyrna and a friend of Ignatius, was martyred by being burned at the stake in 157 CE, his flesh was depicted as "bread being baked."[11]

Ignatius also associates the process of the grains becoming one loaf with the addition of water ("the living water" within him). Commenting on the outpouring of the Spirit on Pentecost, Irenaeus (who as a youth had been instructed by Polycarp) taught that "just as it is not possible for one barley-cake to be made out of dry ground grain without the addition of moisture, nor [is it possible in the case of] one loaf of bread; so also neither we, the many, were able to become one in Christ Jesus without heavenly water."[12] Dry ground grain and water becoming one loaf symbolize the Spirit (heavenly water) poured out on the disciples, making them one (one loaf). In baptism, "our bodies have received unity through that bath which is for immortality, and our souls have received unity through the Spirit."[13]

This baptismal symbol expressed in ground grain, water, and bread might be Irenaeus' own creative insight. But the same elements—grain, water, and bread—are in Ignatius, and the Greek text of Irenaeus (quoted by Eusebius) appears to be the most reliable source for Ignatius' "I am grain

---

11. *Mart. Poly.* 15.2. Ignatius assumed that he would die in the Colosseum by wild animals. But he knew of martyrdoms of fire and crucifixion (cf. *Rom.* 5.3). The prospect of death by any of these means could evoke the image of a fiery ordeal. Ignatius would have known that at Rome (unlike in the eastern Roman empire where corpses were buried) corpses were cremated. Hence, the nature of his death (intense suffering) and disposal of his corpse (cremation) could evoke the image of fire and heat linked to his end.

12. *Adv. haer.* 3.17.2: *Sicut enim de arido tritico massa una fieri non potest sine humore neque unus panis, ita nec nos multi unum fieri in Christo Iesus poteramus sine aqua quae de caelo est.* If *triticum* is a translation of σῖτος (barley, wheat, grain, flour) and *massa* translates μᾶζα (barley-cake, lump, mass), then two meanings are possible. Either: ground grain (σῖτος) cannot be made into one lump of dough (μᾶζα) without adding water; and without dough, neither could the one loaf of bread be made. Or: dry grain/barley flour (σῖτος) cannot be made into a barley-cake without adding water (since the water makes the dry flour hold together as dough during the baking process) and so likewise with regard to making bread out of ground grains. I prefer the latter although both translations agree that the many grains becoming one loaf of bread is not possible without moisture.

13. *Ibid. Corpora enim nostra per lavacrum illam quae est ad incorruptionem unitatem acceperunt, animae autem per Spiritum.*

of God" statement. Perhaps, Irenaeus' symbolic expression of baptism was received from Polycarp, who had received it from Ignatius or the beloved disciple, John.[14]

Ignatius believed that his martyrdom would be a sacrifice of agape offered up to the Divine for the unity of the church (of which the bread is a symbol). For the Ephesians, Smyrnaeans, and Polycarp, Ignatius is a "ransom/expiation" (ἀντίψυχον).[15] That he is a sacrifice for those Smyrnaeans who are obedient to Polycarp (*Poly.* 6.1) suggests that his death will be for the unity of the church. Twice in his Ephesian letter, Ignatius employs the word (περίψημα); it describes his devotion to both the cross—"my spirit is an offscouring of the cross" (18. 1)—and to the Ephesians—"As your sacrifice I also am sanctifying myself in behalf of you Ephesians, a church famous forever (8.1)."

This self-designation as an "off-scouring" is an echo of St. Paul (cf. 1 *Cor.* 4:13), and Ignatius' understanding of his death as a pure sacrifice in behalf of others is not unlike that of the Johannine view of Christ's death as a sacrifice for the unity of the church (cf. *John* 17:18–23). By imitating his Lord's passion, Ignatius will help realize what his Lord's death effected, namely, the unity of agape among his disciples.[16]

In addition, his martyrdom will be "a word of God" and his being "poured out as a sacrificial libation to the Divine."

> For, if you are silent concerning me, I shall be a word of God. . . . Grant me nothing more than to be poured out as a sacrificial libation to God (σπονδισθῆναι θεῷ) while an altar is still prepared so that you, after forming a chorus, may sing with agape to the Father in Christ Jesus because God deemed the bishop of Syria worthy of being found in the West [where the sun sets] after summoning

---

14. *Cf. Poly. ad Phil.* 13; Eusebius, *Hist. eccl.* 3.36.14–15; 5.5.8; 5.8.4; 5.20.5–7 (Irenaeus' letter to Florinus).

15. See *Eph.* 21.1; *Smyr.* 10.2; *Poly.* 2.3.

16. I am persuaded by Willard M. Swartley's argument ("The Imitatio Christi in the Ignatian Letters, " *VC* 27[1973], 81–103) that Ignatius' preoccupation with the unity of the church is shaped by the division in his own church (following his arrest/departure). One can see his difficulty. As bishop, he symbolizes the unity of the church; yet his own church is divided. As martyr he hopes to be a sacrifice of love which promotes unity; but his sacrifice is flawed if offered by a bishop who failed to secure unity. Then, at Troas he learned that peace was restored at Antioch. His shame dissipates and he approaches martyrdom with a cheerful confidence (cf. *Ign. ad Poly.* 7.1). For a critical evaluation of Swartley's view as well as the position of P. N. Harrison (on which Swartley builds), see Thomas A. Robinson, *Ignatius of Antioch and the Parting of the Ways* (Peabody, MA: Hendrickson Publishers, 2009) 163–181. Robinson argues that the division in the Antioch church was due to persecution by civil authorities and the removal of Ignatius and other leaders. Ignatius' "unworthiness" stems not from his sense of having failed to keep the peace as bishop (Harrison had argued that civil authorities had been forced to intervene in the affairs of the Antioch church and to remove Ignatius because of internal conflict that had threatened to produce civil disorder). According to Robinson, the news of peace (which Ignatius received at Troas) refers to the end of persecution, not to the healing of division in the Antioch church.

him from the East [where the sun rises]. Beautiful, may my sunset be: in death, to set my face towards the Divine that I may rise to him.[17]

In this moving passage, Ignatius likens his journey from Antioch towards Rome to that of the sun which rises in the East and journeys across the sky to where it sets in the West before sinking below the horizon and dying only in order to be reborn again in the East. Regarding this passage, Schoedel alludes to a fragment of Melito, bishop (ca. 175) of Sardis (80 km. east of Smyrna) in which baptism is seen in the image of the sun going down in the West (being washed in the ocean) only in order to rise in the East. This solar image symbolizes Christ's baptism in the Jordan; his descent into Hades is represented by the sun's going down under the earth.[18] If Ignatius has in mind a similar tradition, then by identifying his journey with that of the sun across the sky in its movement from birth to life to death to rebirth and that of the Son of God from birth to life to death to resurrection, Ignatius vividly portrays his journey to Rome as an imitation of and participation in the cosmic drama of redemption in Jesus Christ.[19]

Ignatius depicts his martyrdom as a sacrificial libation or drink-offering. The image is drawn from St. Paul (cf. *Phil.* 2: 17) and refers to the custom practiced by both Jews and pagans. In the Tamid service in the temple at Jerusalem, twice a day at sunrise and sunset, a lamb was sacrificed and, together with grain, offered on the altar. The blood of the lamb and a wine libation were poured on the altar as an offering. The wine libation was called "the blood of the grape" (*Sirach* 50:15). Pagans also had the custom of offering wine libations when sacrifices were offered at their temples, of pouring wine on the altar as a sacrificial offering to the Deity before the wine was drunk by the religious devotees.

For Ignatius, the pouring out of the wine symbolizes the spilling of his blood. Ignatius desires as drink the imperishable agape of Christ (symbolized by the blood of Christ); and in union with Christ, the "High Priest" (cf. *Phd.*

---

17. *Rom.* 2.1–2: The last sentence is καλὸν τό δῦναι ἀπὸ κόσμου πρὸς θεόν, ἵνα εἰς αὐτὸν ἀνατείλω. From Smyrna, the next leg of Ignatius' journey will be north to Troas and then boarding a ship to Neapolis, the port of Philippi. In a marine-sunset, the sun appears to sink into the sea—an image of death; and death is a departure "from the world" (cf. John 16:28). Moreover, some sunsets disperse streaks of color across the sky, from the horizon upward or in Ignatius' words—"from the world towards God." My translation, "to set my face towards God," suggests this upward movement of the dying light. But Ignatius may intend more, for some sunsets streak the sky with red light or fill the atmosphere near the horizon with a red glow. When linked to a death where blood is shed and sacrificial agape is expressed, such a sunset could convey the power of poignant beauty and goodness.

18. Schoedel, *Ignatius*, 171.

19. In this context, the solar baptismal symbol suggests also that martyrdom is a second baptism. Ignatius was martyred, ca. 125 CE. See the appendix for the debate on how to date Ignatius. (Cf. *Eph.* 12.2 where Ignatius hopes to follow in the footsteps of Paul the blessed martyr).

9.1), he desires to offer himself (symbolized by his own blood) as a sacrificial libation to the Divine, a sacrificial act of agape for the unity of the church.

In this fellowship of suffering agape, Ignatius will become "a word of God" *(Rom.* 2.1). The shedding of his blood in imitation of his Lord's suffering will be in fellowship with the divine Son and therefore a revelation of God in his death. That "a word of God" refers to a revelation of God in Jesus Christ, is suggested by Ignatius' statement about revelation to the Magnesians: "There is one God who manifested himself through Jesus Christ, his Son, who is his Word who came forth from silence (ὅς ἐστιν αὐτοῦ λόγος ἀπὸ σιγῆς προελθών)" (8.2). The fact that both in *Rom.* 2.1 and *Mag.* 8.2 Ignatius speaks of a word of God coming forth from silence seems more than coincidental.[20] The conclusion seems unavoidable: in the mind of Ignatius, the unity of his fellowship with Jesus Christ in the midst of suffering unto death will be a revelation of God to the spectators in the arena. God had summoned a bishop from the East, where the sun (Son) rises in order that his death in the West might be a manifestation of that light.

A metaphoric rendering of eucharist images illuminates Ignatius' understanding of martyrdom. Do those images also carry a literal meaning in this context? "As drink, I desire his blood which is imperishable agape." An identity between wine and blood would imply that in partaking of the wine one partakes of Christ's blood which conveys imperishable agape. But surely what Ignatius desires is figuratively to drink of Christ's blood, that is, to be in fellowship with him while dying as a martyr—to receive agape and express agape. Figuratively he will drink of the blood and pour out his own blood as a sacrifice of agape. Similarly, in desiring the "bread of God, which is the flesh of Jesus Christ, [the Messiah] of the seed of David," Ignatius desires communion with the crucified, risen humanity of Jesus Christ. The qualifying phrase, "[the Messiah] of the seed of David," underscores the meaning of "Jesus Christ," that is, his human nature. Ignatius desires fellowship with the man, Jesus Christ, who suffered, died, rose, and who has meal fellowship with his disciples.

For Ignatius, bread symbolizes the unity of the church associated with baptism and with the eucharist—a unity based in fellowship with the immortal humanity (flesh) of Jesus Christ (for which bread is also an image). In addition, the blood of Jesus Christ is a symbol of his "imperishable agape," which sounds forth in the "symphonic agape" (cf. *Eph.* 4.1–5.3) of the eucharistic assembly. Ignatius' martyrdom as a fulfillment of his union with Christ and his church is expressed as becoming "pure bread" (since bread is a symbol

---

20. See Virginia Corwin (*St. Ignatius and Christianity at Antioch* [New Haven: Yale University Press, 1906] 126) for noting the correlation of *Rom.* 2.1 and *Mag.* 8.2 via word of God/silence. In *Mag.* 8.2 silence is the silence of God; in *Rom.* 2.1 silence means that the Romans should not intervene and seek Ignatius' pardon. In both cases, a word of God comes forth from silence.

of both Christ's immortal flesh and the unity of his church) and as drinking Christ's blood (a symbol of sacrificial agape). Ignatius' desire to be a libation and become a word of God expresses the hope that his agape-sacrifice can be a vehicle of divine redemption for pagan spectators—a vehicle for revealing the Divine nature as that of suffering, sacrificial love.

His identification with the sunset and with images of being grain of God, becoming pure bread, eating the flesh/drinking the blood of Jesus Christ, being poured out as a drink-offering, and becoming a word of God vividly portray Ignatius' view of martyrdom. Surely, he does not mean that he is literally wheat or will literally become a libation or a word of God. His desire for "the bread of God, that is, the flesh of Jesus Christ" expresses his longing as "grain of God" to become one with Christ and his church as "pure bread." His desire to drink "the blood" expresses his desire to imitate Christ's passion, pouring out his own blood as a libation—an act of agape to God for the sake of the unity of the church. "Bread of God" and "blood" are eucharist/agape images, but their Romans' context is a symbolic one.[21]

2. EUCHARISTIC UNITY AND "THE MEDICINE OF IMMORTALITY" (*EPH*. 20.1–2)

To the Ephesians, Ignatius desires to compose another little book discussing the "plan (οἰκονομία)" about "the new man (ὁ καινὸς ἄνθροπος) " Jesus Christ, "his faith and his agape (αὐτοῦ πίστις καὶ αὐτοῦ ἀγάπη), his passion and resurrection" (20.1). Ignatius would be more inclined to do this if he learns by revelation that the Ephesians gather together

> in one faith (ἐν μιᾷ πίστει) and in Jesus Christ . . . in order that you may be obedient to the bishop and the presbytery with undistracted understanding, breaking one loaf which is the medicine of immortality (ἕνα ἄρτον κλῶντες, ὅ ἐστιν φάρμακον ἀθανασίας), the antidote of not dying, but instead living forever in Jesus Christ. (20.2)

The parallelism—"his faith and his agape . . . in one faith and in Jesus Christ"—suggests that union in Jesus Christ is union in his agape, a union of obedience to the clergy. "Breaking one loaf" refers to the eucharist and reflects Pauline influence.[22] But before assuming that Ignatius is literally

---

21. In regard to "bread of God" in *Rom*. 7.3, Schoedel *(Ignatius,* 55) says that "there, sacramental realism is scarcely in evidence."
22. Ignatius knew 1 Corinthians well. "The one loaf of bread (τὸν ἄρτον) which we break, it is, is it not, a fellowship (κοινωνία) in the body of Messiah"? (10:16). Since in verse 17, Paul is comparing one loaf of bread (εἷς ἄρτος) to one body (ἐν σῶμα) of Christians, the τὸν ἄρτον of 10:16 must connote "the one loaf of bread."

equating eucharistic bread with the food that gives immortality, one should observe his use of plant-food images.

In his letter to the Trallians, Ignatius likens "heresy (αἵρεσις)" to a "strange plant-food" whose teaching is a mixture of "honeyed-wine (οἰνόμελι)" with "deadly poison (θανάσιμον φάρμακον)" (6.1–2). These heretics deny the real suffering of Jesus Christ (10.1); their teaching is a "fruit that embodies death (καρπὸς θανατηφόρος)" (11.1). Just as a physician sugarcoats a bad tasting pill (so the patient can take the medicine and recover health), so likewise the heterodox teaching might taste like honeyed-wine; but in fact such teaching hides not a medicine (φάρμακον) that restores health, but rather a poison (φάρμακον) that brings death.[23] As Robert Grant says—the image of the "medicine of immortality (φάρμακον ἀθανασίας)" in *Eph.* 20.2 is not intended to be any more literal than "deadly poison (θανάσιμον φάρμακον)" in *Trall.* 6.2.[24]

Another reading of this Ephesians' text seems much more plausible. If "breaking one loaf" is a synonym for the eucharist (just as is the term agape), the ὅ ἐστι ("that is") could refer either to the "breaking one loaf" or the gathering together in unity through obedience to the bishop and "breaking one loaf."[25] Since in Acts the phrase "breaking bread" is the term referring to a eucharist[26] and in *1 Cor.* 10:16 "breaking one loaf" refers to the fellowship of believers in the eucharist, Ignatius' "breaking one loaf" connotes the unity of believers in eucharistic worship, and more specifically probably refers to the fellowship of sharing food and drink in the agape meal. Nevertheless, in Ignatius' mind, there is an inseparable connection between eucharistic bread and obedience to the bishop.

In *Eph.* 5.2, "bread of God" is an image associated with an episcopal eucharistic assembly: "unless one is inside the place of worship (ἐντὸς τοῦ θυσιαστηρίου), one lacks the bread of God." Being on the outside is the same as separating oneself from "the bishop and the entire assembly (ὁ ἐπίσκοπος καὶ πᾶσα ἡ ἐκκλησία)" (5.2). *Eph.* 20.2 speaks of gathering "in one faith" and being obedient to the clergy. The "one loaf" is not simply an image for the unity of eucharistic fellowship; it connotes also the episcopal eucharistic unity of the church—being "in one faith and in Jesus Christ . . . obedient to the bishop and presbytery . . . breaking one loaf, which is, the medicine of immortality."

---

23. Depending on context, *pharmakon* can mean either medicine or poison. For a discussion of this medical figure of speech, see Robert M. Grant, *Ignatius of Antioch,* vol. 4 of *The Apostolic Fathers,* ed. Robert M. Grant (New York: Thomas Nelson, 1966), 76.

24. *Ibid.*, 53.

25. Schoedel (*Ignatius,* 98–99) argues that the neuter ὅ ἐστι of the long recension (rather than ὅς ἐστι of the middle recension) is the more likely reading. He points out that the neuter ("which is" or "that is") is in Ignatius a way of connecting two images, neither of which need to be neuter.

26. Henry Chadwick, *The Early Church* (London: Penguin, 1956), 261.

Here, it is important to know that Ignatius thought of the church as an image of a higher reality. Things or objects in the church were a "counterpart/image" (τύπος) of the heavenly world. For him, the bishop is an image (τύπος) of the Father, the deacons are an image of Jesus Christ, and the presbyters are an image of the apostles *(Trall.* 3.1). The divine world is reflected in the earthly church.[27]

Allen Brent sees the threefold clerical order of bishop, presbytery, and deacon as an Ignatian iconography of Father, Spirit, and Son; and he argues that Ignatius believed that by having union with this clerical order "in the drama of a eucharist," a Christian has union with the Divine and with immortality. For Brent, the key text is *Mag.* 6.2: "Be united to the bishop and the ones presiding as an image and teaching of immortality."[28]

The eucharistic unity of "the bishop and the entire assembly" expresses the unity between "the church (ἡ ἐκκλησία) and Jesus Christ" which in turn expresses the unity between "Jesus Christ and the Father"; the agape unity of an episcopal eucharistic assembly embodies and voices the goal of God's work in Jesus Christ: that "all things in unity (πάντα ἐν ἑνότητι) may be symphonic." The agape of Christ's sacrifice creates an assembly (ἐκκλησία) in whose harmony his "symphonic agape" is heard. In that "symphonic agape" (σύμφωνος ἀγάπη) the beautiful melody (μέλος) of Jesus Christ is sung to the Father by the members (μέλη) of his assembly *(Eph.* 4.1–5.3).

I agree with Brent that immortality is dependent upon being in unity with the three-fold clerical order. But this is not the whole picture. I view the eucharist as an agape meal. Brent (29) sees eucharist and agape meal as separate realities. In my view, the "the breaking of one loaf" is fellowship in the episcopal assembly in which through meal, choral song, prayer, ecstatic prophecy, healing and preaching, the risen and crucified Messiah is made known in the harmony of all members (μέλη). Ultimately, "the medicine of immortality" is the unity of "imperishable agape" *(Rom.* 7.3) among all the members of the episcopal assembly.

Before examining the Smyrnaean description of the eucharist (as "the flesh of . . . Jesus Christ," *Smyr.* 7.1), it is crucial to examine a passage *(Phd.* 4. 1) in Ignatius where the image of "flesh of Jesus Christ" signifies an episcopal eucharistic assembly.

---

27. For "counterpart," see Henry Chadwick, "The Silence of Bishops in Ignatius," *HTR* 43 (1950), 169–172. By an analysis of Hellenistic epigraphy, Allen Brent *(Ignatius of Antioch and the Second Sophistic.* [Tübingen:Mohr Siebeck, 2006], 66–85) argues convincingly for a translation of τύπος as "image."

28. *Ibid.*, 85–91.

3. "THE FLESH OF JESUS CHRIST": IMAGE FOR AN EPISCOPAL EUCHARISTIC ASSEMBLY

Ignatius employs the image of "one flesh of Jesus Christ" for the episcopal eucharist/agape unity at Philadelphia where there were Jewish and Gentile Christians. Ignatius had a dispute with a group that used either Mosaic law or the prophets as its authority. Ignatius countered with "the faith" of Jesus Christ centered in "his cross, death, and resurrection" (8.2). While preaching (presumably at a eucharist), Ignatius experienced prophetic inspiration and delivered an oracle of God:

> Do nothing without the bishop. Keep your flesh (τηρεῖτε τὴν σάρκα ὑμῶν) as the temple of God. Continue to love the unity (ἀγαπᾶτε τὴν ἕνωσιν); continue to flee from divisions. Continue to be imitators of Jesus Christ as even he is an imitator of his Father. (7.2)

Ignatius' use of St. Paul is instructive (cf. *1 Cor.* 3:16–17). The assembled body of Christians is a temple. The unity of their agape is an imitation of Christ's agape which in turn is an imitation of the Father. In both writers, disunity desecrates the temple; and no doubt, Ignatius remembers also what St. Paul says in *1 Corinthians* 6: 13–20—how consorting with a prostitute pollutes the body (as a temple of the Holy Spirit) because in sexual intercourse "the two become one flesh (σὰρξ μία)." This is the same Genesis text that is quoted in the Pauline Ephesians (5:31) where the author, while encouraging the Ephesians to love after the pattern of Christ who offered himself as "a sacrifice to God (θυσία τῷ θεῷ)" (5:2), likens the love between Christ and the church to that of conjugal love in which "the two shall become one flesh (σὰρξ μία). This mystery (μυστήριον) is great; however, I say it is about Christ and the church" (5.31–32).[29]

If Ignatius has *1 Corinthians* 6:13–20 in mind, then his admonition to "keep your flesh as the temple of God" would rest on his belief that the church is the "one flesh of Jesus Christ."

Ignatius' oracle of the Holy Spirit, is cited in a context where the image "one flesh of Jesus Christ" appears: "Hasten therefore to use one eucharist. For there is one flesh (μία σὰρξ) of our Lord Jesus Christ and one cup for unity (εἰς ἕνωσιν) of his blood, one altar, as there is one bishop" *(Phd.* 4.1).

The prophetic bishop of Antioch, as a confessor-martyr in chains, commands (through a divine oracle) one eucharist, reminding his hearers that there is only "one flesh of Jesus Christ." The other images denote unity. "One

---

29. Ignatius did know Pauline Ephesians. In *Smyr.* 1.2 he quotes Ephesians 2:16 where "body" is an image of the church. To Polycarp (5.1), he alludes to Ephesians 5:28–29.

cup for unity of his blood" means the agape (blood) of Christ creates unity. "One altar (ἐν θυσιαστήριον)" is an image for one dwelling place of God's people (cf. *Mag.* 7.2; *Eph.* 5.2; *Trall.* 7.2). "One bishop" symbolizes the unity of God and the unity of the church. "One flesh of Jesus Christ" is an image for the episcopal unity of the church as one body of Christ.

Why this image in this letter? In his letters to the Philadelphians and the Magnesians, Ignatius deals with division between Gentile Christians and Jewish Christians. Paul J. Donahue argues that the reason for division is the difference between Jewish and Gentile Christians on restrictions and preparation for participation in the eucharist/agape meal. Some Jewish Christians, for whom the dietary/food regulations of Mosaic law were "a binding expression of God's will," could not share in a non-kosher eucharist/agape meal. They separated and celebrated their own eucharist. Ignatius mandates one episcopal eucharistic assembly.[30]

To the Magnesians, Ignatius commands episcopal unity: "Be subject now to the bishop and to one another . . . in order that the unity may be both physical and spiritual" (13.2). The obvious sense of "physical" is "one assembly" rather than separated groups (each with its own eucharist).Yet within that one assembly, "let no one continue to view one's neighbor according to the flesh but in Jesus Christ love one another always" (6.2). Since circumcision (a mark of the flesh) symbolized the difference between Jew and Gentile, "one flesh of Jesus Christ" is consciously chosen as an image symbolizing the unity of Jew and Gentile.[31]

Indeed, Ignatius probably has in mind the Pauline Ephesian belief that through the death/resurrection of Jesus Christ, the separation between Jew and Gentile was abolished; the "one new man" has the power to incorporate both Jew and Gentile into his one body. After the resurrection of Jesus, distinctions of the flesh, which formerly separated human beings, must give way to the unity of the "one flesh of Jesus Christ," the church.

In Pauline Ephesians, the "one new man" is both individual (the flesh of Jesus Christ) and corporate—Christ is the head of the church, his body; in this body, one grows into the "perfect man" (cf. 1:22; 2:13–16; 4:13–16; 5:23). Likewise, Ignatius is confident that by sharing his suffering with Christ, "the perfect man" will be present empowering him; in martyrdom, he will put on "the new man" (cf. *Smyr.* 4.2; *Rom.* 6.2; *Eph.* 20.1). Ignatius' "new man,"

---

30. Paul J. Donahue, "Jewish Christianity in the Letters of Ignatius," *VC* 32 (1978), 81–93, esp. 84–89. Donahue uses the term "Judaizers" to dennote either Christians who had previously been "God-fearers" (pagans who had been drawn to Judaism before their Christian conversion) or Jews who had converted but still retained observance to Torah food restrictions. For an evaluation of Donahue's "God-fearer" option, see Robinson, *Ignatius*, 58–60.

31. St. Paul's list of Hebrew credentials ("confidence in the flesh," Phil. 3:3–4) began with circumcision.

"perfect man," and "one flesh of Jesus Christ" point to Pauline Ephesians where "the mystery of Christ" is the "one new man" making peace by "his blood" so that Jew and Gentile may be reconciled "to God in one body through the cross" (2:13–16).

The Ephesians' belief of "Jew and Gentile united in the one body, the church" occurs also in a creed-like recital which begins Ignatius' refutation of the docetists at Smyrna:

> I glorify Jesus Christ the God . . . being truly of the race of David according to the flesh, Son of God according to the will and power of God, having been truly born of a virgin, having been baptized by John in order that all righteousness might be fulfilled by him, truly (under Pontius Pilate and Herod, the Tetrarch) nailed, in behalf of us, in the flesh from which we are the fruit of his divinely blessed passion, in order that he might set up a sign for the ages through the resurrection for his saints and believers, whether among Jews or Gentiles in the one body of his assembly (ἐκκλησία). (*Smyr.* 1.1–2).

The fruit of Christ's suffering flesh on the cross are disciples who are members of one body. This looks like the basis for the Trallian passage (cf. 11.1–2) where the "passion" of Jesus summons those who are "his members (μέλη αὐτοῦ)" since "a head is not able to be born without members; for God promises unity, which is, himself." Disciples are "branches of the cross" and their "fruit" is "imperishable."

The phrase "nailed, in behalf of us, in the flesh from which we are the fruit of his divinely blessed passion (καθηλωμένον ὑπὲρ ἡμῶν ἐν σαρκί ἀφ' οὗ καρποῦ ἡμεῖ ἀπὸ θεομακαρίστου αὐτοῦ πάθους)" uses the image of fruit (καρπός) to confess that the church is born from the flesh of the crucified Jesus. [In Luke-Acts, Jesus is the fruit (καρπός) of Mary (*Luke* 1:42) and the Messiah is expected to be a "descendant (καρπός)" of David (*Acts* 2:30).] In Ignatius' "creed," Christians are the fruit of that crucified flesh. The church as the fruit of his suffering flesh ("divinely blessed passion") includes both Jew and Gentile.

This "creed" reinforces the conclusion that "one flesh of Jesus Christ" in the Philadelphian letter is an image for the episcopal unity of the church— one episcopal eucharistic assembly of Jewish and Gentile believers. Thus, although "the flesh of Jesus Christ" denotes his crucified/resurrected humanity, in a eucharistic context "the flesh of Jesus Christ" is also an image of the church, signifying the unity of an episcopal assembly nourished by living with Christ "dwelling in us so that we may be his temples and he, our God, may be in us" (*Eph.* 15.3). The "flesh of Jesus Christ" connotes an episcopal eucharistic assembly (ἐκκλησία) of Christians at Philadelphia.

4. "THE EUCHARIST IS THE FLESH OF OUR SAVIOR, JESUS CHRIST" (*SMYR.* 7.1)

The docetic heterodox at Smyrna, maintaining that the Christ had not really suffered and died, separated from Polycarp's church and held their own "eucharist."[32] *Phd.* 4.1 reveals clearly what Ignatius thought of such action. There is "one eucharist . . . one flesh of Jesus Christ . . . one bishop." If one hears *Smyr.* 7.1 in the context of what Ignatius said to the Philadelphians and one gives to *eucharistia* the sense of "eucharistic assembly," then the Smyrnaeans heard this:

> They [schismatic Smyrnaeans] abstain from a eucharistic assembly (*eucharistia*) and prayer, because they do not confess that the eucharistic assembly (*eucharistia*) [of Polycarp] is the flesh of our savior, Jesus Christ [the flesh] which suffered for our sins, which the Father raised by his goodness. (*Smyr.* 7.1)

This passage points out two errors of the schismatic Smyrnaeans. First, by withdrawing from Polycarp's eucharistic assembly of believers, they have rejected the only assembly in which the immortal man, Jesus Christ, lives and abides. Second, this immortal man is not some disembodied gnostic spirit. He really suffered, died, and rose and now lives in and abides with Polycarp's assembly of believers.

The image, "the flesh of our savior, Jesus Christ," points in two directions. First, it points back to *eucharistia* and expresses an ecclesiological claim: the eucharistic assembly of Polycarp is the true body of Jesus Christ. Just as Ignatius warned the Philadelphians (*Phd.* 4.1) that there is one episcopal eucharistic assembly of believers, so also he tells the Smyrnaeans that only Polycarp's eucharistic assembly is the flesh of Jesus Christ, the body of Christ. This approach to *Smyr.* 7.1 is consistent with Ignatius' ecclesiology, with his approach to the Philadelphians, and with the context of *Smyr.* 7.1; for he follows this by warning the Smyrnaeans to flee from the schismatics, to do nothing apart from Polycarp, and to consider as valid no other eucharist than his. "Wherever the bishop appears, there let the congregation be; just as wherever Jesus Christ is, there is the entire assembly (ἡ καθολικὴ ἐκκλησία)" (cf. *Smyr.* 7.2–8.2).

Second, the image of "the flesh of our savior, Jesus Christ," points forward to the phrases that confess the nature of the immortal man, Jesus Christ—"[flesh] which suffered . . . which the Father raised." This expresses Ignatius' christological refutation of the schismatic docetists, namely, that the Jesus Christ who lives in and abides with Polycarp's assembly of believers is

---

32. Cf. *Smyr.* 4.1–2; 5.3; 7.2–8.2.

the Son of God who (as a genuine human being) suffered, died, and rose (cf. *Smyr.* 2.1; 3.2; 12.2; *Eph.* 19.3). By withdrawing from Polycarp's eucharistic assembly, schismatic Smyrnaeans cut themselves off from the flesh of Jesus Christ, that is, the immortal man (crucified, risen flesh) who lives and abides in the harmony of his disciples (the flesh of Jesus Christ).

"Flesh of Jesus Christ" designates two realities: the crucified, risen Christ ("flesh . . . which suffered . . . which the Father raised") and the harmony of the disciples (members of the body/assembly) with the crucified, risen man (head of the body/assembly). The harmony of the flesh of Jesus Christ is the reality of Jesus' unity with the Father being realized in an assembly, the church (cf. *Eph.* 5.1; *Phd.* 7.2).

An image ("flesh of Jesus Christ") with a double meaning in one sentence should not be surprising. *Mag.* 7.1–2 reflects a similar literary structure and meaning. A eucharistic assembly is "one prayer, one entreaty, one mind, one hope in agape, in blameless joy, which is (ὅ ἐστι) Jesus Christ" (7.1). In *Mag.* 7.2, the unity of the assembly is "one temple of God . . . one altar . . . one Jesus Christ who proceeded from the one Father." The term "one Jesus Christ" designates christological and ecclesial realities. The unity of the eucharistic assembly is the reality of Jesus Christ in the world (7.1), and *Mag.* 7.2 restates this—"one temple of God . . . one altar . . . one Jesus Christ"—but then the "one Jesus Christ" (signifying eucharistic unity) is identified as "who proceeded from the one Father." The context shows that "one Jesus Christ" designates both the unity of the church and the person of Jesus Christ.[33] In *Smyr.* 7.1, "the flesh of our savior, Jesus Christ" functions in the same way as "one Jesus Christ" does in *Mag.* 7.2.

Smyr. 7.1 is Ignatius' application of his "creed" (cf. *Smyr.* 1.1–2) to the struggle of the Smyrnaean church. Ignatius indicts the schismatic Smyrnaeans for their refusal "to confess" (ὁμολογεῖν). The near identity of Christ and his disciples is a central thought of Ignatius' "creed": "I glorify Jesus Christ the God . . . being truly of the race of David according to the flesh . . . nailed, in behalf of us, in the flesh from which we are the fruit of his divinely blessed passion." This is a reference to the suffering agape of Christ giving birth to his church (recall the birth pangs Ignatius suffers as he anticipates his own passion; cf. *Rom.* 6.1); just as a child is a descendant (κάρπος) of its parent (flesh of flesh), so the church is the "fruit of Christ." But the "fruit" is the "imperishable agape" (*Rom.* 7.3) of Christ. The identity of Christ and the

---

33. The word μέλος also designates the unity of the church and the person, Jesus Christ. Through the union of the choral voices of the members (μέλη) of the assembly, the beautiful melody (μέλος) of Christ is sung to the Father. The unity is "symphonic agape" (see *Eph.* 4.1–2). In *Rom.* 7.3, "imperishable agape" is in parallel with "the blood [of Jesus]" and with "corruptible food." The latter contrast shows that "imperishable agape" connotes the love expressed among members in the eucharist/agape as they share food and drink.

church is agape. *Trall.* 11.1–2 takes this thought one step further: Christ's sacrificial agape is the source of the agape which the church lives out in the world, but the "imperishable fruit" (of agape) that the tree (the cross as divinely blessed passion) seeks to produce is dependent on having branches (μέλη). In this sense, Christ the head of the body (assembly) is dependent on his members (μέλη) for the manifestation of his agape to the world (Ignatius' death will be a manifestation of that agape to the Roman world). The Messiah and his church are essential to one another in the plan of God for the world.

For Ignatius, the identity in the eucharist is not between Christ and the elements; it is between Christ the head and the church as his members, between the crucified, risen Lord and "the one body of his assembly" (*Smyr.* 1.2). The immortal power of Christ's sacrificial agape defeating the power of death ("flesh which suffered . . . which the Father raised") is present in the flesh of his disciples, and its essential character is the unity of agape (one assembly). The agape unity of the assembly is the agape between the Son and the Father being realized in community (cf. *Eph.* 5.1; *Phd.* 7.2; *John* 17:20–23). The cross is not simply a manifestation of divine love for the world; it is a manifestation of the unity of agape—the unity of agape between the Father and the Son. And the church is essential to the realization of this unity of agape since its struggle for unity is the process of God's plan being realized in the world. Christology and ecclesiology are inseparable in the plan of God—to create "the one body of his assembly (ἐκκλησία)" (*Smyr.* 1.2). The "the breaking of the one loaf" in an episcopal assembly is "the medicine of immortality" (*Eph.* 20.2).

The heresy of the schismatic Smyrnaeans is not simply christological (that is, a docetism of the passion); it is also ecclesiological—refusing "to confess" that the church is the fruit of the divinely blessed passion, that the divine plan is to realize in community the unity of agape between the Son and the Father that was disclosed in the passion. By producing division, the docetic Smyrnaeans deny the passion in a second way; and ironically, such a denial is their road to death (cf. *Smyr.* 2.1; 7.1; especially *Phd.* 3.2–3).

5. EVALUATION OF ARGUMENTS FOR SACRAMENTAL REALISM IN ST. IGNATIUS

According to Schoedel, *Smyr.* 7.1 is the clearest expression of sacramental realism in St. Ignatius. His argument has three components. First, *eucharistia* refers to a service of prayer and meal with the emphasis on eucharist as meal. Second, flesh refers to the whole meal just as in *Eph.* 20.2 "breaking bread" refers to the whole meal. Third, Ignatius' teaching "presupposes that he could count on wide agreement in Smyrna with a realistic doctrine of the presence of Christ in the elements of the eucharist."[34] Thus, *Smyr.* 7.1 becomes: the food of the meal is the flesh of our savior, Jesus Christ [the flesh] which suffered . . . which the Father raised.

Four observations cast doubt on this view. First, in the only other place where "eucharist" and "flesh of Jesus Christ" appear together ("one eucharist . . . one flesh of Jesus Christ . . . one bishop" [*Phd.* 4.1]), *eucharistia* connotes an episcopal assembly. The contexts of *Smyr.* 7.1 and that of the Ephesians' eucharist show that an "entire assembly" united to the bishop is the basis for a meal that can be called "breaking one loaf" (cf. *Smyr.* 8.1–2; *Eph.* 5.1–2; 20.2). *Eucharistia* as meal presupposes *eucharistia* as episcopal assembly. Second, although "breaking bread" (Schoedel's phrase) in *Eph.* 20.2 refers to the whole meal, the correct phrase is "breaking one loaf"; and it is quite certain that "one loaf" symbolizes the unity of the members of Christ's body (the one flesh) in obedience to "the bishop and presbytery" (*Eph.* 20.2). The images of pure bread, bread of God, and one loaf (*Rom.* 4.1; *Eph.* 5.2; 20.2) signify the eucharistic unity of the church; and bread of God is linked specifically to an episcopal eucharistic assembly ("the bishop and the entire assembly"). Since "flesh of Jesus Christ" can connote an episcopal eucharistic assembly, the connection between the images of "bread" and "flesh of Jesus Christ" in the eucharist surely must have corporate meaning (in addition to bread and flesh signifying the crucified, risen humanity of Christ). Schoedel's reduction of *eucharistia* to meal excludes this important ecclesial dimension of Ignatius' eucharist. Third, even if one granted Schoedel's identity of eucharist and meal, why is the sacramental reality of the meal in the food, per se? Eucharist is synonymous with agape meal (*Smyr.* 8.2) or "breaking one loaf" (*Eph.* 20.2); and what Ignatius stresses "about agape" is caring "for the widow, the orphan . . . the hungry, the thirsty" (*Smyr.* 6.2). Applied to a meal, agape is about sharing food and drink with the needy. Thus, *eucharistia* as meal is not food and drink, per se, but rather the giving/sharing of food and drink—acts of agape. And in the "breaking of one loaf" (*Eph.* 20.2), the emphasis is on "one loaf," that is, the unity of members with one another and obedient to the bishop/presbytery. Hence, in Ignatius, *eucharistia* as meal is agape in which members share food and drink in the unity of an episcopal assembly. Schoedel's reduction of *eucharistia* to food, per se, falls short of Ignatius' *eucharistia*. Fourth, for the claim that Ignatius "could count on wide agreement in Smyrna" in regard to sacramental realism, Schoedel cites 1 *John* 4:2–3 and *Poly. ad Phil.* 7.1. But these texts confess the humanity of Jesus Christ (he "came in the flesh") and say nothing about sacramental realism.

---

34. Schoedel, *Ignatius*, 240.

Schoedel's assertion that Ignatius' teaching "presupposes that he could count on wide agreement in Smyrna with a realistic doctrine of the presence of Christ in the elements of the eucharist"—is crucial to his argument, for it would establish a historical context of sacramental realism within which to understand *Smyr.* 7.1. Yet (apart from *Smyr.* 7.1), there is no evidence for that assertion in the letter to the Smrynaeans or the one to Polycarp. Sacramental realism (as the context of *Smyr.* 7.1) does not exist at Smyrna. The issues there are docetism and schism; and I have shown how 7.1 speaks to both of those issues.

Bradshaw's position is not much different from Schoedel's. "Medicine of immortality" (*Eph.* 20.2) refers literally to the bread, and "the eucharist is the flesh" (*Smyr.* 7.1) is a reference to the bread. Then, by maintaining that *Smyr.* 7.1 is Ignatius' response to a debate with docetists at Smyrna over whether the elements convey the flesh and blood of Jesus Christ, "the eucharist is the flesh" becomes Ignatius' belief that the bread is the flesh of Christ.[35] I have shown that the "one loaf" of *Eph.* 20.2 is probably an image for the episcopal eucharistic unity of the church (cf. also "bread of God" in *Eph.* 5.2). Moreover, there is no evidence for a debate at Smyrna over whether the elements convey Christ. Like Schoedel, Bradshaw's approach to *Smyr.* 7.1 rests on an assumption (a "sacramental realist" debate at Smyrna) that has no historical basis.

The alleged sacramental realist view of Ignatius also has been utilized to argue that *John* 6:51b-58 expresses sacramental realism. This use of Ignatius was put forth by Helmut Koester and developed further by Lothar Wehr (see note 7). Foundational is the hypothesis that *John* 6:51b-58 is the work of a Redactor in distinction from the rest of chapter 6, whose author is the Fourth Evangelist. Thus, there are two views of the image of the bread—that of the Fourth Evangelist where bread is a symbol of the life that Jesus gives to believers and that of the Redactor where bread is the flesh of Jesus (sacramental realism). Through a grammatical analysis, Wehr attempted to show that there is both a figurative and literal sense of *bread* in John, chapter 6. In 6:51b-58, *bread* has a literal sense. Then in order to strengthen his argument, Wehr shows that the language of Ignatius (*Rom.* 7.3; *Smyr.* 7.1) is an echo of 6:51b-58; and since Ignatius was allegedly a sacramental realist, then 6:51b-58 must express sacramental realism. I will examine this use of Ignatius in New Testament scholarship on 6:51b-58 in more detail in the next chapter.

---

35. Bradshaw, *Eucharistic Origins*, 87–88.

6. CONCLUSION

In the last century, the view of scholars was that St. Ignatius' understanding of the eucharist was sacramental realism—the belief that in the bread and wine the communicant receives the flesh and blood of Jesus Christ. This study questions the basis and certainty of that historical judgment.

Interpretations of St. Ignatius' understanding of the eucharist have focused on three texts: *Smyr.* 7.1, *Eph.* 20.2, and *Rom.* 7.3. The approach of Schoedel/Bradshaw is to see *eucharistia* of *Smyr.* 7.1 and "breaking one loaf" of *Eph.* 20.2 as references to the food of the agape meal. Since in *Rom.* 7.3, Ignatius identifies "the bread of God" with "the flesh of Jesus Christ," *Smyr.* 7.1 ("the eucharist is the flesh of our savior, Jesus Christ") is understood as: the food of the agape meal is the flesh of Jesus Christ.

This approach to *Smyr.* 7.1 is questionable because there is no historical basis for sacramental realism at Smyrna. Moreover, in the only other place where *eucharistia* and "flesh of Jesus Christ" appear together (*Phd.* 4.1), "flesh of Jesus Christ" signifies an episcopal eucharistic assembly. In addition, images of bread ("pure bread," "bread of God," and "one loaf" [*Rom.* 4.1; *Eph.* 5.2; 20.2]) also signify the eucharistic unity of the church; and schism was a problem at Smyrna. The ecclesial connotation of these images, in the context of a schismatic-docetic challenge, casts new light on *Smyr.* 7.1: "They [schismatic Smyrnaeans] do not confess that the eucharistic assembly (*eucharistia*) [of Polycarp] is the flesh of our savior, Jesus Christ [the flesh] which suffered for our sins, which the Father raised by his goodness" *(Smyr.* 7.1).

The ecclesiological claim is that the eucharistic assembly of Polycarp is the true body of Christ, "the flesh of Jesus Christ." Only those Smyrnaeans joined to Polycarp's assembly have Christ living in and among them. The phrases following "the flesh of our savior, Jesus Christ" make the christological claim—the Jesus Christ who abides in Polycarp's assembly is not a disembodied gnostic redeemer but rather the Son of God who really suffered, died, and rose ("[flesh] which suffered . . . which the Father raised"). This understanding of eucharistia does not deny its connotation as meal. But *eucharistia* as meal presupposes *eucharistia* as an episcopal assembly.

Since "pure bread," "bread of God," and "one loaf" signify eucharistic unity, *eucharistia* as meal cannot be equated with the food, per se (as Schoedel/Bradshaw do). For although "bread of God" surely refers to the concrete food of the meal, as a link to an episcopal eucharistic assembly (cf. *Eph.* 5.2) it also joins the food of the meal to the assembly of believers, that is, the eucharistic-agape unity of the members with each other and with the immortal humanity of Christ present in worship and meal fellowship.

My view is that Ignatius' language in *Rom.* 7.3 is symbolic. Requesting that the Romans not intervene to save him from martyrdom, he likens himself to "grain of God" that will be milled into "pure bread" by the jaws of wild animals, as a "libation" or "drink-offering" to God, as a sacrifice that will become a "word of God" to pagan spectators in the Colosseum. None of these images make sense if taken literally. This should restrain one from taking his eucharistic images of bread/flesh and blood/agape literally—especially when one sees that his desire to drink the blood of Christ (imperishable agape) expresses his intent to be a libation, and his desire to eat the bread of God (the flesh of Jesus Christ) asserts his aspiration to become "pure bread."

In *Rom.* 7.3, Ignatius conveys with eucharistic images the desire to imitate his Lord's passion (whose martyrdom was a "drinking of the cup"): to drink of the cup and become in his martyrdom one with his Lord and his church (cf. *Phd.* 4.1—"one cup for unity of his blood").

The Romans' letter reveals a shepherd-bishop intent on completing his life of discipleship in martyrdom—an act of sacrificial agape in behalf of the welfare and unity of Christ's flock. His martyrdom follows in the steps of the apostles Peter and Paul. His last meal of "the flesh and blood of Jesus Christ" is his own martyrdom in fellowship with his Martyr-Lord and his church (cf. 6.1–7.3). He will "completely pour out his life in agape" just as eucharistic wine is poured out from "the one cup for the unity of [Jesus'] blood" (cf. *Phd.* 4.1–5.1). He will fully partake of "the bread of God"—the humanity of the new immortal man—and drink of the cup. In doing so he will receive the "imperishable agape" and in that unity, will express his agape for Christ and his church. In death, he will enter fully into the life of his Lord and his heavenly church (cf. *Rom.* 7.3; *Phd.* 9.1).

Martyrdom as a consummation of fellowship with the immortal man, Jesus Christ, is expressed in the images of eating his flesh (receiving his immortal humanity) and becoming "pure bread" (becoming one with Christ and his church). Bread signifies the crucified, risen humanity of Christ ("the flesh of Jesus Christ") and the unity of his disciples. Drinking of the cup is, figuratively, Ignatius' drinking Christ's blood—his "imperishable agape"—and expressing his own agape in the ultimate sacrifice: the offering up of his life to God in behalf of the one flock.

The images of "blood" and "cup" connect the believer to the crucified and risen Christ and his sacrifice of agape as the pattern for Christian life, as the basis for the harmony of the members in the eucharist/agape liturgy (cf. *Phd.* 4.1, "one cup for unity of his blood"). But also, in a hostile environment, these images remind the disciples that the ultimate sacrifice of agape (martyrdom) may be required. Both "bread" and "cup" symbolize the unity of Christ and his disciples, a unity so profound that Ignatius believed his final drinking of the cup would be a manifestation of Christ to a Colosseum of pagan spectators. The bread and the cup express the heart of the eucharist: the unifying reality of the immortal man whose sacrificial agape (more powerful than death) is present in his members and their liturgy of thanksgiving—their self-offerings to God and one another in the harmony of prayer, song, homily/ creed and the sharing of food and drink in an episcopal assembly.

The sacrificial agape of the cross is both a revelation of divine love suffering in the human life of Jesus Christ and a disclosure of the goal of the divine plan: to realize in community the unity of agape existing between the Son and the Father (cf. *Phd.* 7.2). The agape of the risen, crucified Messiah creates and strengthens unity and harmony—the harmony of "symphonic agape singing through Jesus Christ to the Father" in the eucharistic unity of the "one flesh of Jesus Christ"—the worship and agape meal fellowship of Jew and Gentile in one assembly, the unity of congregation obedient to clergy, the unity of imperishable agape. (cf. *Eph.* 4.1–2; *Rom.* 7.3).

Since the unity of agape is at the heart of an episcopal assembly gathered together to give thanks (*eucharistia*, *Eph.* 13.1) and since *eucharistia* and *agape* [meal] are synonyms for that congregational worship (*Smyr.* 8.1–2), from this point on—when I refer to Ignatius' eucharist, my term will be *eucharist/agape*. This judgment is based not only in his letters; but also when Ignatius' thought is compared to that of the other Apostolic Fathers (*First* and *Second Clement, Barnabas, Didache, Polycarp, Martyrdom of Polycarp, Papias,* and *Hermas*), his focus on the unity of agape stands out. The noun for unity occurs eleven times in Ignatius' letters; the verb for unity occurs six times. Neither noun nor verb is found elsewhere in the Apostolic Fathers. *Agape* is used forty-three times in Ignatius, and in all the other Apostolic Fathers it is used a total of thirty-five times.[36]

Eucharistia is used five times. In two passages (in *Phd.* 4.1 and twice in *Smyr.* 7.1), it is associated with the ecclesial sense of "the flesh of Jesus Christ" and connotes an episcopal assembly. In *Phd.* 4.1, it is also in parallel with "one cup for the unity of his blood" where "one cup" signifies the unity of Christ's agape ("blood")—"one eucharist . . . one flesh . . . one cup for the unity of his blood." In *Eph.* 13.1, *eucharistia* probably means "thanksgiving" but implies also an episcopal assembly—"Be eager to come together more

---

36. These statistics are from Robert M Grant, *The Apostolic Fathers*, vol. 1 (New York: Thomas Nelson and Sons, 1964), 138 n. 2 and Grant, *Ignatius*, 33. Ignatius appears to know 1 Corinthians almost by heart and he seems to breathe in the atmosphere of the tradition of the Fourth Gospel (see Percy N. Harrison, *Polycarp's Two Epistles to the Philippians* [Cambridge: Cambridge University Press, 1936], 231–66). The absence of sacramental realism in Ignatius' casts grave doubt on the assumption that either Paul or John was a sacramental realist. Justin Martyr (ca. 150 CE at Rome) is the first witness to the view that "the food is called eucharist" and is received "not as common bread or as common drink" but as "the flesh and blood of that Jesus who was made flesh" (*1 Apol.* 66).

frequently for thanksgiving and glory to God" (συνέρχεσθαι εἰς εὐχαριστίαν Θεοῦ καὶ εἰς δόξαν). And in *Smyr.* 8.1–2, "doing an agape" is a synonym for *eucharistia*.

Chapter 3

John 6:53—The Scandal of a Crucified Messiah as Divine Wisdom, and Martyrdom as "Eating His Flesh and Drinking His Blood"

The purpose of this chapter is to determine the meaning of the saying of the Johannine Jesus to the Judeans: "Truly, truly I say to you—unless you eat the flesh of the Son of Man and drink his blood, you have no life in yourselves" (6:53). My method will be to understand this saying in the context of chapter 6, chapter 6 in the context of the Fourth Gospel, and the Fourth Gospel in the environment of Ephesian Christianity in the last third of the first century.[1]

1. PROVENANCE OF THE FOURTH GOSPEL

Both Polycrates, bishop of Ephesus (ca. 195 CE) and Irenaeus, a bishop in Gaul (ca. 180 CE) refer to the disciple John as "the beloved disciple who reclined on the chest of the Lord."

Polycrates, born ca. 130 CE, probably of Christian parents, knew of John's tomb at Ephesus. If Polycrates' place of birth was Ephesus, then his testimony about John's tomb undoubtedly was known by his parents. This puts the origin of the tomb testimony sometime in the reign of Trajan (98–117 CE) which agrees with Irenaeus' belief that John wrote his Gospel in Ephesus and died early in the reign of Trajan.[2]

---

1. Thanks to David Aune for his helpful critical evaluation of an earlier draft of this chapter.
2. Cf. John 13:23; Eusebius, *Hist. eccl.* 3.23.3; 5.8.4; 5.24.3–4; Irenaeus, *Adv. haer.* 2.22.5; 3.1.1; 3.3.4.

Irenaeus, who in his youth had been a disciple of Polycarp, bishop of Smyrna (forty miles north of Ephesus), remembered vividly "the spot where the blessed Polycarp was sitting when he used to converse . . . how he used to narrate his conversation/association with John" (τὴν μετὰ Ἰωάννου συναναστροφὴν ὡς ἀπήγγελεν). . . .³ The life span of Polycarp (70/1–157 CE) is consistent with the Fourth Gospel being composed at Ephesus in the late first century. If John was twenty in 30 CE, then in 100 CE he would have been ninety. This assumption is also consistent with the last episode in the Fourth Gospel which presupposes the rumor that John would not die but instead remain as a witness until the Parousia (21:21–23). The rumor implies that John lived to an old age and was one of the last disciples to die. I assume that the Fourth Gospel reflects the testimony of a disciple of Jesus who ended up in Ephesus in the late first century. The date of his Gospel in its redacted form is ca. 90–110 CE.⁴

2. JOHN 6:51B-58: THE SACRAMENTAL REALIST VIEW

In the last half of the twentieth century, the predominant scholarly approach to *John* 6:53 assumed that it was part of a redactional unit, 6:51b-58, whose character was eucharistic. This approach goes back to Rudolf Bultmann and entails two assumptions. For the Fourth Evangelist, "faith has no support outside itself." Thus, because 6:51b-8 (allegedly) describes the eucharistic appropriation of "the reconciling death of Christ by faith" through the material means of bread and wine, this section must be the work of a Redactor. The second assumption is that the Redactor has taken from Hellenistic mystery religions the belief that "the food of the sacred meal is God, himself." This theophagic view of the eucharist is (allegedly) reflected in Ignatius' designation of the eucharist as "the medicine of immortality" (*Eph.* 20.2).⁵ Hence, Ignatius' alleged sacramental realism is accepted as supportive of the Redactor's views. Bultmann's view has been prominent in New Testament scholarship.⁶

---

3. Irenaeus' letter to Florinus in Eusebius, *Hist. eccl.* 5.20.5–6.

4. D. Moody Smith (*John* [Nashville, TN: Abingdon, 1999], 36–42) argues also for this date/place. For a discussion of John's identity, see Richard Bauckham, *The Testimony of the Beloved Disciple* (Grand Rapids, MI: Baker Academic, 2007), 49–78.

5. Rudolf Bultmann, *The Gospel of John*, trans. G.R. Beasley-Murray (Oxford: Basil Blackwell, 1971), 219, 224, 232–37.

6. The assumptions of Bultmann are in Günther Bornkamm, "Die eucharistische Rede im Johannes-Evangelium," *ZNW* 47(1956): 161–69; Helmut Koester, "History and Cult in the Gospel of John and in Ignatius of Antioch," trans. Arthur Bellinzoni, *Journal of Theology and Church* 1 (1965): 111–23; Ernst Haenchen, *John 1*, trans. Robert W. Funk (Philadelphia: Fortress, 1984), 296–99; Lothar Wehr, *Arznei der Unsterblichkeit. Die Eucharistie bei Ignatius von Antiochien und im Johannesevangelium* (Munster: Aschendorff, 1987).

According to Lothar Wehr, the Fourth Evangelist stresses belief in the words of Jesus and the Redactor stresses "the eating and drinking of sacramental gifts."[7] In the Redactor, "the gift is no longer Jesus as the Son of God descending from heaven and summoning faith, but rather, eucharist as 'flesh and blood' of Jesus." "What the Evangelist says about faith, the Redactor asserts about the eucharist."[8]

For Wehr, the shift from figurative to sacramental realism is in verse 51: "if one eats of the bread, that one will live forever" is figurative, a metaphor for believing; but sacramental realism appears in the linking of "bread" and "my flesh" in the second part of the verse along with "unless you eat the flesh . . . you have no life in you" (v. 53) and "the one who eats this bread will live forever" (v. 58). The basis for such exegesis is that "to eat" takes the genitive ("of it" and "of this bread") in vv. 50–51; but after the linking of "bread" and "my flesh," "to eat" takes the accusative case of "flesh/bread" (in vv. 53, 54, 56, 58). *Bread* linked to Jesus through the "I am" is figurative (vv. 35, 48, 51a); but after the link to "flesh" (flesh-me-bread) it is literal.[9]

In this view, *John* 6:51b-58 is a homiletic reflection on the eucharist, a corrective to two groups. Against the docetists, it affirms the real incarnation and the eucharist as its extension in the food and drink of the meal. Against the traditionalists of the Johannine community, it counters their magical view. Thus, the Redactor's section resolves a eucharistic conflict in the Johannine community over the connection between Christ and the food/drink.[10]

Wehr's exegetical distinction between bread (accusative) and bread (genitive) does not hold up. Maarten Menken observes that the genitive versus accusative difference is not a criterion for non-eucharistic versus eucharistic meaning. In *1 Cor.* 11:26–28 "to eat" is used with both accusative "bread"

---

7. Wehr, *Arznei der Unsterblichkeit*, 203.
8. *Ibid.*, 203, 228, 235. In a work that predates Wehr, Raymond E. Brown (*The Gospel according to John*, 2 vols. [Garden City, NY: Doubleday, 1986], 1:272–90) sees a similar contrast between 6:35–50 and 6:51–8. Verses 35–50 stress "the necessity of belief in Jesus" while verses 51–58 stress "the necessity of eating and drinking the eucharistic flesh and blood . . ." (290).
9. *Ibid.*, 205–6, 226–30.
10. *Ibid.*, 235, 270–75. Ignatius is employed to show that since his language is similar to that of John 6:53 and since he was (allegedly) a sacramental realist, then 6:53 must also represent sacramental realism. (See Koester, "*History,*" 116–17, 120–23; Wehr, *Arznei der Unsterblichkeit*, 129, 156, 159–62). For Brown, the contrast between verses 35–50 and 51–58 is a "juxtaposition of sapiential and sacramental themes . . . of Jesus' two fold presence to believers in the preached word and in the sacrament of the Eucharist" (*Gospel*, 1.290). But unlike Koester/Wehr, for Brown this sacramental theme represents "true Johannine thought and not a correction to it" (1.286); and like Koester/Wehr, Brown also sees sacramental realism in 6:51–88 although he does not employ Ignatius to prove it (1.292). Rudolf Schnackenburg, *The Gospel According to John*, 3 vols, trans. Cecily Hastings, Francis McDonagh, David Smith, Richard Foley (New York: Seabury Press, 1980, 2: 61–62, 454 n. 173) is uncertain about 6:51b-58 being redactional but has "no doubt" about its "realistic understanding." He cites Ignatius.

and the genitive "of bread" with no apparent change in meaning.[11] Moreover, there is no evidence in the Johannine corpus for inferring the existence of a eucharistic controversy over whether bread and wine convey the presence of the flesh and blood of Christ; and I have shown in the previous chapter that Ignatius was not a sacramental realist.

3. *JOHN* 6:51–58: A TROPE OF CANNIBALISM

J. Albert Harrill argues that the cannibalistic language of 6:53–56 originated in the invective exchanges between the synagogue and the Johannine community.[12] Harrill demonstrates that in Greco-Roman society, metaphors of diet conveyed fears of dissolution of civilized society through seditious acts of tyrants and conspirators. Those who threatened society were condemned in the language of cannibalism. Metaphorically, their seditious acts were described as the "eating of raw flesh" and "drinking of the blood" of their fellow citizens. In Greco-Roman society, the image of cannibalism/anthropophagy was "a fundamental trope in polemics against factionalism and tyranny."[13]

Harrill sees two steps in the evolution of *John* 6:53–37. In the invective exchanges between the synagogue and Johannine Christians, the charge of being cannibals was leveled at John's community because after Jesus' death they continued to follow him—a false messiah who had conspired to incite insurrection against lawful authority and thus bring about the dissolution of Jewish society. This made his followers renegades from Judaism. In step two, John's community accepts the negative metaphor of being cannibalistic and changes it into a "positive affirmation of community self-definition." The invective of cannibalism becomes a "badge of honor." [14]

Harrill's argument is ingenious; but the weakness of this argument is the lack of independent evidence for the assertion that the synagogue had charged Johannine Christians with being cannibals. Without independent evidence for this charge, Harrill's argument is circular and therefore speculative.

---

11. Maarten J. J. Menken, "John 6:51c-58: Eucharist and Christology?" in *Critical Readings of John 6*, ed. R.A. Culpepper (Leiden: Brill, 1997), 183–204, here 196.

12. J. Albert Harrill, "Cannibalistic Language in the Fourth Gospel and Greco-Roman Polemics of Factionalism (John 6:52–66)," *JBL* 127:1 (2008), 133–58.

13. *Ibid.*, 140. Mark Anthony was charged with eating "the raw flesh" and drinking "the blood of Roman citizens." Josephus characterized the leaders of the Jewish Revolt against Rome as "bestial monsters" who "eat raw flesh and gulp down warm blood of fellow citizens they claim to protect" (140, 145–46).

14. *Ibid.*, 153–58.

Another case for the function of the trope of cannibalism is set forth by Meredith J.C. Warren who views 6:51–58 as an integral part of Johannine theology which utilizes the Hellenistic trope of "the consumption of a deity" in order to underscore "Jesus' divinity." According to Warren, 6:51–58 sets forth the claim of Jesus' "expiatory death" (6:51c) which as a sacrifice implies the consumption of his flesh as a meal following the sacrifice.[15]

By examining four Hellenistic novels—*Chaereas and Callirhoe*, *An Ephesian Tale*, *An Ethiopian Story*, *Leucippe and Clitophon*—Warren attempts to show that human sacrifice and the eating of the victim's flesh is a narrative device used to establish the divine identity of the heroine. Likewise, in *John* 6:51–58, the reference to eating the flesh of Jesus (which presupposes his death in 6:51) utilizes this Hellenistic trope in order to underscore Jesus' divine identity.[16]

Since this Hellenistic trope is a narrative device, the reality of eating Jesus' flesh exists only in the text (the narrative world of "Christian imagination") and not in the historical world of the Fourth Evangelist. Hence, the trope accents the divine identity of Jesus but says nothing about the eucharistic rite of the Johannine community.[17]

The persuasiveness of Warren's case rests on the assumption that the literary trope of "eating the flesh of a person sacrificed" was known in the region where the Fourth Gospel originated. However, of the four heroines that Warren discusses—Callirhoe, Anthia, Charicleia, and Leucippe—only Leucippe is sacrificed and eaten.[18] There is no threat of human sacrifice of Callirhoe. Anthia is saved from being sacrificed, as also is Charicleia.[19] Hence, the literary function of "eating the flesh of a sacrificed person" as underscoring the divine identity of the heroine fits only one figure—found in the Hellenistic novel of *Leucippe and Clitophon*; and that novel was composed in the early second century CE, probably at Alexandria, Egypt.[20]

There are other scholarly views of 6:51–58 which I have not yet alluded to. I will address those views as I develop my own position. My thesis is that 6:51b-8 illuminates *John* 6 and underscores two themes—the scandal of the cross and the need to abide. I will argue that the Ephesian Christian

---

15. Meredith J.C. Warren, *My Flesh is Meat Indeed: A Nonsacramental Reading of John 6:51–58* (Minneapolis, MN: Fortress Press, 2015), 64, 210, 217–25.

16. *Ibid.*, 183–86, 236–39.

17. *Ibid.*, 8–18, 83, 189, 231–41, 255.

18. *Ibid.*, 179–181. The reader experiences the horror of Leucippe's sacrifice and being eaten by bandits; however, later in the novel, the reader is relieved to learn that the sacrifice had been staged. Leucippe was still alive.

19. *Ibid.*, 171–76, n. 188.

20. Of the four novels, only *Chaereas and Callirhoe* is datable to the first century CE; it is the only novel in which the trope of sacrifice/cannibalism is absent.

community, expelled from the Jewish synagogue and therefore no longer under the protection of Jewish status, was vulnerable to persecution and martyrdom on account of the name and because it would not participate in the Ephesian festivals associated with the imperial cult. Jewish Christians would have felt a strong impulse to return to the safety of the Jewish synagogue. The Fourth Gospel sets forth the necessity of accepting the risk of martyrdom and appropriating through faith the reality of the sacrificial agape of the Son of Man, a martyrdom that revealed Divine Wisdom: the plan to destroy the power of death and establish a synagogue in which imperishable agape between the Divine and the Son of Man is realized in the reciprocal agape of the members—a synagogue that cannot perish.

The metaphor of the necessity of "eating the flesh and drinking the blood of the Son of Man" asserts the need of overcoming the scandal of Jesus' crucifixion by appropriating his suffering and death as a revelation of Divine Wisdom, and the metaphor expresses that discipleship ending in martyrdom is also an imitation of and fellowship with Jesus' sacrificial death. Martyrdom is an "eating of the flesh and drinking the blood of the Son of Man."

4. EUCHARIST, DIVINE WISDOM, AND THE SYNAGOGUE OF THE SON OF MAN (6:1–48)

According to the Fourth Evangelist, the miraculous feeding of the 5000 was a "sign" (σημεῖον, 6:14); after the meal was over, Jesus commands his disciples: "Gather up the fragments left over, that nothing perishes. So the disciples gathered up and filled twelve baskets of fragments from the five loaves of barley. . . ." (6:12–13).

The meal appears to be a type of "eucharist."[21] The symbolic comment on the remaining fragments of bread—"Gather up the fragments left over (Συναγάγετε τὰ περισσεύσαντα κλάσματα) that nothing perish (ἀπόληται)" (6:12)—is similar to the symbolic meaning of eucharistic bread in the *Didache*: "Just as this fragment (κλάσμα) was scattered (διασκορπίζειν) upon the mountains and after it was gathered (συνάγω) it became one, so let your church be gathered (συνάγω) from the ends of the earth into your kingdom" (9.4). As the gathering of the grains is critical to the creation of the bread, so likewise, the gathering of believers creates the church.

If in *John* 6:12–13, the fragments of bread represent believers, then Jesus is gathering (συνάγω) the believers of Israel—the gathering of Jewish Christians,

---

21. ". . . after Jesus gave thanks (εὐχαριστεῖν), he gave the (bread) . . . (6:11)" suggests a type of "eucharist."

a synagogue (συναγωγή) of believers that cannot perish (ἀπολλύεσθαι).[22] The same verbs, "to gather" and "to perish," are used in the evangelist's narration of the high priest's ironic prophecy—that it is better that one man die for the nation lest "the whole nation perish" (11:50). Unknowingly, Caiaphas had prophesized that "Jesus was about to die . . . not only in behalf of the nation but also in order that he might gather (συνάγω) the scattered children of the Divine (τὰ τέκνα τοῦ θεοῦ τὰ διεσκορπισμένα) into one" (11:51–52). This is a clear parallel to the eucharistic symbolism of bread in the *Didache* (9.4): the verb—"to scatter" (διασκορπίζειν)—is in both Didache and John. But in John, the gathering of the scattered children of the Divine into the one church is realized by the death of Jesus.[23] Probably "the scattered children" are Diaspora Jews.

The Fourth Gospel appears to show that the Johannine community was celebrating the festivals of Hanukkah (10:22–39) and Tabernacles (7:1–9:41) as being eschatologically fulfilled in the suffering, death, and resurrection of Jesus, the Messiah. In Hellenistic Judaism, both of those festivals express the eschatological hope of the Divine gathering (συναγαγεῖν) the Diaspora to the temple (cf. *2 Macc* 1:27; 2:7, 18). Hence, *John* 6:12–13 and 11:51–52 depict the Son of Man realizing the mission which the Divine had given him—"to gather the scattered children of the Divine into one."

The Gospel of John ends with a "second eucharist" beside the sea of Tiberias, prior to which seven disciples, responding to the command of Jesus, cast out their net and caught 153 fish. The fish represent the Gentile mission[24] and symbolize the believers.[25] The verb—"to draw/pull" (ἑλκύειν) the net full of fish—is used twice (21:6, 11); and the same verb appears two other times—in 6:44 to state that "no one is able to come to me unless the Father . . . draws him" and in 12:32—"but if ever I am lifted up from the earth, I will draw all persons to myself." The allusion in the 'second

---

22. The gathering of Christians at Smyrna was a "synagogue" (cf. *Ign. Polyc.* 4.2). Ephesian Christians probably also employed that term. In the Wisdom of Solomon (16:27–29), the ungathered bread of the wilderness was a metaphor for an ungrateful Israelite; for the Fourth Evangelist, the gathered bread of a "eucharist" is a metaphor for a believer.

23. According to Irenaeus *(Adv. haer.* 3.6.1; 5.2.1), because the church (ἐκκλησία) has been "gathered" (συνάγω) to the Divine through the death of the Son, it is called the "synagogue of the Divine" (συναγωγὴ θεοῦ). This belief probably goes back to Irenaeus' teacher, Polycarp, who in turn could have learned it from John, the beloved disciple.

24. Greek zoologists believed there were 153 different kinds of fish. See Edwyn C. Hoskyns, *The Fourth Gospel,* ed. by Francis N. Davey (London: Faber & Faber, 1947), 553–54. By using the technique of gematria, Bauckham *(Testimony,* 279–81) argues that the 153 is an allusion to Ezekiel 47:10 and depicts "symbolically the church's mission of bringing people to faith in Jesus."

25. John 21:9–14 suggests the meal as a type of eucharist—21:13: ". . . Jesus both takes [λαμβάνει] and gives [δίδωσι] the bread to them, and likewise, the fish [ὀψάριον]." Ὀψάριον (cf. 6:9,11) and προσφάγιον [21:5] can indicate fish tidbit/ relish eaten with bread. The "eucharists" are bread meals with fish relish.

eucharist'—that the net, although full, "was not split" (σχίζειν, 21:11) shows that none of the fish were lost (compare 6:12) and that the believers are in unity (cf. 17:11).

In the bread discourse, Jesus describes the believer as one "who comes to me" (6:35) and adds—"All that the Father gives me will come to me; and whoever comes to me, I will never expel (ἐκβάλλειν ἔξω).... This is the will of the One who sent me, that I should lose (ἀπόλλυναι) nothing of all that he has given me . . ." (6:37–39). The same construction (ἐκβάλλειν ἔξω) is used twice in 9:34–35 in order to describe the Pharisees' expulsion of the blind man whom Jesus had healed on the Sabbath. The evangelist adds: "the Judeans . . . agreed that if anyone should confess (ὁμολογεῖν) him [Jesus] to be Messiah, he was to be put out of the synagogue (ἀποσυνάγωγος, 9:22)." Gathering believers is creating a synagogue (6:12; 11:51–52); in 6:37–39, believers are assured of never being expelled from the synagogue that Jesus creates.

Ἀποσυνάγωγος occurs also in *John* 16:1–2 where Jesus prophesies that his disciples will be expelled from synagogues and some will be put to death.[26] The causal link between expulsion and martyrdom is similar to the situation of Jewish Christians in Revelation. There, two groups are contrasted: Christians who did not deny "my name" and another group called "the synagogue of Satan"—"those who say they are Jews and are not, but lie."[27] Whether "the synagogue of Satan" is a Jewish community exempt from participation in the imperial cult, or whether it is a synagogue of Christian Jews who gain exemption by claiming to be Jews—both views presuppose that membership in a Jewish synagogue protects one from provincial prosecution for refusing to worship Roman Deities.[28]

---

26. I am persuaded by Jonathan Bernier's argument (*Aposynagogos and the Historical Jesus in John* [Leiden: Brill, 2013], 74–76) that the passages containing aposynagogos (9:22; 12:42; 16:2) show that both during Jesus' lifetime and after his death, persons who believed him to be Messiah were expelled from the synagogue (public assembly) in Jerusalem. The mechanism for expulsion was not the Birkat ha-Minim but rather mob violence and threat of death. I will argue that 16:2 also describes the situation of the Ephesian church/synagogue, ca. 90–110 CE.

27. The groups are contrasted both at Smyrna (2:9) and Philadelphia (3:9). See Adela Yarbro Collins, "Insiders and Outsiders in the Book of Revelation and its Social Context," in *To See Ourselves as Others See Us,* eds. Jacob Neusner & Ernest S. Frerichs (Chico, CA: Scholars, 1985), 187–218.

28. Julius Caesar exempted Jews from participation in any service associated with pagan Deities. Although Gaius Caligula (37–41 CE) desired to install his statue in the Jerusalem temple, the Jewish War against the Romans (66–73 CE) was not because of Roman pressure to worship Roman Deities but rather over the status of Jews in Caesarea Maritima and the flagrant abuse of power of Roman procurators in Judea. See E. Mary Smallwood, *The Jews Under Roman Rule* (Leiden: Brill, 1976), 126–36, 174–80, 284–92.

Presumably, Jewish Christians were protected from provincial prosecution as long as they were members of a Jewish synagogue. If expelled, they lost that protection and would have been subject to prosecution on account of the name;[29] or, perhaps, because they did not attend festivals associated with Roman Deities and the imperial cult.[30]

In summary, of the four gospel accounts of this feeding, only the Fourth Evangelist's account makes a symbolic statement concerning the twelve baskets of leftover fragments of bread: they had been "gathered" in order that none may "perish." The comments of the Johannine Jesus (6:37, 39) and the Evangelist (11:50–52) express the Johannine belief that Jesus' death "gathers" a "synagogue of God" that cannot "perish." Quite probably, this eucharistic didache addresses the issue of martyrdom at Ephesus and the other six churches of Revelation.

The crowd's response to the miraculous feeding was to acknowledge Jesus as a prophet and attempt to seize him in order to make him a king. Hence, Jesus flees back to the mountain. Evidently, they saw Jesus as a prophet-king who could lead them in a revolt against the Romans.[31]

The crowd and the disciples are left on a hill next to the sea of Galilee. When evening came, the disciples descended, got into a boat, and began to row across the sea to Capernaum. "It was now dark." A strong wind came up, and the sea became rough. After they had rowed for three or four miles, "they behold Jesus as he is walking on the sea and approaching close to the boat; and they were afraid. But he speaks to them: 'I Am (Ἐγώ εἰμι). Cease

---

29. Rev 2:3, 13; 3:8–9.

30. Steven Friesen (*Imperial Cults and the Apocalypse of John* [Oxford: University Press, 2001], 95–104, 116–21, 126–28, 202) shows that the imperial cult was not only for elite provincials. At Ephesus, it was integrated into the cults of Dionysus [God of grapes/wine] and Demeter [Goddess of grain/bread]. It impacted civic religion, entertainment, commerce, government, and household worship. Good news about an emperor's reign occasioned imperial festivals involving sacrificial offerings of animals and libations in order to provide meat and wine for the entire city. Bread could be a component. See S.R.F. Price, *Rituals and Power: The Roman Imperial Cult in Asia Minor* (Cambridge: University Press 1984), 75, 102–14, 209–15, 227–33. Ephesian inscriptions imply "the existence of cult statues" of Augustus, Domitian, Trajan, and Hadrian—honored as "Zeus Olympios" and called "king" (see Sjef von Tilborg, *Reading John in Ephesus* [Leiden: Brill, 1996], 195–96).

31. From 45–66 CE, at least six different Moses-like prophets appeared in Palestine, gathering people in the wilderness and promising divine "signs of liberation" (σημεῖα ἐλευθερίας). These prophetic gatherings were suppressed by the Roman military. In the Jewish War against Rome (66–73 C.E.), the leader of one of the insurgent groups, Simon bar Giora, was acknowledged as king. See Richard A. Horsley ("Jesus and Empire," in *In the Shadow of Empire*, ed. Richard Horsley [Louisville: John Knox, 2008], 75–95, here 79–83) and Richard Bauckham (*The Testimony,* 215–30). Wayne Meeks (*The Prophet-King* [Leiden: Brill, 1967], 63–99, 286–313) argues that Jesus was viewed as a prophet-king like Moses; D. Moody Smith (*John*, 49) notes that this is the only place in the gospels that depicts Jesus' fear of "a popular misrepresentation of his mission or messiahship."

being afraid.'" Then they desired to "receive (λαβεῖν, cf. 1:11–12) him into the boat, and immediately the boat was at the land toward which they were going." (6:16–21).

In both Synoptic accounts (*Mark* 6:45–52; *Matt.* 14:22–33) Jesus rescues the disciples. In Mark, they are distressed by having to row against the wind driven sea waves; and when Jesus gets into the boat, the wind ceases. The common element of all three versions is the terror of the disciples when they see Jesus walking on the sea and his response—"It is me (ἐγώ εἰμι). Cease being afraid." In Mark and Matthew, the terror of the disciples is because they think Jesus is a "ghost" (φάντασμα). Hence, Jesus' ἐγώ εἰμι is a form of personal identification.

Since the Johannine story lacks any mention of the disciples' distress in rowing against the wind driven seas, or the disciples thinking that they saw a "ghost" or of the wind ceasing, Gail O'Day sees it as "a story of theophany, not rescue." The fear of the disciples is generated by their being in the presence of the Divine. O'Day associates the ἐγώ εἰμι with LXX *Isa.* 43:25; 51:12; 52:6 where it appears that the name of Yahweh is "I Am." By walking on the sea and speaking the ἐγώ εἰμι, the Johannine Jesus—in act and word—reveals his unity with God. This continues the theme of *John* 5:19–47: the unity of the Father and the Son who comes in the "name" of his Father. Jesus' walking on the sea is a "revelation of the divine in Jesus."[32]

Catrin H. Williams argues that in Deutero-Isaiah, ἐγώ εἰμι functions as a divine self-declaration and that the evangelist associates this ἐγώ εἰμι with Jesus, thus linking the prophet's testimony to Jesus as an eschatological revelation of Yahweh. In addition, Williams concludes that the Evangelist (based on his understanding of LXX *Isa.* 43:25; 45:19; 51:12) probably sees Jesus' ἐγώ εἰμι as a divine name—a concept which the Evangelist develops further at 8:58 and 18:3–9.[33]

At 18:3–9, ἐγώ εἰμι is the divine name; in its presence, the captors (who have come to arrest Jesus) fall to the ground. The second ἐγώ εἰμι also had power: it protects Jesus' disciples ("I told you that 'I Am'; if you seek me, let them go"). Thus, the Evangelist adds—"This was to fulfill the word which he had spoken—'Of those you gave me, I lost none'" (18:9; cf. 17:12).[34]

The development in 18:3–9 clearly ties ἐγώ εἰμι to 6:12–13 where the fragments of bread are "gathered" so that none may "perish." The divine

---

32. Gail R. O'Day, "John 6:15–21: Jesus Walking on Water as Narrative Embodiment of Johannine Christology," in *Critical Readings of John 6*, ed. R.A. Culpepper (Leiden: Brill, 1997), 149–59, here 153, 155.

33. Catrin H. Williams, *I am He* (Tübingen: Mohr Siebeck, 2000), 221, 288–303, 308. Williams argues that in early Christianity the double ἐγώ εἰμι in Isa. 43:25; 51:12 was probably seen as Yahweh saying—"I am 'I Am.'" Hence the second "I Am" is seen as the divine name. But ἐγώ εἰμι is not an utterance of the tetragrammaton (281–83).

34. *Ibid.*, 281–83, 296–97.

ἐγώ εἰμι revelation of 6:20 is the disciples' dawning realization of what the miraculous feeding revealed: Jesus is the Son who in the "name" of the Father gives life of the age to come (5:24, 39, 43). The crowd sees Jesus as a Moses-like prophet-king who could lead them in a revolt against the Romans; the disciples "desire to receive" (6:21) Jesus as a manifestation of the Divine Name, "I Am."

The next day, the people find Jesus at Capernaum. Aware that they had sought him out because they had eaten a good meal, Jesus commands them; "Stop toiling for the food (βρῶσις) that perishes (ἀπολλύεσθαι) but rather work and continue working for the food that abides (μένειν) to the life of the age to come which the Son of Man will give. For on this one God the Father has set his seal" (σφραγίζειν, 6:27).[35] The people ask for another sign, alluding to the manna in the wilderness by quoting scripture—"Bread from heaven he gave them to eat"—and then they state that in seeing the sign they will be enabled to "trust/believe you [Jesus]" (6:30–31).[36]

What follows is Jesus' midrash on the quotation, consisting of three discourses: one to the Galileans (vv. 32–40) and two to the Judeans (vv. 44–51, 53–58). Jesus' response to the Galileans (vv. 35–40) is the first half of a chiasmic unit (vv. 35–48) that has its mid-point at vv. 42–43 where the Judeans now appear with the grumbling/unbelieving response: how can he say "I am the bread . . ." for surely we know that he is "the son of Joseph."[37] Jesus' response to the Judeans (vv. 44–51) constitutes the second half of the chiasm (vv. 44–48) and then provides an introduction (vv. 49–51) to the next discourse (vv. 53–58).

Jesus' introductory words—"Moses did not give to you the bread from heaven but rather my Father is giving to you the true bread from heaven" (6:32)—reflects the Evangelist's perspective of Jesus addressing disciples of Moses. Nevertheless, "bread from heaven" as a metaphor for Torah and Divine Wisdom is an assumption that Jesus and the Galilean crowd shared.[38] Hence, when Jesus says "the true bread is that which comes down and gives life to the world" (6:33), the response of the crowd—"Lord, give us this bread

---

35. The word βρῶσις can mean food, eating, or meal. Two types of eating are contrasted: one associated with belief and one with unbelief. But 6:12 is also in the background—the symbolism of a food that does not perish; 6:27 shows that "abiding" connotes "not perishing." "Abiding" appears again in 6:56. The word σφραγίζειν signals that Jesus will deliver "Divine Words" in the discourses of chapter 6. The same word is in 3:33–34, where Jesus as "the one sent by the Divine speaks the Divine Words."

36. The quotation appears to be a paraphrase of Ps. 77:24 (LXX) and Exod. 16:4, 15.

37. The chiasmic unit is the insight of John Dominic Crossan, "It is written: Structuralist Analysis of John 6," *Semeia* 26 (1983), 3–21.

38. Susan Hylen (*Allusion and Meaning* [Berlin: Walter de Gruyter, 2005], 101–12, 137–44, 179–80) and Peter Borgen (*Bread from Heaven* [Leiden: Brill, 1965], 6–24, 147–48) assume that in first century Judaism, manna is a metaphor for Torah and Divine Wisdom. In Hellenistic Judaism, "bread from heaven" was a metaphor for the belief that what feeds a human being is the Divine Word (cf. Wisd. 16:20, 26).

always" (6:34)—is a genuine request for Torah and Divine Wisdom. To call "the bread from heaven" the "true bread" is to characterize it as reliable and valid just as Divine Wisdom is true.[39]

The thought that frames the chiasmic unit (vv. 35, 48)—"I Am the bread of life"—and the thought at the mid-point—"I Am the bread that came down from heaven" (vv. 41–42) expresses the premise of the midrash: Jesus, the Son of Man, is the eschatological bread that has come down from heaven. As a sign from heaven, the feeding of the five thousand reveals Jesus as the one designated (σφραγίζειν) by the Divine to execute eschatological justice and give life through his words and deeds (cf. 5:25–30, 36; 6:27).

The "I Am the bread of life" sayings that frame the chiasmic unit (vv. 35, 48) link "bread of life" with "Torah of life"[40] and with the Divine Name that Jesus reveals (I Am). Just as the Divine had been revealed to Moses at the burning bush and had nourished the Israelites in the wilderness with the gift of "bread from heaven," so now was the Divine revealed in the life-giving words and acts of Jesus, the eschatological Moses who reveals the Divine Name and gives Divine Wisdom.

The saying attached to the first "I Am the bread of life" oracle—"the one coming to me shall never hunger and the one believing/trusting in me shall never ever thirst" (v. 35)—is clearly an allusion to Divine Wisdom who made her "dwelling with Jacob/Israel" in the wilderness, who was present in Moses, "the holy prophet," and who offers an invitation—"Come to me, you who desire me and be filled with my produce . . . those who eat me will hunger for yet more and those who drink me will thirst yet for more" (*Sirach* 24:8, 19, 21). In Sirach, Wisdom is identified as "the law that Moses commanded us" (24:23), and what Wisdom gives is "the bread of understanding and water of wisdom" (15:1–3).[41] Hence, the Galilean request to "give us this bread always" (v. 34) is answered by the Evangelist's claim that the Divine Wisdom (given through the Torah of Moses) has been manifested again in Jesus. Jesus gives "the bread of understanding" and "the water of wisdom

---

39. See Hylen, *Allusion,* 141 n. 64. She lists numerous citations from the Hebrew Bible that characterize Divine Word/Judgment as true. If Jesus is the eschatological Moses, then 6:33 ("true bread") is not intended to denigrate the manna in the wilderness. Manna is a metaphor for Torah and Divine Wisdom. The next unit (6:35–48) shows Jesus as the eschatological manna: Divine Wisdom in the flesh who gives life of the age to come.

40. Borgen (*Bread,* 148–49) argues that "bread of life" is modeled after "Torah of Life" and cites Sirach 17:11; 45:5 where "law of life" is an allusion to the giving of Torah to Moses.

41. In the wilderness, both bread and water were miraculous signs (Exod. 16:9–12; 17:1–7). In the Fourth Gospel, Jesus is both "living water" (4:13–15; 7:37–38) and "living bread" (6:51a). As the eschatological fulfillment of the wilderness gifts of bread, water, and Torah, the Johannine Jesus is the Divine Word/Wisdom in the flesh (cf. 1:14)—the fulfillment of the invitation of Wisdom (in Sirach 24)—to come and eat/drink Wisdom.

to drink" (*Sirach* 15:3). And v. 47 (the chiasmic parallel to v. 35) states that those who trust in him will receive his eschatological gift—the life of the age to come, the life that does not perish (ὁ πιστεύων ἔχει ζωὴν αἰώνιον).[42]

Verse 46 echoes the prologue: "No one has ever seen (ἑώρακεν) the Divine. . . . The one being (ὁ ὤν) beside the Father, that one exegeted him" (1:18). The reference there is to "the Divine Word who became flesh (σάρξ) and tabernacled among us" (1:14).

Verses 37–38 and their chiasmic counterpart, verse 45, probably reflect the context of a Jewish-Christian synagogue worship service: "Everyone whom the Father gives me shall come (ἥκειν) to me; and the one coming (ὁ ἐρχόμενος) to me, I shall never expel because I have come down from heaven . . . to do the will of the One who sent me." No believer will be expelled from Jesus' synagogue.

Verses 39–40 expand on the Divine will: that the Son should "lose" no one "who believes in him." Believers "have imperishable life" (ἔχειν ζωὴν αἰώνιον) and "on the last day" will be raised by the Son. The "losing" no one, links verse 39 to Jesus' command at the feeding/bread/sign—"Gather the fragments left over that none perishes." The chiasmic parallel (verse 44) shows that the Divine plays a role in "drawing" (ἑλκύειν) the believer to Jesus. The "drawing" connects the verse to Jesus' death through which he will "draw" all to himself (12:32) and to the 'second eucharist,' which is a kind of parable of the apostolic mission of those sent by the Son to all peoples. There, the catching and "hauling" (ἑλκύειν) of fish to shore (in response to Jesus' command) represents the gathering of believers into unity. And the "beholding" (θεωρεῖν) in v. 40, as a form of believing, links that verse to the disciples' theophany on the sea of Galilee and emphasizes that believers participate in the life of the age to come (ζωὴ αἰώνιος).

The midrash of—"Bread from heaven, he gave them to eat" (6:32–48)—reflects the Christology of the Fourth Evangelist: Jesus of Nazareth is the one whom the Divine sent as the eschatological prophet/king like Moses in order to speak Divine Words, revealing the Divine Name, giving Divine Wisdom and gathering/creating a synagogue (συνάγω) of the children of Israel so that none may perish.

---

[42]. I agree with Craig S. Keener (*The Gospel of John*, 2 vols. [Peabody, MA: Hendrickson, 2003], 1:421) that 1:16 should be translated as "grace added to grace." In 1:16–17, "grace" (given in Jesus Christ) "adds to grace" (given in Torah). In John 6, "Wisdom" links the grace in Torah and in Jesus Christ: the Divine Word/Wisdom by which humans are to live.

5. DIVINE WISDOM AND THE SCANDAL OF A MESSIAH CRUCIFIED (6:48–71)

John 6:48–51 transitions to eating the bread: the contrast is between "your fathers ate the manna in the desert and died" and (I Am) "the bread that came down from heaven that anyone might eat it and not die" (vv. 49–50). The contrast is between life and death; but it is not intended to denigrate the manna. Manna was "bread from heaven," the "bread of angels" (*Ps.* 77:24–25 LXX)—an expression of Divine care of Israel. The Israelites perished in the wilderness because they had "not listened to my [the Divine] voice" but had "grumbled (γογγύζειν) against me [the Divine]" (*Num.* 14:22–23, 27). Hence, "this evil synagogue" (ἡ συναγωγὴ ἡ πονηρὰ αὕτη) received Moses' Divine Oracle that "in the wilderness they shall be utterly exhausted and they shall die."[43] In spite of Divine revelation (Torah) and Divine signs of care (bread, water), the Israelites did not "trust" (πιστεύειν) in the Divine for their "salvation" (*Ps.* 77:22 LXX).[44]

The contrast also underscores the eschatological character of life which Jesus gives. The Divine had given "living words/oracles" (λόγια ζῶντα, *Acts* 7:38) to Moses to give to the Israelites—words that, when obeyed, gave life; so also in Jesus, the Divine speaks the words that give life—a life that cannot perish (cf. *John* 3:34; 5:25–30; 6:12, 68). The "living bread" that came down from heaven is eschatological bread—"if ever one eats of this bread, s/he will live into the age" (ζήσει εἰς τὸν αἰῶνα, 6:51a).

In 6:51b, "living bread" becomes "the bread which I shall give in behalf of the life of the world is my flesh" (ἡ σάρξ μου). "My flesh" refers to Jesus' humanity.[45] The "giving of his flesh" connotes Jesus' humanity in its mortality, in its capacity to suffer and die. Divine Wisdom/Word became flesh (1:14), and the offering of Jesus' flesh is the dying of a human being.[46]

---

43. Cf. Num 14:26–35. The Divine Oracle applies to all Israelites above the age of twenty.
44. The "grumbling" of the Judeans (6:41) over how Jesus can say "I Am the bread . . ." alludes to the "grumbling" Israelites of the wilderness. In discussing manna as a type of eucharist, Paul speaks of the causal link between the "grumbling" (γογγύζειν) of the Israelites and their dying. It is a "warning" for Corinthian Christians "upon whom the end of the ages (τὰ τέλη τῶν αἰώνων) has come" (cf. 1Cor. 10:10–11; 11:29–30). Likewise, the Evangelist is addressing his own community. At 6:61 "the grumbling (γογγύζειν) of many of his [Jesus'] disciples" is a form of "taking offense" (σκανδαλίζειν) at what Jesus has said.
45. Cf. John 1:14; 17:2; Isa. 40:6. Clearly, "flesh" connotes human life.
46. See Menken, "John 6:51c-58," 190.

This evokes the Judean response—"How is this one able to give to us his flesh to eat?"[47] Thus, Jesus said (6:53–57):

> Truly, truly I say to you—Unless you eat the flesh of the Son of Man and drink his blood you are not possessing life in yourselves. The one eating my flesh and drinking my blood possesses the life of the age to come and I shall raise him/her on the last day. For my flesh is true eating (βρῶσις) and my blood is true drinking (πόσις).[48] S/he who eats my flesh and drinks my blood abides in me and I in her/him. As the living Father sent me, and I live because of the Father; so also the one eating me—that one shall live because of me.

The symbolic link between living bread and flesh given for the life of the world is complemented with the necessity of drinking the blood of the Son of Man. The tone is ominous: either assimilate the flesh and blood of the Son of Man (and receive life) or end up like "the fathers" in the wilderness who, because of disobedience, died without any hope of reaching the promised land. The phrase "flesh and blood" expresses the reality of human existence.[49] "Drinking my blood" signifies an assimilation of the fact that Jesus' life will

---

47. The ritual of killing a sacrificial animal and then eating its flesh as a way of participating in the sacrifice is the paradigm for the connection between Jesus' "giving of his flesh" and the Judean question of "how can this one give to us his flesh to eat?" The allusion to the Passover being near (6:4) suggests that Jesus' death (prophesized in 6:51b) has a Paschal connotation. In the Fourth Gospel (unlike the Synoptics) Jesus dies in the afternoon of 14 Nisan as Passover lambs are being sacrificed in the temple. The evangelist understands Jesus' death through the paradigm of the sacrifice of Passover lambs and the Passover meal of bread, wine, and sacrificial lamb in Jerusalem. Hence, it is not surprising that the question about Jesus (giving his flesh to eat) is posed by Judeans.

48. I follow the translation of Jan Heilmann (*Wein und Blut: Das End der Eucharistie im Johannesevangelium und dessen Konsequenzen* [Stuttgart: W. Kohlhammer Gmb H, 2014], 151) who cites many ancient sources, indicating that βρῶσις and πόσις together connote the acts of eating and drinking. Since in 6:51b, Jesus has prophesied his sacrificial death, the transition to a meal (6:53–57) is not an abrupt change of focus. According to Hans-Josef Klauck (*The Religious Context of Early Christianity*, trans. Brian McNeil [Minneapolis, MN: Fortress Press, 2003], 12–13) "sacrificial praxis was a social and religious reality of the first order in the whole of antiquity." It was a feature of life that was "taken for granted." Greeks, Romans, and Jews practiced a form of "slaughter-sacrifice which was followed by a sacrificial meal." Heilmann (*Wein und Blut*, 187–92, 234–37) sees "eating flesh" and "drinking blood" as metaphors of internalizing the teaching of Christ who is the infleshed Word (John 1:14) and who gives Divine Wisdom. The image of "drinking blood" also connotes the acceptance of Jesus' destined violent death (202–6, 238–39). This position is further developed in Jan Heilmann, "A Meal in the Background of John 6:51–58," *JBL* 137.2 (2018), 481–500.

49. Cf. Heb 2:14; Gal 1:16–17; Matt 16:17. Menken ("John 6:51c-58," 190–91) notes that in Eph 2:13–16, the redemptive consequence of Jesus' crucifixion is expressed in images of his flesh and blood.

end in a violent death.⁵⁰ A disciple must assimilate the life and violent death of the Son of Man.⁵¹

The metaphor of eating bread and drinking water of *John* 6:35, which had been associated with fellowship with Divine Wisdom given in Jesus, has shifted to "eating Jesus' flesh and drinking his blood" (which implies his sacrificial death and a meal as a means of sharing in the reality of that sacrifice). The "eating and drinking of Jesus' flesh and blood," as a metaphor for internalizing/digesting his life and violent death, expresses the necessity of seeing that in that life and violent death, Divine Wisdom is revealed.

This conclusion is similar to *1 Cor.* 1:18–25:

> For on the one hand, the word of the cross is foolishness to the ones perishing (τοῖς μὲν ἀπολλυμένοις); but on the other hand it is the power of the Divine to us, the ones being saved (τοῖς δὲ σῳζομένοις) . . . for the Judeans request signs (σημεῖα) and the Hellenes seek wisdom, but we proclaim a Messiah crucified (κηρύσσομεν χριστὸν ἐσταυρωμένον) which is a scandal (σκάνδαλον) to Judeans and foolishness to Gentiles but to those very chosen ones (αὐτοῖς δὲ κλητοῖς), both Judeans and Hellenes, Messiah [crucified is] Divine Power and Divine Wisdom (χριστὸν θεοῦ δύναμιν καὶ θεοῦ σοφίαν). For Divine folly (τὸ μωρὸν τοῦ θεοῦ) is wiser than humans and Divine weakness (τὸ ἀσθενὲς τοῦ θεοῦ) is stronger than humans.

---

50. In Mark 6:30–8:26, the disciples do not see the meaning of bread. In 8:27–33, Simon Peter finally confesses that Jesus is Messiah and is told that the Son of Man must suffer and be killed. In John 6, the teaching about bread ends with the prophecy of Jesus' violent death and the necessity of the disciples "eating his flesh and drinking his blood."

51. In the Fourth Gospel, *the Son of Man* is not a messianic title (cf. 9:36; 12:34). In the canonical gospels, it occurs only once without the definite article (John 5:27) where its meaning is "a human being"—an allusion to Dan 7:13 where one "like (ὡς) a son of man" [a human being] also lacks the definite article. The Greek of John 5:27—καὶ ἐξουσίαν ἔδωκεν αὐτῷ ("and he [the Father] gave authority to him . . . because he is a son of man") is too close to Dan 7:14—καὶ ἐδόθη αὐτῷ ἐξουσία ("and authority was given to him" [the one "like (ὡς) a son of man"]) to be merely coincidental. Jesus is the Son of the Divine who as a human being exercises the eschatological authority to judge the quick and the dead (cf. John 5:25–29; 11:4, 41–47). Barnabas Lindars ("The Son of Man in the Johannine Christology," in *Christ and Spirit in the New Testament*, eds. Barnabas Lindars and Stephan S. Smalley [Cambridge: University Press, 1973], 43–60, here 58, 60) also concludes that 5:27 refers to Dan 7:13–14 but argues that "Son of man" in Daniel is a "mythological figure" and "was not primarily thought to be a man in the strict, earthly sense. He was 'one like a son of man,' a heavenly being." But John 5:27 does not say ". . . because he is one like a son of man." The Greek is clear: ". . . because he is a son of man [a human being]." On the "Son of Man" in John, see Richard Bauckham, *Testimony*, 231–37 and Benjamin E. Reynolds, "The Johannine Son of Man and the Historical Jesus: John 9:35 as a Test Case," in *John, Jesus, and History*, 3 vols., eds. Paul N. Anderson, Felix Just, and Tom Thatcher (Atlanta, GA: SBL, 2016), 3:459–68, here 463–65. I disagree with Reynolds' contention that the title "Son of Man" is not a reference to Jesus' humanity but rather to "a pre-existent, heavenly figure who descends from heaven." I think the Evangelist's view (5:27) that the Divine Son has been given authority to execute justice because he is a son of man (a human being) is presupposed when the Evangelist has Jesus say he is the Son of Man who descends from heaven (6:27, 33, 35, 38, 51, 53). The point is that he is the Divine Son (6:40, 46) who has assumed flesh (1:14).

First Corinthians was written while Paul was at Ephesus, his place of residence for three years. More likely than not, Ephesian Christians had a copy of that letter. It is certain that the letter was utilized by Christians at Antioch in the early second century. Ignatius, martyred at Rome, ca. 125 CE, seems to have parts of it "memorized."[52] Even if there was no copy at Ephesus, (which seems unlikely) surely there were Ephesian disciples of Paul influenced by his teaching. The Pauline Ephesian letter, also known by Ignatius, speaks of the church mission as making known "the many-sided wisdom of God" (3:10; cf. also 1:9–10).[53] It seems certain that by the early second century, Pauline letters were known by some Anatolian Christians and that Paul's teaching was known at Ephesus.

Moreover, the elapsed time between the composition of 1 Corinthians and the Fourth Gospel is probably only forty to fifty years. In other words, some Ephesian disciples (of age twenty) –when Paul resided at Ephesus—would have been in their sixties when the Fourth Gospel was composed. How could they have listened to chapter six without thinking of the wisdom section in 1 Corinthians?

The most prominent similarity of *John* 6 and *1 Cor.* 1:18–25 is the "scandalous" nature of the gospel: Divine Wisdom is revealed precisely in a Messiah crucified (St. Paul); Jesus' flesh offered as a sacrifice in his crucifixion is a revelation of Divine Wisdom (*John* 6). "The Divine Word/Wisdom became flesh" (1:14). In *1 Cor.* 1:23, such a gospel is a "scandal" to Judeans who are seeking a "sign." And in *John* 6:61 many of the disciples are "scandalized" by the word of Jesus—that in order to have life they must "eat the flesh and drink the blood of the Son of Man." In 1 Corinthians, those who are scandalized will "perish" while those who believe will be numbered among "the chosen" (1:18, 24). In *John* 6, believers will not "perish"; they are members of the synagogue that Jesus has created and are of the "chosen" (cf. 6:12–13; 6:70).

The similarity of thought, language, and in some cases, identical imagery in *John* 6 and *1 Cor.* 1:18–25—asking for a "sign," unbelief as "perishing," the "scandalous" message of a Messiah crucified as a revelation of Divine Wisdom, and belief as entrance into the "chosen" messianic community—is too striking to conclude that it is merely coincidental, especially when one recalls that 1Corinthians was composed at Ephesus and Paul lived and taught there for three years.

In light of *1 Cor.* 1:18–25, *John* 6:51b-58 is the Johannine depiction of a prophetic Messiah at a Galilean synagogue gathering, foretelling his violent death by likening it to the slaughter of Passover lambs and employing the

---

52. This is the judgment of Robert M. Grant, *Ignatius of Antioch* (London: Thomas Nelson and Sons, 1966), 24.
53. Even if Ephesians was not composed at Ephesus, it seems certain that Ephesian Christians had a copy.

image of a sacrificial meal of eating and drinking as a metaphor for the necessity of belief—for internalizing his life and violent death as a revelation of Divine Wisdom.[54]

John 6 ends on the note of disbelief and belief. "Many of his disciples left." But the twelve disciples remain. Jesus asks the rhetorical question—"You don't wish to leave, do you?" Simon Peter responds for the Twelve: "Lord, to whom shall we go? You have the words of life of the age to come and we have believed and know that you are the Holy One (ὁ ἅγιος) of the Divine" (6:66–69).[55]

Raymond Brown argues that 6:67–71 "is the Johannine parallel to the Synoptic scene at Caesarea Philippi" and Ernst Haenchen asserts that Peter's "... the Holy One of the Divine" is not "a messianic title."[56] Both judgments probably are correct. In 6:68–69, Peter acknowledges that Jesus is the eschatological prophet/king [like Moses] and has been consecrated by the Divine to give life to Israel. The hearer of the Gospel knows that Jesus is the one "consecrated" (ἁγιάζειν), the one sent on a mission to lay down his life so that none might perish (cf. 10:27–30, 36). The consecration of Jesus refers both to the holy "temple of his body" (2:21) and to the sanctifying power of his sacrificial death for his disciples (17:17–19). The Divine "consecrated" Jesus; and in his death, Jesus consecrated himself.

---

54. I follow Nils A. Dahl ("Paul and the Church at Corinth According to 1 Corinthians 1:10–4:21," in *Christian History and Interpretation: Studies Presented to John Knox*, eds. W.R. Farmer, C.F.D. Moule, R.R. Niebhur [Cambridge: University Press, 1967], 313–35, here 317) in thinking that the images and thought of 1 Cor. 1:18–25 are Paul's and not language he has adopted from an opposition group at Corinth. For an understanding of 1 Cor. 1:18–25 within the context of crucifixion as a legal form of public torture, terror, and execution in the Greco-Roman world, see Martin Hengel, *Crucifixion in the Ancient World and the Folly of the Message of the Cross*, trans. John Bowden (Philadelphia: Fortress Press, 1977), esp. 1–10, 18–21, 31–38, 51–63, 84–85, 88–90. For a study that puts 1 Cor. 1:18–25 in the context of sapiential traditions of Judaism (Sirach, Qumran, Philo) and argues that Paul is responding to Corinthian Christians who claim the Torah as "the pre-eminent locus of divine wisdom," see James A. Davis, *Wisdom and Spirit: An Investigation of 1 Corinthians 1.18–3:20 Against the Background of Jewish Sapiential Traditions in the Greco-Roman Period* (London: University Press of America, 1984), 72–82, here 147.

55. The title of "the Holy One of Israel" is Isaiahan (cf. 41:14, 16, 20; 43:3, 14, 15; 45:11; 47:4; 48:17; 49:7; 54:5; 55:5). The Evangelist believed that Isaiah had seen the heavenly glory of the pre-existent Jesus (cf. Isa 6:1–10; John 12:37–41). Just as Deutero-Isaiah could say that "the Holy One of Israel is faithful and I [the Holy One] chose you [Israel]" (43:3, 10), so Peter also affirms that the Holy One of Israel has been manifested in Jesus; and Jesus responds with a rhetorical acknowledgment that he had "chosen the Twelve" (Israel). Peter's confession (in behalf of the Twelve) is that of Israel, "the chosen one," faithfully receiving the eschatological gift of life in the words and deeds of the Son who reveals the glory of Divine Wisdom, the Divine Name ("I AM"), the Holy One of Israel. In Isa. 43:10, Israel is "the servant whom I [the LORD] chose that you may know and believe me and understand that I AM." After the bread meal, the disciples received a theophany of the "I AM." The next day, they (through Peter) affirm that the Holy One of Israel has been revealed in Jesus, the Son of Man.

56. Brown, *Gospel*, 1.301–2; E. Haenchen, *John 1*, trans. Robert W. Funk (Philadelphia: Fortress, 1984), 307–8.

The image of "consecration" is also associated with Jesus' death as a martyrdom. The washing (νίπτειν) of the disciples' feet during the last supper (13:5–11) expresses symbolically that the sacrificial death of Jesus will wash the disciples, making them clean (καθαροί) and preparing them for consecration by the holy Spirit. Peter's "You are the Holy One of the Divine" is his acceptance, in behalf of the Twelve, of Jesus' self-prophecy (6:51b): that Jesus would offer his flesh as a redemptive sacrifice (as bread for the life of Israel)—that his sanguinary death would be a testimony (μαρτυρία) to the Divine (cf. 18:37; 19:34–37).[57]

6. DIVINE WISDOM AND THE SCANDAL OF MARTYRDOM

Does the disciples' acceptance of Jesus' destined death and their remaining (abiding) with him, imply their acceptance of their own probable martyrdom? Two points deserve consideration. The theme of "abiding" is a red thread in the subsequent farewell discourse of 13:31–16:1. The abiding of the believer and the Son of Man will occur when the Paraclete appears—"the Spirit of Truth" who "abides" (μένω) with the believer (14:15–20). This "abiding" is developed in the discourse about the grape vine and branches (15:1–10). In ten verses, the verb occurs nine times. The Paraclete will enable the believer to abide in the love of the Son, keeping his commandment just as the Son kept the commandment of his Father and abided in that love (cf. 14:15–17; 15:9–10).

The disciples are commanded to love one another just as Jesus had loved them (15:12). Before Jesus exits to his death, he refers to his death as the basis for his commandment: "No one has greater love than this—that one lays down her/his life in behalf of his friends. You are my friends if ever you do what I am commanding you" (15:12–14). His disciples are now "friends" (not his "servants," 15:15). During his last supper, he had washed their feet as a parabolic action pointing to his death as an act of sacrificial love. They are to emulate that sacrificial love in their life with one another (13:1–16). The fact that the "abiding" in 6:56 is linked with 14:15–21 and 15:1–10 suggests that "to abide" in the life of the Son of Man entails not only the acceptance

---

57. Ignatius of Antioch, writing to the Ephesians (ca. 125 CE) says that he desires to walk in "the footsteps" of St. Paul, "the one who has been consecrated" (ὁ ἡγιασμένος, 12.2). This supports my contention that in Ephesian Christianity, martyrdom was a "consecration."

of Jesus' violent death as a revelation of Divine Wisdom but also the risk of a disciple's martyrdom.

At 15:18–27, Jesus tells his disciples that as his witnesses, they too (like him) will be hated and persecuted. And just as the Son of Man had prophesized his own death (6:51b) so at 16.2–3, he prophesizes the martyrdom of some of his disciples: they will be "expelled from the synagogues" and "everyone who kills you will think they are offering worship to the Divine." At 16:1, Jesus gives the reason for the farewell discourse of 13:31–16:1 (with the new commandment, the coming of the Paraclete, the reciprocal abiding, and persecution): "These things I have spoken to you lest you be scandalized/offended (σκανδαλίζεσθαι)." Here is the second point deserving discussion.

The verb—to scandalize/take offense—appears in only one other place in the Fourth Gospel: after the saying on "eating the flesh and drinking the blood of the Son of Man." Jesus knowing that "his disciples are grumbling about this word, said to them: 'Is this word scandalizing you?'" (6:60–61). In 16:1, "to be scandalized" means to fall away because of the threat of expulsion from the synagogue and (lacking the protection of the synagogue) being vulnerable to martyrdom; if in 6:60–61, "to scandalize" connotes the same meaning as in 16:1, then "eating the flesh and drinking the blood of the Son of Man" expresses an abiding with the Son of Man which may result in expulsion from the local synagogue and consequent risk of martyrdom.[58] The prospect of martyrdom makes sense of 6:54—"s/he who eats my flesh and drinks my blood possesses the life of the age to come and I will raise her/him up at the last day." (Martyrdom is a sharing in the crucified, risen life of the Son of Man; and the martyr is raised.) Does this line of thought make sense of the rest of the narrative in *John* 6?

The next two verses allude to Jesus' death and the Spirit who gives life. "What if ever you behold the Son of Man ascending to where he was formerly? The Spirit is the one creating life; the flesh does not profit (ὠφελεῖν) anything. The words which I have spoken to you are spirit and are life" (6:62–63). "The Son of Man ascending" refers to his being lifted up—his crucifixion.[59] And in the context of martyrdom, the saying about "the flesh profits nothing" appears similar to Ignatius' pejorative comment expressing his fear that Roman Christians might intervene and save him from martyrdom.

---

58. Barnabas Lindars ("The Persecution of Christians in John 15:18–16:4a," in *Essays on John*, ed. C.M. Tuckett [Leuven: Leuven University Press, 1992], 131–52) argues that 15:18–16:4a is part of a redactional unit (extending to 16:15) revealing a Johannine community excommunicated from the local Jewish synagogue and fearing a violent form of persecution (136–43).

59. I agree with C.H. Dodd (*The Interpretation of the Fourth Gospel* [Cambridge: University Press, 1958], 441–42) that Jesus is glorified and exalted in his death. "Resurrection is already given in the act of self-oblation" expressing divine ἀγάπη and revealing the glory the pre-existent Jesus had with the Divine before the foundation of the world (17:5, 24)—an "ascending to where he [the Divine Son who is a son of man] was formerly."

Such action would be loving his "flesh." "Neither the ends of the earth nor the kingdoms of this age will profit (ὠφελεῖν) me at all" (*Rom.* 2.1; 6.1).⁶⁰

It is especially poignant that the disciple, speaking in behalf of the Twelve and confessing Jesus as "the Holy One of the Divine" is Simon Peter; for he will betray Jesus, thrice, after vowing to abide with him and die with him (13:36–38). But the Ephesian hearer of the Gospel also knows that Simon Peter, whom the risen Jesus appointed as shepherd of his sheep, suffered the violent end of holy consecration by being burned at the stake in Nero's garden.⁶¹

7. CONCLUSION

In this chapter, I determined the meaning of the saying of the Johannine Jesus to the Judeans: "Truly, truly I say to you—unless you eat the flesh of the Son of Man and drink his blood, you have no life in yourselves" (6:53). By employing the testimony of Polycrates, bishop of Ephesus (ca. 195 CE) and Irenaeus, a bishop in Gaul (ca. 180 CE), I argued for a provenance of the Fourth Gospel as Ephesus, ca. 90–110 CE.

My survey of scholarship on 6:51b-58 demonstrated that the dominant approach was to see that unit as the hand of a Redactor in distinction from the Evangelist. Since the language of that unit was similar to that of Ignatius (cf. *Rom.* 7.3) and Ignatius was allegedly a sacramental realist, then it followed that 6:51b-58 expressed a sacramental realist view of the Johannine eucharist. In chapter 2, I showed that Ignatius was not a sacramental realist. This opens the way to another approach to 6:51b-58.

I have shown that the section 6:32–48, the midrash of "Bread from heaven, he gave them to eat" reveals the Johannine Wisdom Christology. The critical

---

60. James D.G. Dunn ["John 6: A Eucharistic Discourse?" *NTS* 17 (1971), 328–38] sees 6:62–63 as a correction of the Evangelist to a Johannine group who, in combatting docetists, had tied eternal life to a "literalistic interpretation of the Lord's Supper" and an "overemphasis on the physical act" of eating/drinking (337). In response, the Evangelist uses eucharistic language in order to stress that life is given through "union with the exalted Christ" through the Spirit/Paraclete (338). Although docetism was probably an issue in the Johannine community (cf. 1 John 4:2–3), there is no evidence for a sacramental realist group. Hence, Dunn's interpretation is speculative.

61. See the brilliant argument of Timothy D. Barnes (*Early Christian Hagiography and Roman History* [Tübingen: Mohr Siebeck, 2010], 4–9). He shows that ζώννυμι (21:18) must refer to Simon Peter "being wrapped" with a flammable garment, that is, being "clothed by another" for the purpose of being burned to death. Tacitus in the early second century (*Ann.* 15.44) describes the deaths of Christians in Nero's garden. The traditional belief that St. Peter was crucified, head downward, is mentioned in Tertullian (early third century). However, Barnes observes that when a person was crucified under Roman rule, that victim always was stripped naked—signifying her/his vulnerability, shamelessness, and helplessness. Simon Peter was clothed by another, tied to a cross with his arms outstretched, and burned to death. Tacitus is closer to the event than Tertullian, and his account explains John 21:18.

verse is 6:35—"I Am the bread of life; s/he who comes to me shall never hunger and s/he who believes in me shall never thirst." This is clear allusion to Divine Wisdom who offers an invitation—"Come to me, you who desire me and be filled.... Those who eat me will hunger [long] for more and those who drink me will thirst for more" (*Sirach* 24:8, 19, 21). Just as the Divine had been revealed to Moses, had given gifts of bread and water to Israel in the wilderness and in the Torah gave "bread of undetstanding and water of wisdom" (*Sirach* 15:1–3) so in Jesus, Divine Wisdom was present in the flesh (*John* 1:14) as "living water" (4:13–15; 7:37–38) and "living bread" (6:51a).

The Johannine Jesus is the one whom the Divine sent as the eschatological prophet/king like Moses in order to speak Divine words (3:33–34; 6:27), revealing the Divine Name ("I Am," 6:20), giving Divine Wisdom (6:35), and creating a synagogue of the children of Israel so that none may perish (cf. the use of συνάγω with regard to "gathering" the remains of the bread into 12 baskets, lest any fragment perish, 6:12–13; and see 11:51–51 where Jesus' death will "gather the scattered children of the Divine").

The Fourth Gospel shows that the Johannine community was celebrating the festivals of Hanukkah (10:22–39) and Tabernacles (7:1–9:41) as being eschatologically fulfilled in the suffering, death and resurrection of Jesus, the Messiah. In Hellenistic Judaism, both of those festivals express the eschatological hope of the Divine gathering (συναγαγεῖν) the Diaspora to the temple (cf. *2 Macc* 1:27; 2:7, 18). Hence, John 6:12–13 and 11:51–52 depict the Son of Man realizing the mission which the Divine had given him—"to gather the scattered children of the Divine into one."

In 6:51b-58, the metaphor of eating bread and drinking water (6:35) associated with fellowship with Divine Wisdom given in Jesus has shifted to "eating Jesus' flesh and drinking his blood"—which implies his violent sacrificial death and a meal as a means of sharing in the reality of the sacrifice. Here, the Evangelist understands Jesus' violent death through the paradigm of the slaughter of a Passover lamb and the Passover meal of bread, wine, and lamb. The "eating and drinking of Jesus' flesh and blood," as a metaphor for internalizing/digesting his life and violent death, expresses the necessity of seeing that in his life and death, Divine Wisdom is revealed.

Concerning Divine Wisdom, the similarity of *John* 6 and *1 Cor.* 1:18–25 is striking. Prominent is the "scandalous" nature of the gospel: Divine Wisdom is revealed precisely in a Messiah crucified (St. Paul); Jesus' flesh offered as a sacrifice in his crucifixion is a revelation of Divine Wisdom (*John* 6); the Divine Word/Wisdom became flesh (1:14). In *1 Cor.* 1:23, the gospel is a "scandal to Judeans" who are seeking a "sign." In *John* 6:61 many disciples are "scandalized" by the word of Jesus—that in order to have life they must "eat the flesh and drink the blood of the Son of Man." In 1 Corinthians, those who are scandalized will "perish" while those who believe are among "the chosen" (1:18, 24). In *John* 6, believers will not "perish"; they are members of the synagogue Jesus has created, are of the "chosen" and will never be "cast out" (6:12–13, 37, 70).

The similarity of thought, language, and imagery is too striking to be coincidental, especially when one recalls that 1 Corinthians was composed at Ephesus and the apostle Paul resided and taught there for three years. *John* 6:51b-58 is the Johannine depiction of a prophetic Messiah at a Galilean synagogue, foretelling his violent death by likening it to the slaughter of a Passover lamb and employing the image of a sacrificial meal of eating and drinking as a metaphor for the necessity of belief—for internalizing his life and violent death as a revelation of Divine Wisdom.

When the Fourth Gospel was written (90–110 CE), the confession of Jesus as Messiah resulted in being expelled from the local synagogue (9:22). Membership in a synagogue protected one from being prosecuted for refusing to worship Roman Deities or refusing attendance at a festival of the imperial cult. Expulsion of Christian Jews from a local synagogue entailed the loss of protection and the risk of being put to death (16:1–2).

Those Christian Jews who gave up their Messianic/Divine Wisdom belief in the crucified Jesus and remained members of the synagogue were said "to be scandalized," that is, they were so threatened by the fear of persecution, prosecution, and death that they fell away. The verb "to be scandalized" occurs only twice in the Fourth Gospel—at 6:60–61 (disciples being scandalized by the need "to eat the flesh and drink the blood of the Son of Man") and at 16:1–2 (disciples falling away under threat of persecution and death). It is highly probable that the "scandal" of the Johannine gospel is that of belief in Jesus as the Messiah whose crucifixion is a revelation of Divine Wisdom and the scandal that belief resulted in expulsion from the synagogue and martyrdom. The necessity of "eating the flesh and drinking the blood of the Son of Man" is the necessity of sharing his martyrdom.[62]

Chapter 2 showed that Ignatius understood his martyrdom as "the eating of Jesus' flesh and drinking of his blood"—"an imitation" and sharing in Jesus' passion (*Rom.* 6.3; 7.3). Ignatius uses Johannine eucharistic language— "eating the flesh and drinking the blood of Jesus Messiah"—in order to express the meaning of his own death as a sacrificial act. The next chapter will show that Ignatius utilizes another eucharistic metaphor—sacrificial libation—as a way of describing his death as an imitation of Jesus' passion. I will

---

62. I agree with Paul N. Anderson ("The Sitz im Leben of the Johannine Bread of Life Discourse and Its Evolving Context," in *Critical Readings of John 6*, ed. R.A. Culpepper [Leiden: Brill, 1997], 1–59, here 5 n.11; 6) that the scandalizing message of John 6 is the cross. The Johannine Christians are "portrayed as understanding full well what it means to ingest the flesh and blood of Jesus"—martyrdom as "the cost of discipleship." Concerning John 6:53–58, Paul S. Minear (*John: The Martyr's Gospel* [New York: Pilgrim, 1984], 98) says: this expresses the "totality of sacrifice demanded of the disciples . . . to drink of his blood . . . is to share his martyrdom."

show that it is quite probable that the eucharist/agape of Ignatius contained the ritual act of a sacrificial libation—the act of pouring wine into a dish or bowl that rested on the altar where the food and drink of the eucharist/agape was placed. That ritual act of sacrificial libation symbolized the shedding of Jesus' blood in his crucifixion—a way of remembering the redemptive power of his sacrificial act of love in behalf of his disciples.

Chapter 4

Martyrdom, Sacrificial Libation, and the Eucharist/Agape of Ignatius

In this century, two important foci in the study of the eucharist in early Christianity have been the relation of the eucharist to martyrdom and the eucharist understood within the framework of a Greco-Roman supper (δεῖπνον) and symposium.[1] But there is no study that deals with sacrificial libation (the sacrificial offering of wine that precedes the symposium) as an image and ritual act which links martyrdom to the eucharist.

This image appears in Ignatius of Antioch and is a continuation of a theme in first century Christianity. Martyrdom as a sacrificial libation exists in Paul (*Phil.* 2:17) in Revelation (6:9–11; 16:4–7; 17:1–6) and is implied in the account of Stephen's death (*Acts* 7:59–8:1; 22:20). In the Synoptic Gospels, sacrificial libation is associated with Jesus' death and the eucharistic cup (*Mark* 14:23–24; *Matt.* 26:27–28; *Luke* 22:19b–20).

On the basis of Revelation and Ignatius, I will show that, quite probably, an altar-table was employed in a eucharist at Antioch, Ephesus, Smyrna, Pergamum, Thyatira, Sardis, Philadelphia, Laodicea, Magnesia, Tralles, and Rome—in house-churches and/or at martyr altar shrines in the cemetery. Pouring a sacrificial libation into a dish on the altar-table appears to have been an essential element of a eucharist/agape.[2]

---

1. Dennis E. Smith, *From Symposium to Eucharist* (Minneapolis: Fortress Press, 2003); Albert G.A. Horsting, "Transformation of Flesh: Literary and Theological Connections between Martyrdom Accounts and Eucharist Prayers," in Maxwell E. Johnson (ed.), *Issues in Eucharistic Praying in East and West* (Collegeville, MN: Liturgical Press, 2010), 307–25; Matthias Klinghardt, "Der Vergossene Becher: Ritual und Gemeinshaft in Lukanischen Mahlbericht," *EC* 3.1 (2012), 33–58.

2. I am very grateful to Jan Heilmann for his peer review of an earlier version of this chapter. His careful, thorough, and insightful evaluation made this final form significantly better.

1. MARTYRDOM, SACRIFICIAL LIBATION, AND THE EUCHARIST/AGAPE OF IGNATIUS

Ignatius, while at Smyrna (forty miles north of Ephesus)—in chains as one of the prisoners in the custody of ten Roman soldiers awaiting the departure to Troas (whence they would cross the Aegean for Neapolis, the port of Philippi in route to Rome where he would die in the Colosseum, ca. 125 CE)—wrote to Christians at Rome, requesting that Roman Christians not attain his release and expressing his desire to be "the food of wild animals" so he can "attain God"; for "I am grain (σῖτος) of God and through the teeth of wild animals I am ground in order that I may be found to be pure bread" (καθαρὸς ἄρτος, 4.1). Roman Christians should "pray to the Messiah in behalf of me" that the wild animals become the instruments of "a sacrifice" (θυσία, 4.2).

Bread symbolizes the unity of the members of the church with the flesh/body of Messiah Jesus (cf. *Smyr.* 1.2; *Eph.* 20.2). The wild animals will grind Ignatius into a substance (flour) which by the fiery ordeal of his martyrdom will be baked into one loaf. This symbol appears again in Polycarp, bishop of Smyrna and a friend of Ignatius, who was martyred by being burned at the stake. His flesh was an offering of "bread being baked" (*Marty. Poly.* 15.2).[3]

Ignatius' sacrifice is imagined also as "a libation poured out to the Divine":

> Grant me nothing more than to be poured out as a libation (σπονδισθῆναι Θεῷ) to the Divine while the altar is still prepared so that you, after forming a chorus may sing with agape to the Father in Messiah Jesus because the Divine (ὁ θεὸς) has deemed the bishop of Syria worthy of being found in the West [where the sun sets] after summoning him from the East [where the sun rises]. Beautiful may my sunset be: in death, to set my face towards the Divine in order that I might rise to Him. (*Rom.* 2.2)

A wine libation is the ritual act of pouring wine on the altar as a sacrificial offering to a Deity before the wine is drunk by the religious devotee. The pouring of the wine signifies the shedding of Ignatius' blood. Ignatius desires as drink "the blood" which is the "imperishable agape" of Messiah (*Rom.* 7.3); and in union with Messiah, the "High Priest" ("to whom has been entrusted the Holy of Holies," *Phd.* 9.1), he will offer himself as a libation, a sacrifice of agape for the unity of Philadelphian Christians: "I am overflowing with agape for you—like a sacrificial libation offered in your

---

3. Polycarp (age 86) was martyred at Smyrna on 23 Feb. 157 CE. See Timothy Barnes, *Early Christian Hagiography and Roman History* (Tübingen: Mohr Siebeck, 2010), 367–78. For Polycarp's martyrdom as a eucharistic offering ("bread being baked") see Horsting, "Transformation," 314–18.

behalf" (λίαν ἐκκέχυμαι ἀγαπῶν ὑμᾶς, *Phd.* 5.1).[4] For Ignatius, "the agape of offering up oneself to the Divine is the way" (ἡ ὁδός, *Eph.* 9.1); and the unity of Messiah's blood in the eucharist/agape assembly is the unity of agape (*Eph.* 4.1–5.3).

In Ignatius' expression of agape towards the Philadelphians (5.1), I construe ἐκκέχυμαι as an intensive perfect. Hence, as such, it emphasizes not a pouring out (libation) that has already happened but rather the state that Ignatius presently exists in as a result of of a process that was going on from the past to the present, namely, his journey, in chains, from Syria to his martyrdom at Rome where he will pour himself out as a sacrificial libation for other Christians (*Rom.* 2.2).

The context of *Phd.* 5.1 supports a libation sense of ἐκκέχυμαι. In *Phd.* 4, Ignatius had encouraged the Philadelphians to demonstrate their unity by employing "one eucharist" since there is only "one flesh [body] of our Lord, Jesus Messiah and one cup for the unity of his blood. . . ." In this chapter, I will show that a sacrificial libation was a component in Ignatius' eucharist/agape at Antioch. Hence, when he thinks of eucharist/agape and his martyrdom, he thinks of his death as a libation of agape.

In this Philadelphian passage, the image of eucharist/agape cup evokes the unity of Christ's blood; and in Ignatius, "drinking Christ's blood" is an image of being united with his "imperishable agape" in a death like his (*Rom.* 7.3). After referring to "one cup for the unity of his blood," Ignatius uses the verb ἐκχέω to express his agape for the Philadelphians. I think a translation should convey the eucharist/agape libation sense of Ignatius' agape. Robert Grant acknowledges the probability that Ignatius is thinking of "his being poured out as a sacrifice for the Philadelphians"; nevertheless, he chooses a translation of "I overflow with love for you."[5] I think the sense could be more accurately expressed as—"I am overflowing with agape for you—like a sacrificial libation offered in your behalf."

Wine libations were a common feature of Greco-Roman culture and were offered in situations where wine was drunk—whether at a family meal, a gathering of members of a club/association, a festive celebration of a birth, a rite of initiation or a marriage. They were also a component of animal

---

4. According to Walter Burkert (*Greek Religion*, ET John Raffan [Cambridge: Harvard Univ. Press, 1985], 70), the two verbs expressing libation are σπένδειν and χεῖν. Ignatius uses both verbs.
5. Grant, Robert M. *Ignatius of Antioch*, vol. 4 of *The Apostolic Fathers*, ed. Robert M. Grant (New York: Thomas Nelson, 1966), 102.

sacrifice or a ritual for initiating civic events/games. They were employed in a cremation ritual and in the making of a peace treaty or taking an oath.[6]

The cemetery was also a prominent place for a libation. Probably four times a year, family and friends would gather at the tomb of a loved one for a picnic of food and drink, for prayer and remembrance of the departed one. As wine was poured on the tomb, one hoped to make contact with the beloved through prayer and libation. Departed souls were believed to be nourished by such libations.[7]

The invocation of a Deity with prayer and supplication is an essential component of a wine libation. A cup/bowl is filled with wine, and the supplicant pours some of the wine into a dish on the table where members are eating or on the hearth of the home or on the altar of a temple or club/association or on the ground while invoking/praying to the Deity.[8]

In the ritual of animal sacrifice, a libation completes the sacrifice when wine is poured on the flame of the altar where the flesh of the animal is being burned. Thus, libation and sacrificial flesh on the altar are intimately linked in the religious imagination. A prominent iconographical theme in painting and vase figures is the devotee holding a libation cup/bowl in his/her hand stretched outward over the flames of an altar.[9]

Sacrificial libations had special meaning in the cult of Dionysus, the God of grapes/wine. Euripides says that the God Dionysus "is poured out [in the wine] as a sacrificial libation (σπενδέσθαι) to the Deities."[10]

In Judaism, a wine libation is a significant feature of the Tamid temple service: the twice daily (at sunrise and sunset) congregational worship in which there was a whole burnt offering of a lamb and a grain offering together with the blood of the lamb and a wine libation poured on the altar. In Hellenistic Judaism, this wine libation was called "the blood of the grape" (*Sirach* 50.15).[11]

For Ignatius, a wine libation is a metaphor for the shedding of blood in the Roman Colosseum (*Rom.* 2.1–2). The ancient image of libation is transformed

---

6. Cf. Burkert, *Greek Religion*, 70; Smith, *Symposium*, 27–42, 68–78, 87–92, 106–9; Hans-Joseph Klauck, *The Religious Context of Early Christianity*, ET Brian McNeil (Minneapolis: Fortress, 2003), 44–50, 59–68, 71–78.
7. Burkert, *Greek Religion*, 193–94.
8. *Ibid.*, 71; Smith, *Symposium*, 28–30; Klauck, *Religious*, 60–61.
9. Burkert, *Greek Religion*, 71.
10. For the complete text of Euripides, see Klauck, *Religious*, 108–9. Jan Heilmann (*Wein und Blut: Das End der Eucharistie im Johannesevangelium und dessen Konsequenzen* [Stuttgart: W. Kohlhammer Gmb H, 2014], 68) cautions about reading too much into this text: it indicates "a direct association of the God [Dionysus] with the wine," but the pouring out of the wine is not a metaphor for self-sacrifice. This may be the case for Euripides' text; but it seems to me that in Ignatius, the libation of wine does express self-sacrifice.
11. Cf. Exod. 29.38–41; Num. 28.1–8; Sirach 50.5–21; M. Tamid 3.3; 4.1–3; 7.1–3. Fearghas Fearghail ("Sir 50:5–21: Yom Kippur or the Daily Whole Offering," *Biblia* 59.3 [1978] 301–16), argues convincingly that Sirach 50.5–21 describes the Tamid service.

in his eucharist/agape understanding of Jesus' sacrificial agape: the pouring/ drinking of wine from the eucharist/agape cup is a symbol of both expressing the "imperishable agape" [of Christ; cf. *Ign. Rom.* 7.3] and receiving it in a life that ends in martyrdom. The response of Roman Christians should be to form "a chorus and sing with agape to the Father in Messiah Jesus"—the same thought that Ignatius expresses in praising the eucharist/agape unity of Ephesian Christians (*Eph.* 4.1–5.3). His martyrdom will be a "ransom/expiation" (ἀντίψυχον) for the Ephesian church (21.1).[12]

The same word (ἀντίψυχον) is used three times to describe Ignatius' sacrificial death in behalf of Polycarp and those Smyrnaeans who are obedient to Polycarp (*Smyr.* 10.2; *Poly.* 2.3; 6.1). Hence, Ignatius' sacrifice will be for the unity of the churches at Ephesus and Smyrna—a view similar to that of the Fourth Evangelist's understanding of Jesus' death as a sacrifice for the unity of the Johannine community at Ephesus (*John* 17:18–23). Ignatius will offer his flesh as a "sacrifice" (θυσία), becoming "pure bread," and shed his blood as a libation offering of agape (σπένδεσθαι). His flesh sacrifice and libation of blood will be a ἀντίψυχον for preserving the unity of the church.[13]

In desiring "as drink . . . his [Messiah's] blood which is imperishable agape," Ignatius will drink figuratively of Messiah's blood, that is, be in fellowship with him while dying as a martyr (receiving and expressing agape). The parallelism of *Rom.* 7.3 shows that "imperishable agape" is associated with "his blood." But there is another parallel. "Imperishable agape" is contrasted with "perishable food." Hence, "imperishable agape" connotes two realities, christological and eucharist/agape/ecclesial: the love of Jesus Messiah shown in the shedding of his blood, and his love experienced in the "symphonic agape" of eucharist/agape fellowship (see *Ign. Eph* 4.1–5.3). [14]

---

12. "Ransom/expiation" (ἀντίψυχον) also describes the redemptive consequence of the deaths of the martyrs of Judaism in 4 Macc. 6:29; 17:21. For the significant influence of 4 Maccabees on Ignatius, see Othmar Perler, "Das vierte Makkabaerbuch, Ignatius von Antiochien und die altesten Märtyrerberichte," *RAC* 25 (1949): 43–72.

13. In Judaism, ἀντίψυχον is based on *Lev.* 17:11—the blood of the animal "instead of your life (ἀντὶ τῆς ψυχῆς) shall make propitiation." In the temple cult, the life of the animal resided in its blood and that blood was offered (instead of the life of Israel). Cf. also 1 John 1:7–2.2. Twice (Eph. 8.1; 18.1), Ignatius uses the Pauline word περίψημα (1 Cor 4.13)—which can have a conventional connotation (lowly, humble, contemptible) or a sacrificial connotation (devoted, dedicated, consecrated). Since in *Eph.* 21.1 Ignatius says "I am your expiation" (ἀντίψυχον), *Eph.* 8.1 and 18.1 probably are expressing his sacrificial relation to the Ephesians ("I am indeed consecrated as your sacrifice" [περίψημα, 8.1]) and his devotion to the cross ("My spirit is devoted to the cross" [18.1]).

14. In *Trall.* 8.1, the blood of Jesus symbolizes agape; in *Smyr.* 8.1–2, "eucharist" and "agape" are synonyms for the same liturgical event (There is no "valid eucharist" without the bishop, without whom "it is not lawful . . . to baptize or to do an agape" [ἀγάπην ποιεῖν]). Andrew B. McGowan ("Naming the Feast: Agape and the Diversity of Early Christian Meals," *SP* 30[1997], 314–18) concludes that in Antioch and western Asia Minor of the second century, the "agape" meal and "eucharist" were synonyms for the same event. Lothar Wehr (*Arznei der Unsterblichkeit. Die Eucharistie bei Ignatius von Antiochien und Johannesevangelium* [Münster: Aschendorff, 1987], 133–40) sees in "imperishable agape" a term for the eucharist.

A "drinking of blood" and a "pouring out of blood" are both metaphors of participation in Messiah's martyrdom. The context in both *Rom.* 7.3 and *Phd.* 4.1–5.1 is eucharist/agape. In *Rom.* 7.3 the contrast is between earthly food and bread/drink of the eucharist/agape; in *Phd.* 4.1–5.1 the concern is for the unity of a eucharist/agape assembly—"one eucharist . . . one flesh . . . one cup for unity with his [Messiah's] blood . . . one altar . . . one bishop. . . ." And to the Romans, Ignatius speaks of his sacrificial libation of martyrdom "while the altar is still ready" (*Rom.* 2.2). In short, Ignatius—in unity with Messiah Jesus—will offer a redemptive sacrifice of his flesh (becoming pure bread) and a eucharist/agape libation of his blood in behalf of preserving the unity of Christians at Smyrna, Philadelphia, and Ephesus.[15]

My view of a bread/flesh sacrifice and a wine libation/blood sacrifice in Ignatius differs from that of Andrew McGowan who argues that since θυσία in the LXX can designate either a cereal/grain offering or an animal offering, in Ignatius one can argue that martyrdom is a cereal/grain/bread offering associated with a eucharist meal whose shared cultic participation maintains the integrity and purity of community identity, much in the same way as the eucharist meal does in the *Didache*. Hence, Ignatius' death is a bread offering with a correlation of bread and flesh (but devoid of any association of his flesh as a flesh-blood sacrifice with propitiary power as are the flesh-blood sacrifices of the martyrs in *4 Maccabees* 6:28–29; 17:20–22. There, ἀντίψυχον describes the martyrs' bloody deaths as "purification" [καθαρίζεσθαι] and "propitiation" [ἱλαστήριον] for the sins of Israel, based on Lev 17:11).

McGowan argues that Ignatius' libation reference is not intended to underscore the propitious character of his blood but rather simply a reference to a wine drink offering. Thus, Ignatius imagines his martyrdom as a cereal offering and as a wine libation—a pure sacrifice remembered through a eucharist/agape meal of bread and wine which maintains the integrity and purity of Christian community. His libation sacrifice need not imply as analogue a flesh-blood offering with propitious character.[16]

---

15. William R. Schoedel (*Ignatius of Antioch* [Philadelphia: Fortress Press, 1985], 171 n.8) thinks the libation image excludes a eucharistic interpretation. Sergio Zañartu ("Les concepts de vie et mort chez Ignace d'Antioche," *VC* 33 [1979], 324–41) thinks the libation image links martyrdom to eucharist: "an assimilation to the passion of the Savior." The eucharist makes present the "life-giving power of Christ's passion-resurrection . . . a life which brings the strong demand of following and imitating Christ" (see 327, 337 n. 12). Peter Meinhold (*Studien zu Ignatius von Antiochien* [Wiebaden: Steiner, 1979], 15–16) thinks libation/altar depicts Ignatius' death as a sacrifice offered to God for the unity of the church.

16. Andrew McGowan, "Eucharist and Sacrifice: Cultic Tradition and Transformation in Early Christian Ritual," *Mahl und Religiöse Identitat in Fruhen Christentum/Meals and Religious Identity in Early Christianity*, eds. Matthias Klinghardt and Hal Taussig (Tübingen: Francke, 2012), 191–206 at 196–200.

McGowan's case depends on translating ἀντίψυχον as "substitute/ ransom" and περίψημα as "off-scouring," while arguing that in Ignatius, ἀντίψυχον does not connote "expiation."[17] He makes a good case for "bread" as a cereal offering by putting Ignatius in the historical trajectory of *Didache*, Justin Martyr, and Irenaeus. But he avoids any discussion of the *Martyrdom of Polycarp*. There, Polycarp's sacrificial offering is imagined both as a bread offering and as an animal burnt offering (14.1; 15.2). Since Ignatius (while in chains) conversed with Polycarp at Smyrna, later wrote a letter to the church of Smyrna as well as one to Polycarp from Troas (and then Polycarp initiated the collection of Ignatius' letters after his martyrdom), the influence of Ignatius on Polycarp is certain. (Recall that Ignatius' use of ἀντίψυχον occurs at *Poly.* 2.3; 6.1 and *Smyr.* 10.2). It seems plausible that Ignatius' use of ἀντίψυχον is a reference to his martyrdom as the offering of a flesh-blood sacrifice with propitious character because when Smyrnaean Christians depicted Polycarp's martyrdom they employed a flesh/blood libation image.[18]

Ignatius reflects the influence of Johannine and Pauline thought. His belief that his death will be for the unity of the church is similar to the Johannine prayer for Christian unity (cf. *John* 17:18–23); and Ignatius' understanding of martyrdom as "eating the flesh and drinking the blood" of the Messiah Jesus (*Rom.* 7.3) is an echo of *John* 6:53–56. His death as a libation is similar to Paul's description of his own martyrdom—"a libation poured out (σπένδεσθαι) on the priestly sacrificial offering of your [Philippian's] faith" (ἐπὶ τῇ θυσίᾳ καὶ λειτουργίᾳ τῆς πίστεως ὑμῶν, 2:17).[19]

Paul employs cultic language in order to describe the Philippian act of kindness in his time of need.[20] If Paul's imprisonment should end in martyrdom, his death will be, figuratively, a libation poured on the Philippian offering—a libation offering of gratitude as a response to their offering to him while he was in prison. Paul probably thought that his sacrificial offering given in his

---

17. *Ibid.*, 198 n. 24.
18. Polycarp was burned at the stake; when the fire could not kill him, he was stabbed. Blood and a dove (Holy Spirit) came forth from his body. His sacrificial blood put out the fire: his blood libation completed his burnt flesh offering, and the redemptive power of his sacrificial death put an end to the fire of persecution and martyrdoms at the church at Smyrna (cf. *Mart. Poly.* 1.1; 14.2; 16.1).
19. I follow Paul Holloway (*Philippians* [Minneapolis: Fortress, 2017], 137) in thinking that θυσία καὶ λειτουργία is a hendiadys and refers to the things which the Philippian, Epaphroditus, brought to Paul when he was in prison. Paul calls these gifts—"a fragrant offering, an acceptable sacrifice pleasing to God" (4.18). Epaphroditus' aid is called "a priestly work" (λειτουργία, 2.30).
20. The language of sacrifice was employed to express the character of virtue, kindness, and prayer in Hellenistic Judaism and early Christianity. See Everett Ferguson, "Spiritual Sacrifice in Early Christianity and Its Environment," *ANRW*, eds. W. Haase and H. Temporini, II 232 (Berlin: Walter de Gruyter, 1980), 1152–90.

death could be offered in behalf of the Philippian Christians. Just as Messiah Jesus had offered his life for Paul (cf. *Gal.* 2:20; *Rom.* 5:8) so Paul would offer his life for the Philippian Christians.[21] Although libation and sacrifice are employed as metaphors expressing the affectionate relationship between Paul and the community he founded, do these metaphors also presuppose that there was a ritual act of libation in the Philippian eucharist which Paul had established? In order to determine the likelihood of this, I will examine other New Testament traditions in which the image of libation depicts martyrdom and/or in which libation is associated with a eucharist.

2. MARTYRDOM AND SACRIFICIAL LIBATION: STEPHEN AND REVELATION

Lest one conclude that St. Paul is unique in imagining martyrdom as a libation, two other traditions of apostolic Christianity deserve attention—Acts of the Apostles and Revelation. When Acts depicts the stoning of the first Christian martyr, Stephen, the narrator notes that Saul [Paul] was present; although he threw no stones, he consented to Stephen's death. Stephen's last words before he died were—"Lord Jesus, receive my spirit. . . . Lord do not hold this sin against them" (7:59–8:1).

Later in Acts, when Paul is defending himself against the charge of polluting the temple, he recounts his early history as a persecutor, his Damascus road experience, his baptism, his vision of Jesus, and Jesus' warning to leave Jerusalem. Paul's response to that warning is to restate his involvement in Stephen's death: "And when the blood of Stephen, your witness (μάρτυς), was being shed (ἐξεχύνετο), I too was standing by and approving . . ." (22:20). If the blood of a martyr is a sacrificial libation to the Divine, that is, a prayerful act which has redemptive power for others, then it is reasonable to infer that whenever a martyr's death is described with ἐκχεῖν or σπένδειν and redemptive consequences follow, the narrator must have intended the death to be seen as a sacrificial libation. As Stephen was dying, he prayed for forgiveness for his enemies (7:59–60); and later on, Saul—who was an enemy and who had consented to Stephen's death—receives grace. Stephen's prayer joined to his own death as a sacrificial libation had redemptive power: it brought about Saul's change of heart and mind.

---

21. Polycarp knew the Philippians' letter as well as 2 Timothy where St. Paul's death was imagined as a "libation" (σπένδομαι, 4:6). See Paul Hartog, *Polycarp and the New Testament* (Tübingen: Mohr Siebeck, 2002), 171, 177–79.

In *Acts* 22:20, Paul has described Stephen's death from a Christian perspective (martyrdom as a sacrificial libation with redemptive power). Therefore, in this context, the translation should be—"And when the blood of Stephen, your witness, was being poured out as a sacrificial libation. . . ."²²

In the Apocalypse of John, a composition directed to seven churches in western Asia Minor, the deaths of martyrs are also libations. The prophet John describes what he saw after his heavenly ascent: a heavenly throne and a "lamb standing as one having been slaughtered/sacrificed" (ἀρνίον ἑστηκὸς ὡς ἐσφαγμένον, 5:6). The prophet saw "under the [heavenly] altar the lives of those who had been slaughtered/sacrificed on account of the Divine Word and on account of the witness they had given" (ὑποκάτω τοῦ θυσιαστηρίου τὰς ψυχὰς τῶν ἐσφαγμένων διὰ τὸν λόγον τοῦ θεοῦ καὶ διὰ τὴν μαρτυρίαν ἣν εἶχον, 6:9).

Later, the prophet hears a voice commanding the angels to effect judgment. The third angel "pours out" (ἐκχεῖν) the "golden libation bowl (φιάλη) of wrath" (15:7–16:4) on rivers and streams, turning water into blood, and then says, "You [God] are just . . . for they [the whore and worshipers of the beast] poured out/shed (ἐκχεῖν) the blood of the holy ones and prophets, and you have given them blood to drink" (16:5–6). Then a voice (identified as "the altar") chimes in, "Yes, Lord God Almighty, true and just are your judgments!" (16:7). The voice [from under the heavenly altar] is the blood of martyrs affirming the Divine judgment upon imperial Rome, the whore of Babylon—"holding . . . a golden cup . . . drunk with the blood of the holy ones and the blood of the witnesses of Jesus" (17:4–6).

The prophet John could be using the trope of cannibalism/anthropophagy to depict the violence of Roman tyranny against Christians.²³ Nevertheless, the use of ἐκχεῖν with regard to "blood" of the martyrs beneath the altar and the picture of imperial Rome as a whore drunk with their blood, holding a

---

22. In the next section (Eucharistic Cup and Sacrificial Libation in the Synoptic Gospels) I will demonstrate that Jesus' death is viewed as a sacrificial libation. For example, in Matthew's last supper, the ritual cup formula is—"my blood of the covenant, that is, the blood poured out as a sacrificial libation for the many for the forgiveness of sins" (26:28 τὸ αἷμά μου τῆς διαθήκης τὸ περὶ πολλῶν ἐκχυννόμενον ἄφεσιν ἁμαρτιῶν). In Matthew's community, Jesus' death was viewed as a sacrificial libation that effects the forgiveness of sins. In Acts, Stephen's martyrdom is understood as an imitation of Jesus' redemptive sacrifice. It (like Jesus' death) brings forgiveness to those (Saul/Paul) who took part in or approved of Stephen being stoned to death. Was Paul the first Jewish Christian who imagined his own martyrdom as a sacrificial libation? Had he told Luke that Stephen's death was the sacrificial death that had changed his understanding of the Jesus movement, or is Luke dependent on a non-Pauline tradition for his understanding of Stephen's death? It seems to me that the former option is more likely.

23. Cf. J. Albert Harrill, "Cannibalistic Language in the Fourth Gospel and Greco-Roman Polemics of Factionalism (John 6.52–66)," *JBL* 127.1 (2008), 133–58.

"golden cup" suggests that a sacrificial libation had been poured on the altar.[24] Martyrdom is a libation of blood and the pouring of wine on an altar is a symbol for that martyrdom.[25]

In Revelation, the martyrs' blood is under the altar and cries out for divine judgment on the whore of Babylon (imperial Rome) who holds a cup and is drunk with the blood of the martyrs. What is implied is that the whore had offered a sacrificial libation (wine poured out on the altar) and then has drunk from the cup of wine. Recall that in the cultic world of Judaism, the wine libation, offered at the altar in the Tamid service, is called "the blood of the grape" (*Sirach* 50:15). The wine that had been poured on the altar and spilled beneath it is a symbol for the blood of the martyrs. Their deaths are conceived as sacrificial libations.

The prophetic vision reveals that the martyrs' Deity will bring judgment on imperial Rome in response to the blood of the martyrs which cries out for justice. An angel pours out (ἐκχέω) from the libation bowl of wrath a libation of blood on rivers and streams, turning water into blood. Then the angel says, "You [the Divine] are just . . . for they [the whore and worshippers of the beast] poured out (ἐκχέω) the blood of the holy ones and prophets, and You have given them [the whore and her followers] blood to drink" (16:5–6).

This passage describes two libations. The first one is viewed from two perspectives—imperial Rome is killing Christians (the whore had been offering wine libations at the altar; she is drunk with the wine); but from a Christian perspective since the shed blood in a martyrdom is a sacrificial libation (the wine of the libation symbolizes blood), the whore is drunk with their blood and the wine that spilled off of the altar is blood which calls out for divine justice. The second libation is the blood which the Christian Deity pours out on imperial Rome (changing water which is essential for life—plant growth

---

24. Ramsay MacMullen (*The Second Church: Popular Christianity A.D. 200–400* [Atlanta: SBL Press, 2009], 9) argues that the vision of Rev 6:9–10 ("under the altar, the lives of those who had been slaughtered/sacrificed . . .") presupposes that in western Asia Minor, "altars for divine worship were placed directly above the resting place" of martyrs buried in the cemetery. If MacMullen is correct, then martyr shrine altars of Christians existed in the cemeteries of the seven churches of Asia Minor (Smyrna, Ephesus, Philadelphia, Pergamum, Sardis, Thyatira, Laodicea) in the late first century. Among Greco-Roman pagans, the cemetery was a place for sacrificial libations. As wine was poured on or into the tomb, one hoped to make contact with the dead through prayer. The pouring of a sacrificial libation on the shrine altar tomb of a Christian martyr will be examined in chapter 6.

25. In the imperial cult the sacrificial wine libation poured on the altar is an act of worship to Roman Deities and to/for the emperor. But worshipful obedience to Roman Deities and the emperor also is expressed in executing Christians (who worship a crucified insurgent as Divine and who imagine their martyrdoms as sacrificial libations offered to the true Deity). The whore (imperial Rome) drinks of the cup whose libation was the execution of Christians. Thus, she becomes drunk with their blood. One is reminded of John 16:2: "The time is coming when everyone who puts you to death will think s/he is offering worship to the Divine (λατρείαν προσφέρειν τῷ θεῷ)."

and drinking water for humans—into blood). This is a blood libation of wrath and death poured out on those who are persecuting and killing Christians.

If Revelation was composed after 70 CE[26] then the libation blood under the heavenly altar could be expressing that both Jesus and the martyrs (like Antipas), who had been a "faithful witness" (cf. ὁ μάρτυς ὁ πιστός, 1:5; 2:13) and had been "slaughtered/sacrificed" (ἐσφαγμένοι, 5:6; 6:9), were an eschatological fulfillment of the Tamid (the sacrificial offering of a lamb, its blood and a wine libation): Jesus, the Lamb, was the pre-eminent sacrifice who conquered death; Antipas and his companions were the libations that completed the sacrifice. "They had washed their clothes and made them white in the blood of the Lamb." They, too, had conquered death (7:14).[27]

But what if Revelation was composed before 70 CE? Timothy Barnes has argued that Revelation was composed in the reign of Galba, probably the winter of 68 CE[28] when Jerusalem was under siege by the Roman Legions and the temple was still intact. In this framework, the martyrs' blood under the heavenly altar could presuppose a Christian Judaism in western Asia Minor loyal to temple worship at Jerusalem. The implied contrast is noteworthy: a Tamid service being performed twice a day in the temple of Jerusalem (a city under siege and on the verge of being destroyed) and Christian Jews in the diaspora imagining their bloody deaths as libations poured on the heavenly altar and believing that they had conquered by the blood of the Lamb (cf. 7:14–17). The sacrifices of Jesus ("the slaughtered Lamb of God") and his "faithful witnesses" were an eschatological fulfillment of the Tamid.

In either dating of Revelation, it appears highly probable that *Rev.* 6:9–10 shows martyrdom as a sacrificial libation that completes the sacrifice of the lamb in the Tamid service. And given the spiritual crisis produced by the destruction of the temple in 70 CE for both Jews and Jewish Christians, the appearance of martyr altar shrines in the cemeteries of western Anatolian Christians or house-church table-altars in the late first century would not be surprising.[29]

---

26. Irenaeus' date (*Adv. haer.* 5.30.3) is the latter part of the reign of Domitian (81–96 CE).

27. With temple and altar destroyed in 70 CE, Tamid services ended; if Revelation was composed after 70 CE, then *Rev.* 6:9–10 shows that Christian Jews in western Asia Minor thought of the sacrifices of their martyrs as a completion of the Tamid at the heavenly altar.

28. Barnes, *Hagiography,* 38–40.

29. I follow Jan Lambrecht [" 'Synagogues of Satan' (*Rev.* 2:9 and 3:9): Anti-Judaism in the Book of Revelation," *Anti-Judaism and the Fourth Gospel*, eds. R. Bieringen, D. Pollefeyt, and F. Vandecasteele-Vanneuville (Louisville: Westminster John Knox Press, 2001), 279–92 at 286–91] in assuming that the majority of Christians in western Asia Minor were Christian Jews and that the reference to the "synagogue of Satan" in Rev. 2:9; 3:9 presupposes a bitter conflict between Jews and Christian Jews over the issue of Jewish identity. The destruction of the Jerusalem temple in 70 CE must have been a spiritual trauma for both groups.

Thus far, in this chapter I have shown that martyrdom is conceived of as a sacrificial libation offered in behalf of other Christians and as a witness of the gospel to outsiders. Sacrificial libation is a cultic way of affirming that martyrdom bears witness to and communicates the redemptive power of Jesus Christ's sacrificial death. Ignatius offered his libation of sacrificial death in order to preserve the unity of Christians at Smyrna and Ephesus and to "safeguard" (ἀσφαλίζεσθαι) the Christians at Philadelphia.[30] When Polycarp was burned at the stake, he was also stabbed and the outpouring of his blood put out the fire. His blood was a libation which completed his burnt flesh offering, and the redemptive power of his sacrificial death put an end to the fire of persecution and the martyrdoms at the church at Smyrna.[31] In the case of the martyrdoms of Antipas and his fellow Christians at Pergamum, their blood libations call forth Divine judgment on imperial Rome. Although this effect of a blood libation is different from that of Stephen's blood libation (Divine wrath poured out on imperial Rome, the enemy of Christians versus Divine forgiveness bestowed on an enemy, Saul/Paul), there is a common theme: martyrdom as a sacrificial libation is a powerful prayer to the Christian Deity for protection, safety, and welfare of the church. It is also a powerful witness to the gospel of Jesus Christ—to the power of his agape embodied in his suffering and death in behalf of others. Through the power of Stephen's sacrificial libation of agape, Saul/Paul will become an apostle to the Gentiles; and Ignatius' sacrificial libation of agape in the Roman Colosseum is "the Divine Word" to all who witnessed his death (*Rom.* 2.1).

I have provided enough background now for examining the Synoptic Gospels' depiction of the last supper and for understanding the function of the image of sacrificial libation in the depiction of that meal.

3. EUCHARISTIC CUP AND SACRIFICIAL LIBATION IN THE SYNOPTIC GOSPELS

All four gospels portray Jesus' passion as "his cup" (*Mark* 10:38; *Luke* 22:42; *Matt.* 26:39; *John* 18:11). In *Mark*, Jesus tells the sons of Zebedee that the Son of Man came in order "to give his life as a ransom for the many" (λύτρον ἀντὶ πολλῶν, 10:39, 45). At the last supper, he refers to "my blood of the covenant, that is, the blood being poured out as a sacrificial libation in behalf of the many" (τὸ αἷμα μου τῆς διαθήκης τὸ ἐκχυννόμενον ὑπὲρ πολλῶν, 14:24).

---

30. *Smyr.* 10.2; *Polyc.* 2.3; 6.1; *Phd.* 5.1.
31. *Mart. Poly.* 1.1; 14.2; 16.1.

The repetition of "the many" suggests that "blood" refers to Jesus' imminent sacrificial death. His blood as a ransom will establish a covenant between him and the twelve disciples, but the covenant will be extended to others ("the many"). The disciples' drinking from the common cup unites them in a covenantal bond with Jesus. The association of the cup with the imminent sacrificial death of Jesus implies the risk that they too may suffer a martyr's death;[32] in 10:39, the sons of Zebedee were told of their destined martyrdom, namely, that they would "drink of the cup."

In Matthew's last supper, the ritual cup formula is—"my blood of the covenant poured out as a sacrificial libation for the many (περὶ πολλῶν) for the forgiveness of sins" (26:28). "To pour out (ἐκχεῖν) blood" can describe murder, that is, the shedding of innocent blood. In both Mark and Matthew, the verbal adjective—"to pour out"—is attached to "blood," indicating that the blood which will be "shed/poured out" in Jesus' death is likened to a sacrificial libation. And although this formulaic statement is spoken while Jesus is holding a cup of wine and in the context in which his death is understood as a "drinking of his cup," the libation verbal adjective is attached to "blood"' and not to the cup which Jesus is holding. By adding "for the forgiveness of sins," Matthew makes clear the redemptive effect of Jesus' shed blood, underscoring in his death the meaning of the angel's announcement of his birth name—"you shall call his name Jesus, for he will save his people from their sins" (1:21). In Matthew's community, Jesus' death was a sacrificial libation that effects the forgiveness of sins.[33]

There is nothing in Mark or Matthew indicating that a libation has been poured from the cup. In Mark the ritual word concerning the blood (14:24) is bracketed by all the disciples drinking from the cup (14:23) and Jesus' statement that he would not drink again of "the fruit of the vine until that day . . . in the kingdom of God" (14:25). Although a link between "blood being poured out" and a cup from which one drinks could be implied, the "τουτο ἐστιν" is ambiguous and implies a range of possibility; it could refer to cup, blood, or the drinking from the cup which preceded the ritual word.

Matthew Klinghardt sees in the Matthaean narration a description of a *proposis*—the ritual act after a libation but before mixing of wine in the first bowl, in preparation for a symposium. In a *proposis* each participant takes a

---

32. On this point, see Hal Taussig, *In the Beginning Was the Meal* (Minneapolis: Fortress Press, 2009), 50–51.
33. Daniel C. Ullucci (*The Christian Rejection of Animal Sacrifice* [Oxford: Oxford University Press, Inc., 2012], 72–79, 90–95, 97) argues that St. Paul and the canonical Gospels have "no sacrificial interpretation of Jesus' death" (94). For Ullucci, only Hebrews understand Jesus' death as a sacrifice that forgives sin. A critique of Ullucci's view of St. Paul would take us too far a field, but Matthew's depiction of the last supper clearly expresses the belief in Jesus' death as a sacrificial libation which effects the forgiveness of sins.

small sip from unmixed wine; and if the *proposis* has a toast, it is for each participant a wish for "well-being, luck, and health."[34]

In Matthew, all participants drink from the same cup. Klinghardt notes the connection of *Matt.* 26:28 with *Exod.* 24:8 where sacrificial blood is sprinkled on the people as a ritual expressing their membership in the Mosaic covenant. In Matthew, the disciples are constituted as a covenantal community by drinking from a common cup—a ritual signifying the unity and equality of members.[35]

I agree with Klinghardt that the "τοῦτο ἐστιν" of 26:28 refers neither to the cup nor what the cup contains but rather to the drinking of all members from a common cup. The custom of *proposis* supports this interpretation; however, I disagree with his claim that the imminent death of Jesus is not implied in 26:28. The image of wine being poured in a libation as a symbol of death is in St. Paul and the martyrs of Revelation. It seems highly probable that the image of libation in 26:28 implies Jesus' imminent death.

In the longer version of Luke the ambiguity of the "τοῦτο ἐστιν" is clarified: the libation character of Jesus' death is explicitly tied to the eucharistic cup.[36] It is not the blood that is being poured out but rather the cup that is being poured out: "This cup is the new covenant in my blood—the cup being poured out as a sacrificial libation in behalf of you" (22:20).[37] The pouring of wine from a cup (a libation) is the image for the shedding of Jesus' blood in

---

34. Matthias Klinghardt, "Bund und Sündenvergebung: Ritual und literarischer Kontext," *Mahl und religiöse Identitat im fruhen Christentum*, eds. Matthias Klinghardt and Hal Taussig (Tübingen: Francke, 2012), 159–80 at 167–71.

35. *Ibid.*, 171–79.

36. In Mark/Matthew the participle, τὸ ἐκχυννόμενον, modifies "the blood"; but to translate it as "being shed" is to disregard the context, that is, the association with a cup of wine and the fact that in Hellenistic Judaism, the wine libation of the Tamid Temple service was called "the blood of the grape." It is highly probable that Jesus' imminent death is being expressed as a sacrificial libation which has redemptive power. The longer version of Luke reinforces this libation connotation of τὸ ἐκχυννόμενον by attaching it to "the cup." It makes clear that Jesus' death is likened to the pouring out of wine in a sacrificial libation. As in Revelation, the verb ἐκχεῖν is a libation verb. Given the fact that the canonical gospels were written after the destruction of the temple and that the crucified and exalted Jesus was worshipped as "the Lamb of God" (cf. John 1:29, 36; Rev. 5:6–14), it appears that the institution narratives teach that Jesus is the eschatological fulfillment of the Tamid and the Passover festival. He is the slaughtered lamb whose bones were not broken and whose blood was shed as a libation on the altar of the temple, his body (cf. John 2:19–21; 19:32–36).

37. All Greek manuscripts (except D, codex Bezae) witness to the long version. If it is a scribal addition, its date is uncertain and depends on the paleographic dating of Papyrus Bodmer XIV-XV (Papyrus 75). See B. Nongbri ("Reconsidering the Place of Papyrus Bodmer XIV-XV [Papyrus 75] in Textual Criticism of the New Testament," *JBL* 135.2 [2016], 405–37) who questions the traditional date of P 75 (175–225 CE) and argues that the early fourth century is "equally likely, if not more likely" (437).

his violent death. Jesus' death is a sacrificial libation, and the ritual of libation is explicitly connected to the eucharist/agape cup.[38]

"This cup is the new covenant in my blood . . ." appears to be an allusion to the "new covenant" of *Jeremiah* 31 [38 LXX]:31–34. Jesus' death as a sacrificial libation will seal a covenant of peace between himself and his disciples. The pouring of wine from the cup not only seals this covenant of peace; the libation also signifies how this covenant will be established—through the pouring out of Jesus' blood in his sacrificial death.

It is certain that among ancient Greeks, a wine libation not only was a component in the cultic ritual that seals a peace agreement between two parties; it also could signify some aspect of the terms of the agreement. For example, in the *Iliad*, the peace treaty between the Trojans and Achaeans is sealed by oaths, the blood of a sacrificial lamb and wine libations (σπονδαί) poured (ἐκχέω) on the ground—ritual acts offered to "Zeus, the highest, and to other immortal Deities (ἀθάνατοι Θεοὶ ἄλλοι)." The terms of the agreement were clear. Whoever broke the truce, "may his brain flow on the ground in the same way as the wine (ὧδέ σφ' ἐγκέφαλος χαμάδις ῥέοι ὡς ὅδε οἶνος)." [39]

The word ἐγκέφαλος is usually translated as "brain," but one should not give a clinical scientific sense to what it means in Homer. It refers to the inside of the head, the part above the mouth. In warfare, a spear thrust that penetrates the part of the head near the brain results in blood flowing out from the head. For example, when Idomeneus (an Achaean) thrust his spear through the mouth of Erymas (a Trojan), the spear went "under the brain" (νέρθεν ὑπ' ἐγκεφάλοιο) and "both eyes were full of blood" (ἐνέπληθεν δέ οἱ ἄμφω αἵματος ὀφθαλμοί). "Gaping in shock (χανών), Erymas spewed (πρῆσε) forth blood through his nose and mouth; and the dark cloud of death enshrouded him (θανάτου δὲ μέλαν νέφος ἀμφεκάλυψεν)."[40] In a later battle scene, when Aias (an Achaean) thrust his spear through the helmet of Hippothous (a Trojan): "[his] blood soaked brain burst forth from the wound, along the socket of the spearhead (ἐγκέφαλος δὲ παρ' αὐλὸν ἀνέδραμεν ἐξ

---

38. I am indebted to Matthias Klinghardt ("Vergossene Becher," 40–46) for his understanding of the libation character of the cup-word. I agree with him that "the new covenant" is an allusion to Jeremiah 31 (38 LXX):31–34 and that the libation sealed a covenant of peace. I differ in thinking that the libation offering expresses the sacrificial character of Jesus' death (50–54). Klinghardt argues (54–58) that this feature does not appear until the early third century when the focus becomes the sacramental presence of Jesus' body and blood offered as an expiatory sacrifice.

39. *Iliad* 3.296–300; cf. 4.155–62. For the Greek text, I am using the Loeb Classical Library critical edition. The translations are mine.

40. *Ibid.*, 16.345–50.

ὠτειλῆς αἱματόεις); and immediately, his life force was destroyed" (τοῦ δ' αὖθι λύθη μένος) . . . he died and fell forward onto the corpse of Patroclus.[41]

A spear thrust to the mouth, just below the brain, results in blood filling the eyes and gushing forth through the nose and mouth; a spear wound in the head can be the source of a blood soaked brain spewing forth and immediate death. Almost certainly, the brain that is spilled on the ground as a result of the truce being broken is a brain soaked in blood. The wine libation that sealed the truce signified the bloody death which would befall anyone who broke the truce.[42]

The contrast between what the wine libation symbolizes in the Homeric covenant of peace and the Judeo-Christian covenant of peace is striking. In Homer, the wine libation signifies what will happen to anyone who violates the peace agreement, namely, the mortal shedding of his blood. In the Judeo-Christian covenant of peace, the wine libation signifies the mortal shedding of Jesus' blood in a sacrificial death in behalf of others. That sacrificial libation of blood bestows divine forgiveness, peace, and immortality.

Scholars, who accept *Luke* 22:19b–20 as original, understand the two libation cups as emphasizing the future and past dimensions of the eucharist—a forward looking towards a future kingdom (vv. 16, 18) and a present remembrance of Jesus' expiatory death (v. 20).[43] But this view is problematic because a sacrificial libation implies an altar on which the libation is poured; and in pre–70 CE Judaism, sacrificial libations were offered only at the temple.

Perhaps Luke is anachronistic in projecting into the narrative a practice of the late first century in which a libation was poured into a dish on an altar-table where the food had been placed. On the other hand, if 22:19b–20 is a scribal addition and papyrus 75 is the earliest witness to it, then *Luke* 22:19b–20 reflects a practice of the late second century or perhaps even later.

However, although papyrus 75 is the earliest Greek manuscript containing *Luke* 22:19b–20, Joachim Jeremias has argued convincingly that Justin Martyr (at Rome, ca. 150 CE) knew *Luke* 22:19b–20. Jeremias observed that Justin's eucharistic practice (1 *Apol.* 66.3) agrees with the long version's single dominical command to repeat the rite, and the command comes after the ritual word about the bread. Mark and Matthew have no such command; and in Paul, there are two commands (after the bread ritual and after the cup ritual). Moreover, the word order (καὶ τὸ ποτήριον ὁμοίως) of Justin's gospel version is the same word order as *Luke* 22:20. Hence, the evidence of

---

41. *Ibid.*, 17.295–303.
42. Thanks to Jan Heilmann for encouraging me to ponder the symbolic meaning of wine poured on the ground in association with a soldier's brain flowing onto the ground.
43. See François Bovon, *Luke 3: A Commentary on the Gospel of Luke 19:28–24:53*, ET James Crouch (Minneapolis: Fortress Press, 2012), 152–59.

Justin Martyr is conclusive: the tradition of *Luke* 22:19b–20 existed at Rome, ca. 150 CE.[44]

In addition, Jeremias observed that Tertullian used *Luke* 22:20 in order to refute Marcion's understanding of Christianity.[45] Hence, it appears that *Luke* 22:20 was known in both the catholic Carthaginian and Marcionite versions of Luke. Since Marcion was expelled by the Roman presbyters in 144 CE, his edited Lukan-Pauline Epistles canon and Antitheses had to be completed before then. Almost certainly, *Luke* 22:20 was known by Marcion and Roman Christians by at least 140 CE. In addition, since the earliest literary evidence for Luke/Acts is in *1 Clement*, whose provenance is late first century at Rome,[46] it seems quite probable that Roman Christians used the longer version of Luke by the late first century.

In summary, in the Synoptic Gospel narratives of the last supper, "sacrificial libation" plays a significant role in understanding Jesus' death and the ritual through which that death was remembered. The pouring out of wine in a libation is the analog for Jesus' sacrificial death (the shedding/pouring out of his blood). The wine in the cup is a symbol for the blood of Jesus.

Sacrificial libation was practiced in pagan Greco-Roman society and in the Jewish ritual of libation in the twice daily Tamid Temple Service in pre–70 CE Judaism.[47] It seems quite probable that whenever the last supper narratives of Mark/Matthew were read in a Christian assembly or in a class for catechumens, a Greek-speaking Jewish or Gentile Christian or catechumen would have understood that Jesus' death was a sacrificial libation and that the eucharist/agape cup was associated with that libation.

Luke 22:20 makes this word-picture sharper by attaching the libation verb to the cup. The ritual act of pouring wine from a cup was a way of conveying and remembering that Jesus' death was an act of sacrificial agape which established a covenant with his disciples—a covenant that effected divine forgiveness, peace, and immortality. Sacrificial libation, as a way of expressing

---

44. See Joachim Jeremias, *The Eucharistic Words of Jesus*, ET Norman Perrin (New York: Charles Scribner's Sons, 1966), 139 n. 5.

45. *Ibid.*, 139 n. 4. The reference is *adv. Marc.* 4.40.4 (CCSL). In arguing against the docetic view of Marcionites, Tertullian says: "And thus, in mentioning the cup while establishing a covenant sealed with his blood, he [Jesus] confirmed the reality of the body" (*Sic et in calicis mentione testamentum constituens sanguine suo obsignatum substantiam corporis confirmavit*). Only Luke 22:20 and St. Paul (1 Cor. 11:25) place "cup" in the ritual word. Both say—"This cup is the new covenant in my blood." But Luke adds the phrase "[the cup] poured out as a sacrificial libation for you." Hence, Tertullian's "a covenant sealed with his blood" is his understanding of "a cup being poured out as a sacrificial libation."

46. See the appendix, "The Dating of Ignatius," n. 45.

47. In Hellenistic Judaism, the wine libation of the Tamid service was called "the blood of the grape" (Sirach 50:15).

the redemptive power of Jesus' sacrificial death, appears to be essential in the eucharist/agape.[48]

However, when Paul states the tradition of the last supper, he does not use a libation verb (cf. *1 Cor.* 11:23–25); but he is writing fifteen years before the destruction of the temple, and the Synoptic Gospels were written sometime after the temple's destruction. It seems not implausible that with the destruction of the temple and its altar in 70 CE, the Pauline-Johannine community of Ephesus and/or the Petrine community of Antioch developed a eucharist/agape meal in which "breaking one loaf" and the pouring of a libation into a dish on an altar-table were ritual gestures of the meal which expressed the fellowship and unity of the members with the crucified and exalted Messiah Jesus, whose exalted body was the temple of the Divine (cf. *John* 2:19–22; 19:34).[49]

When Ignatius expressed his desire to be poured out as a libation in the Roman Colosseum "while the altar is still prepared/ready (ὡς ἔτι θυσιαστήριον ἑτοίμον ἐστιν, *Rom.* 2.2) in order that you [Romans], by becoming a chorus of agape might sing to the Father in Messiah Jesus . . .," he was imagining a eucharist/agape at Rome and its response to his act of sacrificial love. A straight forward reading of *Rom.* 2.2 would lead one to conclude that Roman Christians employed an altar-table in worship. How probable is this conclusion?

4. THE PAGAN INDICTMENT OF CHRISTIANS: NO TEMPLES OR ALTARS

Origen in his work, *Against Celsus*, written ca. 248 CE, cites Celsus' claim (made ca. 175 CE) that because Christians have no "temples, images, or

---

48. The long version of Luke reflects the influence of Paul's account of the Lord's Supper but with one difference: both Paul and Luke describe the cup as being "the new covenant in my blood," but Luke adds—"that is, the cup poured out as a libation in behalf of you." The similarity of Luke and Paul shows that Luke knew the Pauline account and assumes that it described a historical event. Luke's cup/libation addition looks like a clarification of Mark's account. I accept the consensus of liturgical scholarship that there is insufficient evidence to assert that the so-called "words of institution" in the Synoptic accounts of the last supper were used in the rite of the eucharist/agape in the first or second centuries of early Christianity. My focus is not on the words but rather the ritual act of pouring a libation in the eucharist/agape meal.

49. Christian Jews continued to worship at the Jerusalem temple, presumably until Roman Legions invaded Israel in 66 CE (cf. Luke 24:52–53; Acts 2:44–47; 3:1; 21:26; 24:11–18; 25:8). When Christian Jews dispersed, almost certainly—some would have migrated to Antioch. The beloved disciple, John, ended up in western Asia Minor where he died in the late first century, probably at Ephesus. The destruction of the temple and altar was a crisis for both Jews and Jewish Christians. It should not be surprising to discover that at Antioch and Ephesus, Christians were using an altar-table in the late first century. That feature could be explained as a response to the crisis evoked by the temple's destruction in 70 CE.

altars," the Christian movement must be an "obscure and secret society." Origen responds by quoting *Rev.* 5:8 and *Ps.* (LXX) 140:2, maintaining that a Christian lives a life of virtue and that his/her "prayers" issuing forth "from pure conscience" are "the incense of sweet savour" that rise to God from the "altar" which "is the mind of a righteous person."[50]

Why does Origen respond with the figurative sense of "altar" without indicating that Christians used altars? For it is certain that at Carthage, ca. 200 CE, altar-tables were used when a eucharist was conducted. In regard to whether a Christian should break a fast by partaking of a eucharist, Tertullian advised receiving the bread, taking it home, and eating it after the fast day had ended (mid-afternoon). Fasting could be even more solemn if one "stands before the altar of God (*stare aram Dei*)" [where the eucharist is conducted].[51] Cyprian, bishop of Carthage (248–258 CE), chose to use the word *altare* for the table on which the eucharistic food was placed and where a holy sacrifice was offered.[52]

The evidence of Tertullian and Cyprian shows that Christians used altar-tables. The absence of Origen's acknowledgment probably reflects his fear that such an admission would imply the worship of Christ as Divine, and this would leave Christianity vulnerable to the charge of neither worshipping Roman Deities nor offering sacrifices for/to the emperor.

When Minucius Felix—a Carthaginian Christian apologist of the early third century—responded to the pagan critique that Christians had no temples or altars, his answer addressed the Christian refusal to propitiate Roman Deities with animal sacrifice. His defense was that Christian sacrifice is the offering of prayer and living a just life.[53]

In both Celsus and the opponents of Minucius Felix, the indictment concerning no temples and no altars appears to be that the Christian cult did not offer propitiating animal sacrifices to the Roman Deities. Neither exchange is pertinent to whether Christians used an altar-table in a eucharist/agape meal—a meal held in house-churches or at cemeteries and available only to those who had undergone baptism.

Tertullian appears to take for granted the use of an altar-table. Had this been an innovation of his generation, one would expect him to comment either

---

50. C. *Cels.* 8.17. I am paraphrasing the translation of Henry Chadwick, *Origen: Contra Celsum* (Cambridge, UK: Univ. Press, 1965), 464.

51. *Orat.* 19.1–4 (*CCSL* 1.267–68). See Nathan Mitchell, *Cult and Controversy* (New York: Pueblo Publishing Co., 1982), 14–15; J. Patout Burns Jr. and Robin Jensen (*Christianity in Roman Africa* [Grand Rapids, MI: Wm. B. Eerdmans Publishing Co., 2014], 234–35, 238 n. 41) observe that Tertullian used *ara* for the Christian altar; and *ara* was the word which denoted "the traditional Roman altars of sacrifice."

52. *Ibid.*, 254–55. For the association of Christ's sacrifice with the eucharistic offering in Cyprian's thought, see Paul F. Bradshaw and Maxwell E. Johnson, *The Eucharistic Liturgies: Their Evolution and Development* (Collegeville, MN: Liturgical Press, 2012), 57–59.

53. *Oct.* 32.1–5 (*CSEL* 2.45–46).

positively or negatively since there seems to be little about Carthaginian church practice that escapes his attention. Hence, it seems not implausible that an altar-table predates Tertullian by at least a generation, ca. 175–180 CE.

5. THE CASE FOR AN ALTAR-TABLE IN THE EUCHARIST/AGAPE OF IGNATIUS

Irenaeus, writing at Lugdunum (Gaul), ca. 180 CE, says that Christians direct their prayers and sacrificial offerings to the altar (θυσιαστήριον) of the heavenly temple (ναός). [54] However, St. Paul referred to the church as "the temple of the Divine" (*1 Cor.* 3:16); and Ignatius spoke an oracle of the Spirit at Philadelphia, encouraging those Christians to "keep your (plural) flesh as the temple of the Divine" (7.2). Hence, Irenaeus' "heavenly temple" does not mean that "temple" had no earthly representation in apostolic Christianity. Could the same be true of "altar"?

Ignatius thought of the church as a type of a higher reality. Things or objects in the church were a "counterpart/image" (τύπος) of the heavenly world. For him, the bishop is a "counterpart/image" of the Father, the deacons are a "counterpart/ image" of Jesus Christ, and the presbytery is a "counterpart/image" of the apostles (*Trall.* 3.1). The divine world is reflected in the earthly church. [55]

In visualizing the heavenly world, Ignatius believed that the exalted Messiah was "the high priest to whom has been entrusted the Holy of Holies" (*Phd.* 9.1); and Ignatius urged Christians "to run with each other (συντρέχω; cf. *1 Cor.* 9:24) towards one temple (ἕνα ναόν), one altar (ἓν θυσιαστήριον), one Jesus Christ . . ." (*Mag.* 7.2). Since Ignatius believed that the church was an image (τύπος) of the heavenly church, did he also employ in his worship at Antioch an altar as an image (τύπος) of the heavenly altar? From his letters to Roman and Philadelphian Christians, one can make a case for Ignatius' use of an altar-table at Antioch.

Ignatius desires "to be poured out as a sacrificial libation to the Divine while the altar is still prepared/ready (ὡς ἔτι θυσιαστήριον ἕτοιμόν ἐστιν) in

---

54. *Adv. haer.* 4.18.6. I am indebted to Maxwell Johnson for pointing me to this passage.

55. For "counterpart," see Henry Chadwick, "The Silence of Bishops in Ignatius," *HTR* 43 (1950) 169–72. By an analysis of Hellenistic epigraphy, Allen Brent (*Ignatius of Antioch and the Second Sophistic*. Studien und Christentum 36 [Tübingen: Mohr Siebeck, 2006], 66–85) argues convincingly for a translation of τύπος as "image." Brent sees the threefold clerical order (bishop, presbytery, and deacon) as an Ignatian iconography of Father, Spirit, and Son; Ignatius believed that by having union with this clerical order "in the drama of a eucharist," a Christian has union with the Divine and with immortality. The key text for Brent's view is *Mag* 6.2: "Be united to the bishop and the ones presiding as an image (τύπος) and teaching of immortality."

order that you [Roman Christians], becoming a choir of love might sing to the Father in Messiah Jesus . . ." (2.2). A plausible explanation for Ignatius linking his libation to the altar of Roman Christians [56] is the assumption that if his death occurs "while the altar is still ready/prepared" it could coincide with the moment in which Roman Christians are enacting their eucharist/ agape with a sacrificial libation.

The same pattern of linking his libation to a eucharist/agape can be seen in his letter to Philadelphian Christians:

> Be careful therefore to employ one eucharist (for there is one flesh of our Lord Jesus Messiah and one cup for unity of his blood, one altar, as there is one bishop together with the presbytery and the deacons, my fellow servants) in order that whatever you do, you may do according to the Divine. My brethren, I am overflowing with agape for you—like a sacrificial libation (Ἀδελφοί μου, λίαν ἐκκέχυμαι ἀγαπῶν ὑμᾶς) and exceedingly happy in safeguarding you (καὶ ὑπεραγαλλόμενος ἀσφαλίζομαι ὑμᾶς). (4.1–5.1)

His anticipated death as a sacrificial libation of agape expresses his passion for the unity of agape given in "one eucharist . . . one flesh of our Lord Jesus Messiah . . . one cup for the unity of his blood, one altar, as there is one bishop . . . with presbytery and deacons." Sacrificial libation and a eucharist/ agape appear to be inseparable aspects of an organic reality.

In this passage, the sequence of "one eucharist . . . one flesh . . . one cup . . . one altar as there is one bishop . . . with presbytery and deacons . . ." suggests that the figurative connotation of "one altar" is "one bishop, presbytery, and deacons." [57] Nevertheless, a figurative sense of "altar" does not necessarily exclude a literal "altar" (just as the figurative sense of "one cup for the unity of his blood" does not exclude the use of a cup in a eucharist/agape).

Likewise, when Ignatius encourages unity at Ephesus, "bread" connotes an assembly loyal to the clergy. Ignatius urges the Ephesians to gather together "in one faith and in Jesus Christ . . . in order that you may be obedient to the bishop and the presbytery with undistracted understanding, breaking one loaf

---

56. Robert M. Grant (*Ignatius,* 87), and Schoedel (*Ignatius,* 171), see here an allusion to the pagan altar in the Roman Colosseum on which a libation would be offered prior to spectacle/games. But why would Ignatius draw the attention of Roman Christians to a pagan altar? Christian apologists of the second century were unanimous in condemning the sadistic cruelty of Roman spectacles in the Colosseum as demonic and idolatrous. (See Elizabeth A. Castelli, *Martyrdom and Memory: Early Christian Culture Making* (New York: Columbia Univ. Press, 2004), 112–19.) Had Ignatius been referring to the pagan altar in the Coliseum, he would have used the word βωμός (a pagan altar); but he uses θυσιαστήριον (a Jewish or Christian altar). Clearly, the reference—"while the altar is still prepared"—is to a Christian altar-table employed in Roman worship.

57. Cf. *Trall* 7.2: "The one within the sphere of the altar is pure (ὁ ἐντὸς θυσιαστηρίου ὢν καθαρός ἐστιν); but the one being outside of the altar (ἐκτὸς θυσιαστηρίου) is not pure, that is, whoever does anything apart from/without the bishop, presbytery, and deacons is not pure in conscience."

which is the medicine of immortality" (ἕνα ἄρτον κλῶντες, ὅ ἐστιν φάρμακον ἀθανασίας).⁵⁸ For Ignatius, being one with the clergy is "an image (τύπος) and teaching of immortality" (διδαχὴ ἀφθαρσίας, *Mag.* 6.2). The thought of *Eph.* 20.2 is similar, and there it is tied to "breaking one loaf."⁵⁹

The unity of a eucharist/agape assembly sings forth the divine goal in Jesus Messiah: that "all things in unity may be symphonic" (σύμφωνα, *Eph.* 5.1). The agape of Christ's sacrifice creates an assembly (ἐκκλησία) in whose harmony (ὁμονοία) his "symphonic agape" (συμφώνη ἀγάπη) is heard and the beautiful sound [μέλος] of Jesus Christ is sung to the Father by the members (μέλη) of his assembly (4.1–2).⁶⁰

To be in unity with "the bishop and the entire assembly" (ὁ ἐπίσκοπος καὶ πᾶσα ἡ ἐκκλησία) is to have "the bread of God" and to be "within the sphere of the altar" (ἐντὸς τοῦ θυσιαστηρίου, 5.2). Here, both "bread of God" and "altar" are used figuratively, not literally. Nevertheless, using "altar" figuratively does not necessarily imply that there is no concrete physical altar-table employed by Ephesian Christians. Indeed, the context suggests that here the figurative use of "altar" presupposes a literal altar-table since it is in parallel with the figurative sense of "bread of God" and Ephesian Christians surely used real bread in their eucharist/agape meal. Presumably, both bread (along with other food) and cup would have been placed on an altar-table.

The most important conclusion of this section is the association of sacrificial libation with eucharist/agape assembly, bread, cup, altar, and martyrdom. In the Romans' passage, martyrdom as a sacrificial libation is explicitly tied to "the altar still prepared/ready" and the anticipated response of Roman Christians—worshipping and singing as a "choir of agape to the Father in Messiah Jesus." Likewise, in the Philadelphian passage, Ignatius'

---

58. I follow J.B. Lightfoot (*The Apostolic Fathers*, Pt. 2: S Ignatius, S Polycarp [London: Macmillan, 1889], 87) and Schoedel (*Ignatius*, 98–99) in thinking that the ὅ ἐστιν of the long recension (rather than ὅς ἐστιν of the middle recension) is the more likely reading.

59. At Antioch, "breaking one loaf" was probably a ritual term designating the entire eucharist/agape meal. The ritual act of breaking one loaf into fragments would have signified the participation of the gathered assembly in the unity of the one body of the crucified and risen Messiah Jesus. Compare 1 Cor. 10:16–17 and Gerard Rouwhorst, "The Roots of Early Christian Eucharist: Jewish Blessings or Hellenistic Symposia?" *Jewish and Christian Liturgy and Worship: New Insights into its History and Interaction*, eds. Albert Gerhards and Clemens Leonard (Leiden, 2007), 295–308 at 306 and Stephen R. Shaver, "A Eucharistic Origins Story Part 1: The Breaking of the Loaf," *Worship*, 92 (May, 2018) 204–21 at 211–14. My thesis is that there was also a ritual act of libation, the pouring of wine from a cup into a dish on the altar-table—signifying the divine agape of the Son made known in his death (cf. 1 Cor. 10:16).

60. I agree with Brent (*Ignatius*, 85–91) that immortality is dependent upon being in unity with the threefold clerical order. But this is not the whole picture. I view the eucharist as an agape meal. Brent (29) sees eucharist and agape meal as separate, independent events. In my view, the "breaking of one loaf" is fellowship in the assembly in which through meal, choral song, prayer, ecstatic prophecy, healing and preaching, the risen-crucified Messiah is made known in the harmony of all members (μέλη). Ultimately, "the medicine of immortality" is the unity of "imperishable agape" (*Rom.* 7.3) among all the members (μέλη).

"overflowing in agape—like a sacrificial libation for you" is a way of preserving/safeguarding the unity of their assembly. This is expressed through the figurative/ecclesial/corporate sense of "one cup" and "one altar."

Although one finds no liturgical text in Ignatius' description of the event of the eucharist/agape meal fellowship, a liturgical act of a sacrificial libation poured into a dish on an altar-table would be an appropriate expression of *Luke* 22:20: "This cup is the new covenant in my blood—the cup being poured out as a sacrificial libation in behalf of you" (and that text was known at Rome). In fact, such a liturgical act could express both the meaning of Jesus' sacrificial death and the meaning of Ignatius' death.[61] In the Roman Colosseum, Ignatius' sacrificial act of libation will be a proclamation of the "the Divine Word" (λόγος θεοῦ, *Rom* 2.1) to the spectators.[62]

6. A SACRIFICIAL LIBATION "WHILE THE ALTAR IS STILL PREPARED/READY"

Ignatius' hope to be a sacrificial libation—while the altar-table of Roman Christians was "still ready/prepared"—appears to be a request to the Roman church. They are to synchronize a eucharist/agape with Ignatius' death. Ignatius is in some sense "staging"[63] his own death. His self-identification as the "the bishop of Syria . . . summoned (μεταπέμπω) [by God] from the East

---

61. Ullucci (*Christian Rejection*, 99) acknowledges that Ignatius understands his martyrdom as a sacrificial libation; but for Ullucci, its connection to the death of Jesus is "undeveloped." I disagree. The connection between Ignatius' sacrificial death and that of Jesus is well developed in Ignatius' letters. Jesus Messiah "suffered for our sins" and martyrdom is "suffering with him" (συμπάσχω αὐτῷ, *Smyr.* 4.2; 7.1). The association of Ignatius' death with Jesus' death is conveyed through the image of suffering. Ignatius is prepared for burning to death, crucifixion, being chewed to death by wild animals, or tortured to death by knife slashings, mangling of the limbs of the body or crushing of the bones (*Rom.* 5.3). A further association with Jesus' "passion" (πάθος, *Rom.* 6.3) is conveyed through the language of sacrifice as applied to both Ignatius' body and blood. He hopes that his body will be ground by the teeth of wild animals and they will make him a cereal-bread offering "sacrifice" (θυσία) since he hopes to attain "pure bread" (4.1–2). And in his bloody death, he will pour out himself as a "sacrificial libation" of "imperishable agape" (*Rom.* 2.2; 7.3; *Phd.* 5.1).

62. According to Virginia Corwin (*St. Ignatius and Christianity at Antioch* [New Haven: Yale Univ. Press, 1960], 126), Ignatius identifies himself with Jesus as the Divine Word. In *Mag* 8.2, "there is one God who revealed himself through Jesus Messiah, his Son, who is his Word (λόγος) who came forth from silence" (ἀπὸ σιγῆς). In *Rom* 2.1, if the Roman Christians remain silent (σιωπάω), that is, do not seek to attain a pardon for Ignatius, then Ignatius will be "the Divine Word" in the arena. In both passages, "the Divine Word" comes forth from silence and reveals the one true God.

63. This is Schoedel's judgment (*Ignatius*, 12) who elaborates (213) on the various aspects of Ignatius' "staging." I agree with Robin Darling-Young (*In Procession before the World: Martyrdom as Public Liturgy in Early Christianity* [Marquette, WI: Marquette Univ. Press, 2001], 1–64) that from the time of Ignatius to Origen, Christians "trained for martyrdom as a public ritual" (30). "Persecution was expected . . . and martyrs had trained for it" (36). The sacrificial death of the martyr was associated with the eucharistic sacrifice (33). Young notes that Ignatius imagined himself as becoming a eucharistic bread sacrifice through the teeth of the wild beasts, but she does not discuss the eucharist/agape image of sacrificial libation (15–18).

[where the sun rises] in order to be found in the West [where the sun sets]. Beautiful may my sunset be: in death, to set my face towards the Divine in order that I might rise to Him" (*Rom.* 2.2)—has a kind of mythic/cosmic quality. He desires to die in the Roman Colosseum because his God has "summoned" him [from the East] to be in his death "the Divine Word" to the spectators [in the West].

Why the request to synchronize Ignatius' death with a Roman eucharist/agape? If a martyr's death is a sacrificial libation in imitation of Jesus' death and if the eucharist is an agape meal which contains the ritual act of pouring a sacrificial libation into a dish on an altar-table, then it follows that a martyr's death is in some sense a re-enactment of the eucharist/agape. Ignatius hopes that his death, as a sacrificial libation, coincides with the time in the Roman worship service when a sacrificial libation is poured from the cup. This makes sense of the phrase—"while the altar is still prepared/ready."[64]

If the Christian altar was an altar-table employed in a eucharist/agape meal—on which food and drink were placed in "preparation" for the meal—then "while the altar is still prepared/ready" implies that some portion of the food and drink is still on the table—that portion which remains after the meal is over and which would later be distributed to shut-ins and other members who could not be present. In Greco-Roman society, sacrificial libation is the ritual act that connects the end of the food-meal to the time for the drinking (the symposium).[65] Hence, if Ignatius dies at that moment, his death corresponds with that eucharist/agape ritual act that represents the sacrificial death of Jesus Messiah. His death in the arena, as a re-enactment of Messiah's death, will be a eucharist/agape libation and a drinking of the cup: an offering of and a participation in "imperishable agape."

---

64. Recall that sacrificial libations were ritual prayers. Ignatius was offering his sacrificial libation in behalf of the safety of the Roman church, and Roman Christians were offering prayers for him as he faced the wild animals. The synchronization of sacrificial libations express "in time" the prayers of Ignatius and Roman Christians in union with each other. Ignatius' death will express his passion for unity with the church, the flesh of Jesus Messiah—that unity of "imperishable agape" which is "the medicine of immortality."

65. In the accounts of the last supper in St. Paul and Luke, the ritual cup-word is spoken "after the meal" (μετὰ τὸ δειπνῆσαι, 1 Cor. 11:25; Luke 22:20). In Mark/Matthew, it is during the meal. One other similarity is noteworthy. A wine libation was the last sacrificial act in the Tamid service. Just as the libation was being poured on the altar, the Levite choir sang forth with a psalm hymn (cf. Sirach 50.15–19; M. Tamid 7.3). Likewise, Ignatius hopes that when he pours his libation, Roman Christians will respond—singing in "a choir of agape to the Father in Messiah Jesus" (2.2). This similarity suggests that however the Jewish Christian understanding of Tamid was transformed by the consciousness of a crucified-exalted Messiah Jesus, the Tamid link between a wine libation and the choral response of thanksgiving had been retained in the eucharist/agape of post–70 CE Christian Judaism. Ignatius' desire to synchronize his libation with the choral response of thanksgiving in a Roman eucharist/agape assembly appears to presuppose that link.

7. CONCLUSION

Wine libations were a common feature of Greco-Roman culture and were offered in situations where wine was drunk—whether at a family meal, a gathering of members of a club/association, a festive celebration of a birth, a rite of initiation, or a marriage. They were also a component of animal sacrifice or a ritual for initiating civic events/games. They were done in a cremation ceremony, the commemoration of the dead in a cemetery, and in the making of peace treaties or the taking of an oath.

The invocation of a Deity with prayer and supplication is an essential component of a wine libation. A cup/bowl is filled with wine, and the supplicant pours some of the wine into a dish on the table where members are eating or on the hearth of a home or on the altar of the temple or club/association or on the ground while invoking/praying to the Deity.

In the ritual of animal sacrifice, a libation completes the sacrifice when wine is poured on the flame of the altar where the flesh of the animal is being burned. Thus, libation and sacrificial flesh on the altar are intimately linked in the religious imagination.

In Judaism, a wine libation was a significant feature of the Tamid temple service: the twice daily (at sunrise and sunset) congregational worship in which there was a whole burnt offering of a lamb and a grain offering together with the blood of the lamb and a wine libation poured on the altar. In Hellenistic Judaism, the wine libation was called "the blood of the grape" (*Sirach.* 50.15).

Among some Christians in apostolic Christianity, the sacrificial wine libation was a red thread in their fabric of understanding the death of Jesus, martyrdom as an imitation of his death, and the eucharist/agape which proclaimed the redemptive power of his death. The apostle Paul understood his imminent death as a libation that would be offered in behalf of the Philippian Christians who had given him aid in his imprisonment (*Phil.* 2:17). According to Acts, Paul's change of heart and mind, from being a persecutor of the church to his summons as an apostle, was produced by the redemptive power of Stephen's sacrificial libation of blood offered as a prayer of forgiveness for his enemies (cf. *Acts* 7:59–8.1; 22:20).

The prophet John understood the death of Jesus (the slaughtered/sacrificed lamb) in light of the Tamid service and the deaths of Antipas and his fellow martyrs as sacrificial libations (poured on the altar) that completed Jesus' sacrifice (*Rev.* 5:6; 6:9–10; 16:5–7; 17:4–6). The Apocalypse of John shows that Christian Jews did depict martyrdom as a libation poured on a heavenly altar (6:9–10). When the Jerusalem temple and altar were destroyed in 70 CE, martyr altar shrines probably evolved in the cemeteries of the seven churches of Revelation; and the practice of using an altar-table probably evolved in the house-churches of those communities.

In the Markan (14:24) and Matthaean (26:28) depiction of Jesus' last meal with his disciples, his death is viewed as a sacrificial libation which seals the covenant he established with them. In Matthew, Jesus' blood is poured out as a sacrificial libation for the forgiveness of sins. The path Jesus chooses, leading to his suffering and death is his "drinking of the cup" and the cup of wine from which he drinks in the last supper is a libation cup expressing "the new covenant in my blood, that is, the cup poured out as a sacrificial libation in behalf of you [his disciples]" (*Luke* 22:20). The pouring of wine from a libation cup is the analog for expressing the shedding of Jesus' blood in his death: the sacrificial wine libation symbolizes the offering of sacrificial love embodied in Jesus' shedding his blood in laying down his life for others.

The link between martyrdom as a sacrificial libation and the eucharist/agape is prominent in Ignatius of Antioch (ca. 125 CE). While in route to Rome (chained to other prisoners in the custody of ten Roman soldiers), Ignatius wrote to Roman Christians, expressing his desire to face the wild animals in the Colosseum, to be ground into "pure bread" as a "sacrifice" and "to pour out himself as a libation to the Divine while the [Roman] altar is still prepared in order that you [Roman Christians], as a choir of agape might sing to the Father in Messiah Jesus . . ." (2.2; 4.1–2).

The assumption seems to be that Ignatius hopes his own martyrdom as a sacrificial libation will coincide with the moment in which Roman Christians are enacting a sacrificial libation in their eucharist/agape. A similar link between martyrdom and eucharist/agape is evident in Ignatius' letter to the Philadelphians in which he encourages unity in their eucharist/agape assembly—"for there is one flesh of our Lord Jesus Messiah [cf. Pauline *Eph.* 5.31–32] and one cup for unity of his blood [cf. *1 Cor.* 10.16], one altar. . . . My brethren, I am overflowing with agape for you—like a sacrificial libation . . ." (4.1–5.1).

It seems quite probable that the cluster of "eucharist/agape assembly—cup—altar—sacrificial libation" are held together in Ignatius' imagination because at Antioch, the character of a eucharist/agape contained the ritual of pouring wine from a cup into a dish on an altar-table as a memorial of the redemptive, sacrificial death of Jesus Messiah. This conclusion makes sense of Ignatius' desire to be poured out as a libation in the Coliseum "while a [Roman Christian] altar is still prepared," and it is consistent with the Synoptic Gospels' depiction of the last supper where Jesus' death is imagined as a drinking of his cup and a sacrificial libation that seals his covenant with his disciples—a covenant that brings forgiveness of sins and peace.

I am not suggesting that pre-Nicene liturgy contained an institution narrative of the Synoptic Gospels or that the ritual of "eucharist/agape libation" was a universal practice. Liturgical practice was diverse: some churches used only bread; some churches used water rather than wine.[66]

Nevertheless, the ancient ritual of sacrificial libation[67] redirects our focus, and that focus is surely worth discussing by liturgical scholars, systematic theologians, and the priesthood of all believers. For example, was "eucharist/agape libation" a stopping place on the road towards the evolution of sacramental realism, that is, the belief that when one receives the bread and wine, one receives the body and blood of the crucified-risen Messiah? Could "eucharistic libation" be a fruitful paradigm today for those Protestant traditions which reject sacramental realism?

8. TRANSITION TO CHAPTERS 5 AND 6

I have presented my argument for the proposition that in Ignatius' eucharist/agape there was a libation. I would describe the probability of this being the case with the phrase—"quite probable." In historical studies, various phrases are used in stating probability—the flip of a coin, more likely than not, quite probable, very probable, almost certain, absolutely certain. In this progression, probability is increasing. Two of the phrases have exact numbers—"the flip of a coin" is .50 and "absolutely certain" is 1.00. The numbers assigned to the other phrases are not precise.

"More likely than not" (better than the flip of a coin) signifies a probability greater than .50 but less than "quite probable." If one says that by "quite probable" one means .60 or more, then "more likely than not" signifies .51–.59; if "very probable" means .70 or more, then "quite probable" signifies .60–.69; and if "almost certain" means .80 or more, then "very probable" signifies .70–.79. If absolutely certain means 1.0, then almost certain means .80–.99. Since the discipline of history is not a natural science, exact numbers have never been given to the phrases in our progression of probability (except for "flip of a coin" and "absolutely certain").

What I hope to accomplish in the next two chapters is to increase the probability for the truth of the proposition that at Antioch, there was a "eucharist/agape libation" during the episcopate of Ignatius. If the reader, at this point, thinks the probability is less than the flip of a coin (less than .50), hopefully the next two chapters will increase that probability to "flip of a coin" or "more likely than not"; if the reader thinks that the probability of a "eucharist/agape libation" is "more likely than not" (.51–.59), hopefully by the end of chapter

---

66. See Andrew McGowan, *Ascetic Eucharists* (New York: Oxford Univ. Press, 1999).
67. In the ancient world, the ritual of sacrificial libation is older than Homer.

6 they will think the probability of a "eucharist/agape libation" is "quite probable" (.60–.69) or "very probable" (.70–79).

One of the obstacles for the reader to overcome in understanding my thesis about a "eucharist/agape libation" is that in the English translations of the Synoptic Gospel accounts of the last supper, the verb ἐκχεῖν—(which appears in all three accounts) to describe either the blood of Jesus "poured out" (*Matt.* 26:28; *Mark* 14:24) or the "cup being poured out" (*Luke* 22:20)—is not translated in English translations as a "sacrificial libation." I have attempted to correct this by showing how important the image of sacrificial libation was in understanding the death of Jesus and the deaths of martyrs like Stephen, Paul, Antipas, and his companions, Ignatius and Polycarp.

What I will attempt to do in chapters 5 and 6 is to show that sacrificial libation was a ritual act that Christians performed in the cemetery at the grave site of their martyrs through the funerary custom of a *refrigerium*. In the ancient Greco-Roman world, in both the eastern and western parts of the Roman empire, the common funerary custom for pagans was that—four times a year, family and friends would gather at the tomb of a loved one for a meal of food and drink, for prayer and remembrance of the departed one. By pouring a libation of wine into the tomb, one hoped to make contact with the beloved through libation and prayer. Departed ones were believed to be nourished and "refreshed" by such libations. Hence, this funerary custom is referred to as a *refrigerium* (refreshment).

In chapter 6, I will argue that it is quite probable that Ignatius had incorporated the custom of *refrigerium* into the funerary practice of Christians at Antioch, and *refrigeria* were held at the tombs of martyrs. I also examine the *Martyrdom of Polycarp* and show the high probability that a *refrigerium* was held at Polycarp's tomb.

But before assuming those tasks in chapter 6, I prepare the ground in chapter 5 by showing that in the Gospel of John (the favorite gospel of Asia Minor Christians), Jesus' death is understood as a sacrificial libation of blood which bestowed the Divine Spirit on his disciples. The model for Polycarp's martyrdom is the Johannine portrait of Jesus' death as a sacrificial libation of blood. Hence, when Smyrnaean Christians gathered at Polycarp's tomb (*Mart. Poly.* 18.1–3) for a eucharist or *refrigerium*, the image of sacrificial libation played an important role in the imagination and practice of those Christians: they "worshipped the Son of God" whose death was a sacrificial libation of blood; they "loved" his disciple Polycarp who "imitated the Lord" in a martyrdom that was a sacrificial libation; and they almost certainly poured libations into the tomb of Polycarp in order to have fellowship with him. Compare 17.3 and 18.2–3.

By arguing the case for a *refrigerium* at Polycarp's tomb and Ignatius' funerary practice of a *refrigerium* at the tombs of martyrs at Antioch, I attempt to increase the probability of a eucharist/agape libation at Antioch by showing that the act of sacrificial libation is broader in scope than simply the eucharist/agape worship life at Antioch or Smyrna. And since Christians were known to assemble and worship in the cemetery, it seems quite probable that sacrificial libation was part of the lives of Anatolian and Syrian Christians in both their eucharist/agape worship life and in their remembrance of their departed loved ones in a *refrigerium*.

When a pagan converted to Christianity, they would have been initiated into a community in which sacrificial libation was part of its ritual meal remembrance of the Divine Son (whose sacrificial libation of agape brought redemption) and a remembrance of those martyrs and saints who followed him in living lives of sacrificial agape and in some cases, sealing that witness with their own blood. The offering of a wine libation in eucharist/agape worship and in a *refrigerium* were important components in expressing and strengthening the solidarity that Christians had with each other and with their Lord in both life and death.

Chapter 5

John 19:34—The Death of Jesus as a Sacrificial Libation and "Living Water"

In order to lay a foundation for my thesis that in the Fourth Gospel, the death of Jesus is understood as a sacrificial libation offered by a martyr, I need to remind the reader of what was argued in chapter 3—that the Gospel was written at a place (Ephesus) and time (90–110 CE) when Christians were experiencing persecution and martyrdom.[1]

1. THE DEATH OF JESUS AS A SACRIFICIAL LIBATION

In the Fourth Gospel, "living bread" and "living water" are images for Jesus as the fulfillment of the pilgrim festivals of Passover (ch. 6) and Tabernacles (chs. 7–9). Jesus, as "living bread" and "living water," is the eschatological fulfillment of the manna and water which God gave to the Israelites during their forty years in the wilderness.[2] "On the last day, the great day of the festival of Tabernacles (Ἐν δὲ τῇ ἐσχάτῃ ἡμέρᾳ τῇ μεγάλῃ τῆς ἑορτῆς)[3] Jesus stood up and shouted—'If anyone thirsts, let her/him come to me; and let the one believing in me drink, just as the scripture said—'rivers of

---

1. This chapter is a reworking of my essay, "'Living Water' and Sanguinary Witness: John 19:34 and Martyrs of the Second and Early Third Centuries," *JTS* 66.2 (Oct., 2015): 553–73.
2. The miracle of water springing from the rock in the wilderness was a prototype of the Tabernacle water ceremony. *T. Sukk.* 3:11–12; Exod. 17:1–7; Num. 20:8–13; Ps. 77:15–16 [LXX]; Gale A. Yee, *Jewish Feasts and the Gospel of John* (Wilmington: Michael Glazier, Inc., 1989), 75.
3. If Aileen Guilding (*The Fourth Gospel and Jewish Worship* [Oxford: Clarendon Press, 1960], 105) is correct in her suggestion that the lectionary reading for Tabernacles may have included Isa. 44:3 ([LXX]—"I will give water to quench the thirst of the ones walking in the desert; I will put my spirit upon your offspring . . ."), then the Johannine Jesus is claiming to be an eschatological fulfillment of Tabernacles.

living water shall flow out of his stomach'" (7:37–38).[4] The scripture quotation points to the passion narrative where the soldier with a spear stabs the side of the crucified Jesus, and "blood and water" come forth from his side. The evangelist adds—"And the one who saw this has testified (ὁ ἑωρακὼς μεμαρτύρηκεν) and true is his testimony (ἀληθινὴ αὐτοῦ ἐστιν ἡ μαρτυρία); and that one knows that he speaks truthfully in order that you also might believe" (19:34–35).

John 7:38 alludes to the eschatological hope of Tabernacles in Zechariah and Ezekiel—when "living water" shall flow from the temple, forming a river and giving life to fish, plants, and humans. In that day, "the Lord will be king over all the earth." (cf. *Ezek.* 47:1–12; *Zech.* 13:1; 14:8–9). Tabernacles was an eight-day festival in which on each of the first seven days a libation of water and a libation of wine were poured into respective bowls which sat on the altar. From the perforated libation bowls, the water and wine then flowed onto the altar.[5] The libation bowl of water signified the water God had given to the Israelites in the wilderness and the eschatological hope of the life-giving presence of God dwelling with Israel as King. The libation bowl of wine linked the Tabernacles' ceremony of water libation with the daily sacrifice of a lamb (in the Tamid service). Crucial for understanding John 19:34 in the light of 7:38 is the association of water and blood issuing from the side of Jesus (whose body is the temple of God; cf. 2:19–21) with the libation bowls of water and wine that flow onto the altar of the temple.[6]

John 19:36–37 sees Jesus' death as that of a servant figure (cf. *Zech.* 12:10 and *John* 19:37), a death understood to be the true Paschal sacrifice (cf. *John* 1:29; 19:36 and *Exod.* 12:46); the blood of the Passover lamb protected Israel from the angel of death (cf. *Exod.* 12:21–27). Furthermore, congregational worship in the temple throughout the year was the twice daily (at sunrise and sunset) sacrifice of a lamb as a whole burnt offering and a grain offering together with the lamb's blood and wine poured on the altar or at its base.[7] This represented the daily sacrificial offering up of Israel's life in worship to God (the Tamid service).

---

4. I follow Bultmann's punctuation of 7:38 in which "the one believing in me" is the subject of πινέτω. See Rudolf Bultmann (*The Gospel of John*, ET G.R. Beasley-Murray [Oxford: Basil Blackwell, 1971], 303, n. 2). Raymond E. Brown (*The Gospel According to John*, vol. 1 [Garden City: Doubleday & Co., Inc.: 1986], 319–25) accepts this view, based on the chiastic parallelism of one thirsting/coming and one believing/drinking. For an argument in support of the RSV translation, see Mary L. Coloe, *God Dwells with Us* (Collegeville, MN: Liturgical Press, 2001), 125–34.

5. *M.* Sukk. 4:1, 9. For the animals sacrificed and the libations offered on each day of Tabernacles, see Num. 29:12–38.

6. As a harvest festival, Tabernacles had rituals pertaining to prayers for rain (water) and sunlight (light). The claim of being "living water" (7:37–38) and "light of the world" (8:12) shows Jesus as the eschatological fulfillment of those prayers. *M.* Sukk. 4:9; 5:1–3.

7. *M.* Tamid 3:3; 4:1–3; 7:1–3; Exod. 29:38–42; Num. 28:1–8.

Significant for my argument is the fact that when the festival of Tabernacles was celebrated, its daily water ceremony was made part of the Tamid morning service. Each morning an assembly of priests, Levites, and worshippers went to the pool of Siloam (about one kilometer from the temple), collected some water and processed to the temple.[8] A priest approached the altar upon which there were two libation bowls. He poured the water into one of the bowls and poured wine into the other one. The libation of wine was part of the daily worship (Tamid); the libation of water was part of the Tabernacles' service.[9] Thus, on each morning of Tabernacles, the wine libation of Tamid was linked to Tabernacles. In other words, during the festival of Tabernacles, each morning of congregational worship at the temple consisted of the sacrifice of grain and burnt offering of a lamb, the sprinkling of its blood on the altar, and two libations—one of water (Tabernacles) and one of wine (Tamid)—flowing onto the altar. Given the ancient cultic association of wine with blood, the water ceremony of Tabernacles is clearly linked with the sacrificial burnt offering of a lamb and its blood sprinkled on the altar along with wine/blood flowing onto the altar. In the Tamid service, the wine libation was called "the blood of the grape" (*Sirach*. 50:15). [10]

Therefore, in the context of Tabernacles and Passover (two very important pilgrim festivals) and the daily worship life of Israel (Tamid), the water and blood issuing from Jesus' side express the Johannine gospel, that is, in Jesus' sacrificial death (blood issuing forth on the altar of the temple, since Jesus' body is the temple [cf. 2:19–21]), the power of death has been destroyed and the life of the Holy Spirit ("living water" on the altar) is present for anyone who believes in Jesus.[11]

Sacrificial symbols applied to Jesus' death are drawn also from the festival of Hanukkah (10:22–39), a festival clearly linked with Tabernacles. Jesus is the one "whom the Father consecrated (ἁγιάζειν) and sent into the world" to

---

8. The healing of the man born blind (9:1–41) demonstrates Jesus' claim to give light through a process involving his own saliva (water) and water from the pool of Siloam. He smeared the blind man's eyes with mud he had made by spitting on the ground. Then he commanded the man to wash his eyes with water from the pool of Siloam. Hence, the man received his sight by coming in contact with water from Jesus' mouth (saliva) and water from the pool of Siloam. This healing is a fitting conclusion to the Tabernacles section in John, expressing its theme of God giving life through water and light (the water/saliva of Jesus joined to the water of Siloam which gives light to the blind man).

9. *T. Sukk.* 3:16; Jeffrey L. Rubenstein, *The History of Sukkot in the Second Temple* (Atlanta: Scholars Press, 1995), 118–20; Håkan Ulfgard, *The Story of Sukkot* (Tübingen: Mohr Siebeck, 1998), 247–50.

10. An explicit link between Tabernacles and Jesus' death is also in John's narrative transition. Jesus leaves Galilee for his final trip to Jerusalem when he goes to the festival of Tabernacles. In Jerusalem he will manifest himself to "the world" while knowing that some Judeans want to kill him (cf. 7:1–13).

11. My exposition of 19:34–35 in light of 7:37–38 was stimulated by Craig Keener's (*The Gospel of John*, II [Peabody, MA: Hendrickson Publishers, 2003], 1154) suggestion that 19:34–35 may be linked with the fact that "the water libation for Tabernacles was poured out at the time of daily offering." The link between blood, water, and Spirit is also in 1 John 3:24; 4:13; 5:6–8.

do works in the name of God (10:36, 38). These works bear witness to the unity of God and Jesus and the unity of Jesus and his disciples: "I am the good shepherd. I know my own and my own know me as the Father knows me and I know the Father. And I lay down my life for the sheep" (10:14–15).

The Father has consecrated his Son for the mission of laying down his life for the other children of the Father.[12] None are to perish (10:27; cf. 17:12). In eight verses (10:11–18), the image of the shepherd sacrificing himself for the sheep appears five times.[13]

Probably in this Hanukkah section, Jesus is both "the eschatologically new altar"[14] where God dwells with Israel and the sacrifice that is offered in order to gather the children to the temple. The complete name for Hanukkah is "Inauguration of the Altar" which refers to the new altar constructed for the temple under Judas Maccabaeus 164/5 BCE.[15] That altar had to be consecrated before it could be used for sacrifice.

By attaching the analogy of shepherd/sheep to the reality of Jesus' death as a consecration of the altar,[16] the evangelist employs both images to illuminate the significance of the sacrifice. As the sacrificial lamb, Jesus' blood issuing from his side sanctifies the altar. The shepherd metaphor underscores the voluntary character of his sacrificial death and its power to gather Israel to the holy place; the lamb metaphor underscores its purifying, sanctifying power. He is the "lamb of God who takes away the sin of the world" (1:29).

The cleansing power of Jesus' death is expressed also in the account of Jesus washing the feet of his disciples. Foot-washing as a signifier of his death underscores his death as sacrificial, as an act of a servant. Just as he performs the act of a slave in a household by washing the feet of the guests prior

---

12. Cf. John 1:12. In the resurrection appearance to Mary Magdalene, Jesus says: "Go to my brothers and say to them 'I am ascending to my Father and your Father, to my God and your God'" (20:17).

13. Hanukkah is mentioned at 10:22. John 7:1–9:41 reflects Tabernacles. Both festivals employ symbolism of light; and originally, Hanukkah was likened to Tabernacles, based on Solomon's dedication of the temple during Tabernacles (cf. 2 Macc. 1:9, 18; 2:9–12; 2 Chron. 7:8–10). Guilding (*Fourth Gospel*, 129–32) argues that the lectionary readings for Hanukkah contained the theme of God as Shepherd, David as a king/shepherd, and the sanctification of Israel through the altar of the temple (cf. Ezek. 37:15–28). This, together with the fact that Hanukkah was likened to Tabernacles, explains why the good shepherd theme (10:1–18) is sandwiched between Tabernacles (7:1–9:41) and Hanukkah (10: 22–39). Hanukkah (2 Macc. 2:16–18) celebrates God's "purification" (καθαρισμός) of the temple, the gift of kingship, "the consecration" (ἁγιασμός) and the hope that God "will gather" (ἐπισυνάξει) Israel "to the holy place" (εἰς τὸν ἅγιον τόπον). All of these themes are in John.

14. The phrase is that of Bauckham (*The Testimony,* 264) who sees 10:36 as a consecration of Jesus "as the new altar of burnt offering."

15. 1 Macc. 4:56, 59. Bauckham (*Ibid.*, 257–62) argues convincingly that the meaning of ἐγκαινίζειν "to inaugurate" and the original title of the festival was "Inauguration of the Altar."

16. Jesus is "consecrated" by the Father. But Jesus (the altar) also "consecrates" (17:19) himself in his death. Recall that the altar and Aaronic priesthood of the tabernacle are consecrated by the blood of sacrificial animals (cf. Exod. 29:1–37). For John, Jesus is the Passover lamb (who died in the afternoon of Nisan 14 as Passover lambs were being sacrificed) whose blood, being poured out, consecrates the altar where God dwells with Israel. His death as a sacrificial libation (blood issuing forth) has a cleansing power.

to the meal, so likewise his death on the cross is a sacrificial act of humbling himself, dying the death of a condemned slave.[17] Moreover, Jesus' comment (in response to Peter's hesitation in being washed)—"unless I wash (νίπτειν) you, you have no share in me" (13:8) and his reference to the disciples being "clean" (καθαροί, 13:10) highlights that, figuratively, his death will wash/cleanse the disciples.[18]

The theme of washing and purification in 13:1–11 appears to complete a theme that began the narrative of the Galilean ministry. In the first sign that manifested Jesus' glory and created his disciples' belief, he changed water which was used for "Jewish purification rites" (κατὰ τὸν καθαρισμὸν τῶν Ἰουδαίων) into wine to be drunk at a wedding (2:1–11). If that narrative is programmatic, the evangelist must intend it to illuminate events, discourses, and/or metaphors which are connected to purification and/or wine.[19]

The miracle at the wedding, if connected to Jesus' death as a washing/purification of his disciples, signifies Jesus' death as an act of pouring out his blood as a means of purifying his disciples so they might share in his life. "The good wine" (ὁ καλὸς οἶνος) which is "the blood of the grape" (cf. the messianic prophecy of *Gen.* 49:11) comes last (the eschatological wine), and it brings purification which water signified in Jewish life (2:6–10).[20] Later on in the gospel (15:1–27), the metaphors of vine/grape/wine/blood/agape will be utilized to express the necessity of the disciples abiding in Christ in time of persecution and imminent martyrdom.

John 2:1–11 looks like a Jewish-Christian version of the myth of Dionysus, the God of grapes/wine, who revealed himself through the miraculous

---

17. John 13:1–16. Cf. Phil. 2:5–11; John 15:1–3, 9–15.
18. My understanding of John 13:1–20 is indebted to Bauckham's treatment (*The Testimony*, 194–97). For a cultural anthropology approach, see Jerome H. Neyrey, *The Gospel of John in Cultural and Rhetorical Perspective* (Grand Rapids: Wm. B. Eerdmans Publishing Co., 2009), 358–76. Neyrey argues (364–65) that in 13:6–11, Peter is a representative disciple undergoing a "status transformation ritual" which symbolizes his purification prior to facing the danger of public confession of the name and risk of martyrdom (16:1–2).
19. The theme of purification is reflected in John's baptism with water (1:31, 33), Jesus' exchange with Nicodemus ("unless one is born of water and Spirit . . ." 3:5), and in the debate between John the Baptist and the Judeans over "purification" (καθαρισμός, 3:25). The man born blind receives his sight by obeying Jesus' command and "washing" (νίπτειν) in the pool of Siloam (9:7–11), the same pool from which the water for the Tabernacles' festival is drawn.
20. Three bits of evidence point to grapes/wine as important symbols of the messianic-eschatological age. The messianic prophecy of Gen. 49:11 describes the fecundity of that age in the image of "washing" (πλύνειν) one's garment in "wine . . . the blood of grapes." Papias, who had received through the elders the teaching of the elder John, spoke of a coming time when each vine would have "10,000 shoots, each shoot 10,000 branches, each branch 10,000 vine-shoots, each vine-shoot 10,000 clusters, each cluster 10,000 grapes and each grape [would give] 25 measures of wine" (quoted by Irenaeus, *Adv. haer.* 5.33.3). The Jewish revolts of 66–73 and 132–5 CE against Rome reflected messianic-eschatological hopes, and the coins struck show images of wine cups and grapes. I owe these references to Martin Hengel, "Interpretation of Wine Miracle at Cana: John 2:1–11" in *The Glory of Christ in the New Testament: Studies in Christology in Memory of George Bradford Caird*, ed. L.D. Hurst and N.T. Wright (Oxford: Clarendon, 1987), 83–112 (at 100).

appearance of wine.[21] Given the mix of Jewish and Gentile population in Galilee and the Hellenization of Palestine by the first century, one cannot rule out the influence of a Dionysian ethos.[22] But the distinguishing mark of John 2:1–11 is the focus on the water of purification, its symbolic link to the death of Jesus and the symbols of grape/wine/blood/agape as an expression of the transforming power of Jesus' death for the disciples' life with him.

In Revelation, the martyr "washes" (πλύνειν) his/her garment in the blood of Jesus (7:14) and is thereby consecrated so s/he can serve in the heavenly temple. The image of washing one's garment in wine (which had been an image of fecundity of creation in the messianic age of *Gen.* 49:11), is changed in the Jewish-Christian consciousness of martyrdom as a means of establishing the kingdom vis-à-vis an imitation of Jesus' passion—the drinking of his cup.[23]

A significant parallel to this Johannine view of death is in 4 Maccabees, a Jewish work, probably of the mid-first or late first century.[24] There also, a martyr's death possesses purifying and saving power for Israel.[25] Two passages are noteworthy. Eleazar the priest, described as "the holy man" (ὁ ἱερὸς ἀνήρ, 6:30), had been scourged and was dripping with blood. He offered

---

21. Residents of Teos, a seaport town of Ionia, boasted of being the birthplace of Dionysus. As proof, they claimed that on certain days at their sanctuary Dionysus manifested his presence in wine flowing out the ground (cf. Diodorus 3.66.2 and the comments of Marcel Detienne, *Dionysos at Large*, ET Arthur Godhammer [Cambridge: Harvard Univ. Press, 1989] 41, 53). Pausanias (6.26.2) knew a tradition about the Greek island of Andros (north of Delos, birthplace of Apollo) where (on a day known as Theodosia, "gift of God") wine sprang from the sanctuary of Dionysus.

22. By the early second century BCE, Hellenization of Palestine under the Seleucids entailed the worship of Zeus and Dionysus (cf. 2 Macc. 6:1–9; 14:3). The festival of Hanukkah celebrates the victory of the Maccabean revolt and the purification of the land of Israel and the temple at Jerusalem. For Jewish-Christians, Jesus as Messiah consecrates himself in his death (a purification of the temple), purifies his disciples, and prepares them to receive his holy Spirit. As victorious Son of Man, he will incorporate them into himself, gathering and creating a synagogue of the eschatological Israel. Both Hanukkah and Tabernacles express the eschatological hope of God gathering (συναγαγεῖν) the diaspora to the temple (cf. 2 Macc. 1:27; 2:7, 18).

23. Different verbs for "washing" are used because in John 9:1–12 and 13:1–11 the washing is of a person while in Revelation 7:14 and Gen. 49:11 it is the washing of clothing. Cf. νίπτειν and πλύνειν in *A Greek-English Lexicon*, (eds.) Henry G. Liddell and Robert Scott (Oxford: Clarendon Press, 1966), 1175-77, 1423.

24. The style of the work is "Asianic." The burial formula of 7:9–10 is similar to Jewish funerary inscriptions in Phrygia, Lycaonia, Lycia, Ionia, and Galatia. At 4:2 there is a reference to Syria, Phoenicia, and Cilicia being under one governor. This was the case only from 19–72 CE; the author is probably anachronistic in reading this administrative grouping back into the historical situation of the second century BCE. Finally, about 5 percent of the words in 4 Maccabees are not used until the first century CE. All of this points to a provenance of mid-first or late first century CE in a diaspora community of, or close to, Antioch. For the above evidence, see David A. de Silva, *4 Maccabees: Introduction and Commentary on the Greek Text in Codex Sinaiticus* (Leiden: E. J. Brill, 2006), xiv-xviii, who argues for some time in the latter part of 19–72 CE, and Jan Willem van Henten (*The Maccabean Martyrs as Saviors of the Jewish People* [Leiden: E. J. Brill, 1997], 58–82) who dates it, ca. 100 CE.

25. The word *martyr* (μάρτυς) does not appear in 4 Macc.; my usage is anachronistic and designates a Jew who is executed because they refuse to violate the Torah.

a prayer in behalf of Israel just as he died: "Be merciful to your people. . . . Make my blood their purification (καθάρσιον) and take my life as their ransom" (ἀντίψυχον, 6:28–29).

In a second passage,[26] the author—after confessing that the reward for the martyrs (Eleazar, the mother and her seven sons) is consecration and standing before the throne of God, living forever—describes what their noble deaths accomplished for Israel:

And thus they themselves having been sanctified (ἁγιαζέσθαι) . . . have been honored . . . with this—that through them the enemies did not prevail over our nation, and the tyrant [Antiochus IV] was avenged and the the fatherland was purified (καθαρίζεσθαι) as if they had become a ransom (ἀντίψυχον) for the sin of the nation; and because of the blood of those devout ones and the propitiation (ἱλαστηρίον) of their death, divine providence saved (διασώζειν) Israel. (17:20–22)

In both passages the martyr's death is offered to God as a purification/ransom for the sins of Israel. The sense of ἀντίψυχον is based on Lev. 17:11: the blood of the animal "instead of your life (ἀντὶ τῆς ψυχῆς), shall make propitiation." In the temple cult, the life of the sacrificial animal resided in its blood and that blood was offered (instead of the blood of Israel). After 70 CE, with the loss of the temple worship and sacrifice, the blood of the martyr is offered as a ransom exchange in order to make propitiation and purification, pleading for God's mercy and saving act in behalf of Israel.

The redemptive power of the martyr's blood in 4 Maccabees is similar to 1 John's understanding of Jesus' sacrificial death: ". . . the blood of Jesus his Son cleanses (καθαρίζειν) us from every sin. . . . If we confess our sins, he is faithful . . . and will forgive our sins and cleanse (καθαρίζειν) us from all wrongdoing. . . . we have an advocate (παράκλητος) with the Father, Jesus Christ the righteous one (δίκαιος) and he is the propitiation (ἱλασμός) for our sins." [27]

Whether "propitiation" and "cleansing/purification" are synonymous in 4 Maccabees and in 1 John can be debated; but it is certain that both traditions use identical images to portray the redemptive significance of a martyr's sacrificial death.[28] Moreover, the washing of the disciples' feet expresses figura-

---

[26]. I am using the critical edition of David A. de Silva, *4 Maccabees* (Leiden: E. J. Brill, 2006). The translation is mine.

[27]. 1 John 1:7–9; 2:1–2. Cf. also 4:10. The author is either the Evangelist or a disciple. 1 John reinforces the importance of the images/symbols/festivals of sacrificial temple worship in understanding the meaning of Jesus' death in the Johannine community; 4 Maccabees shows a similar process going on in Judaism with regard to its martyrs.

[28]. For the argument that ἱλάσκεσθαι means καθαρίζειν in 1 John 2:2; 4:10, see C.H. Dodd, "ΙΛΑΣΚΕΣΘΑΙ, Its Cognates, Derivatives, and Synonyms in the Septuagint," *JTS* 32 (1931), 352–60 (esp. 360).

tively that Jesus' sacrificial death will wash the disciples, making them clean, and preparing them for the consecration of the Holy Spirit (*John* 13:5–11). The Gospel of John, 4 Maccabees, and 1 John reflect a common theme: the use of identical sacrificial temple images (purification, propitiation, and consecration through blood) in order to express the redemptive power of the martyr's death.

The correlation of blood and water issuing forth from Jesus' side with the water and wine libations in the Tabernacle service in the temple strongly suggests that Jesus' death is understood as a libation of blood poured on the altar (Jesus' body). This, together with the sacrificial cultic language of 1 John and its parallel in the portrayal of the deaths of the Maccabean martyrs, strengthens my thesis, namely, that Jesus' death in the Fourth Gospel is understood as a sacrificial libation of blood that destroys the power of death and brings the life of the Divine Spirit ("living water").

2. "LIVING WATER" AND THE SACRIFICIAL DEATH OF JESUS

In the Fourth Gospel, the sacrificial death of Jesus is a revelation of God's love for Israel and the unity of love of Father and Son (cf. 10:15, 17, 30, 36, 38). The consecrated Son, through his sacrificial death, makes possible the consecration of his disciples through the Spirit of Truth (14:15–21; 17:19). The indwelling Spirit gives the disciples an experience of the Son's love for them and of being loved by a God who is their "holy Father" (14:20–24; 17:11, 21–26). Empowered by the Spirit of Truth, the disciples continue the mission of the Son. As he bore witness (μαρτυρία) to the Father so they will bear witness (μαρτυρεῖν) to the Son (15:26–27).

The Evangelist's community is undergoing persecution and martyrdom.[29] The themes of testimony (μαρτυρία), bearing witness (μαρτυρεῖν), and hostile response are strands interwoven in its story. Jesus never is called a martyr; but in Revelation, both Jesus Christ and Antipas, a Christian executed at Pergamum (1:5; 2:13), are called "the faithful witness" (ὁ μάρτυς ὁ πιστός).

---

29. The repeated reference to the Holy Spirit as the Paraclete (14:16, 26; 15:26; 16:7) in the farewell discourse (an Advocate for those on trial) together with 16:1–3 and mention of Simon Peter's destined martyrdom (21:18–19) are sufficient evidence.

Martyr still means "witness"; but in both cases the witness dies because he remains faithful in witnessing to divine truth.[30]

In his trial before Pilate, Jesus defines his royal destiny: "I have been born for this, and for this I have come into the world—to bear witness (ἵνα μαρτυρήσω) to the truth" (18:37). After his death, the Paraclete, the Spirit of Truth, will bear witness (μαρτυρεῖν) to Jesus in and through the disciples;[31] and some of them will be put to death (15:26–16:2). Jesus' sacrificial death is the climax of his witnessing: a revelation of the Divine love for Israel and the world (3:16; 15:13). His sacrificial death is a "sanguinary witness."[32] In this sense, the Evangelist depicts Jesus' death as a martyrdom (μαρτυρία) even though the word μαρτυρία does not yet have this connotation.[33] When I use *martyr* or *martyrdom*, the connotation is sanguinary witness.

When the observation of the Evangelist (of water and blood issuing from Jesus' side when he died) is understood in the context of 7:38 (of Jesus being "living water" flowing from the temple [Jesus' body] in the eschatological age) and the context of Jesus' sacrificial death as a martyrdom that washes and purifies his disciples so they might receive the indwelling Holy Spirit, then Jesus' claim to give water that will become in the believer "a spring of water welling up to eternal life" (4:14) takes on a martyrial connotation. In Revelation, the martyrs (who had "washed their robes and made them white

---

30. The description of Antipas—"my witness, my faithful one who was killed in your presence"—is a witnessing which results in death. With regard to Jesus, the cluster of "the faithful witness, the first born of the dead, and the ruler of the kings of the earth" reflects the events—death, resurrection, lordship of Jesus. Thus, "the faithful witness" must designate a witnessing that culminates in the death of Jesus. I owe this insight to David E. Aune, *Apocalypticism, Prophecy, and Magic in Early Christianity* (Grand Rapids: Baker Academic, 2008), 196–97.

31. One could argue that 19:34–35 is the Paraclete speaking through the Evangelist, testifying (μαρτυρεῖν) that what was seen (blood and water issuing from the side of Jesus) "is true testimony" (ἀληθινὴ αὐτοῦ ἐστιν ἡ μαρτυρία).

32. G.W. Bowersock (*Martyrdom and Rome* [Cambridge: Univ. Press, 1995], 6–16) argues that in the New Testament, only in Revelation and Acts (where Stephen as a witness shed his blood, 2:20) does *martys* connote a witnessing given in death. Although Ignatius of Antioch yearns "to pour out his blood as a libation" in the Roman Colosseum and be "a word of God,'" he never employs *martys* in the self-perception of his death as a divine "summons" (cf. Ign. *Rom.* 2.1–2). The term "sanguinary witness" is my own construction, but it was evoked by Bowersock's description of Ignatius' desire to die as the sense of his "sanguinary mission" (17).

33. The earliest document in which μαρτυρία connotes the modern sense of martyrdom, that is, the execution of one who refuses to renounce their religion is *The Martyrdom of Polycarp*. Still, the term does not exclude the sense of faithful witnessing. Polycarp's martyrdom (μαρτυρία) is likened to his stamping a seal (ἐπισφραγίζειν) on the eleven martyrdoms (οἱ μαρτυρήσαντες) that had preceded his, thus putting an end to the persecution at Smyrna (1:1; cf. 19:1). (A σφραγίς on a document marks it as genuine and can also seal or close it.) The eleven martyrdoms are testimonies sealed and confirmed by the testimony/martyrdom (μαρτυρία) of Polcarp. (In John 6:27, God the Father set his seal [σφραγίζειν] on the Son of Man.)

in the blood of the lamb," 7:14) will be led by the lamb/shepherd and receive as a reward "springs of living water" (7:17).[34]

The image of water connotes both "purification/washing" and "life-giving" (the liquid essential for plant growth and for human life); the image of blood that issues forth connotes death as a sacrificial libation. Taken together, water and blood connote the Spirit of life given through sacrificial death. "Living water" is an image closely associated with Jesus' death as a cleansing sacrifice and a life-giving sanguinary witness. Jesus' death is understood as a sacrificial libation of blood that destroys the power of death, washes away sin, and gives the life of the Divine Spirit ("living water") to his disciples.

This conclusion is confirmed by martyrdoms of the second century. Anticipating martyrdom, Ignatius of Antioch (ca. 125 CE) is aware that his "eros has been crucified and the fire of loving maternal things is no longer within him." It has been replaced by "the living water . . . speaking within me, saying 'Come to the Father'" (*Rom.* 7.2). Similarly, in his letter (from the churches of Lugdunum and Vienne [Gaul]) to the churches of Asia and Phrygia (ca. 177 CE), Irenaeus depicts the confessor-martyr Sanctus, a deacon from Vienne, as one who, although tortured by having plates of hot brass attached to his body, was refreshed by "the heavenly spring of living water proceeding from the body of Christ."[35]

Also, when Polycarp, bishop of Smyrna, was martyred (157 CE) by being burned at the stake, his body could not be consumed by the blazing fire and he had to be stabbed. Although "living water" is not mentioned, perhaps its presence is implied. (See *Mart. Poly.* 13.3; 15.1–16.1.)

3. CONCLUSION

In the Fourth Gospel, "living bread" and "living water" are images for Jesus as the eschatological fulfillment of the pilgrim festivals of Passover (ch. 6) and Tabernacles (chs. 7–9). Jesus, as "living bread" and "living water," is the eschatological fulfillment of the miraculous manna and water the Israelites received during their forty years in the wilderness.

---

34. Irenaeus dated Revelation in the reign of Domitian (81–96 CE). See *Adv. haer.* 5.30.3; Steven Friesen (*Imperial Cults and the Apocalypse of John* [Oxford: Univ. Press, 2001], 135–51) dates Revelation, ca. 80–100 CE. Timothy Barnes (*Early Christian Hagiography and Roman History* [Tübingen: Mohr Siebeck, 2010], 38–40), argues convincingly for a date of 68 CE, in the reign of Galba, when Jerusalem was under siege by Roman Legions and the temple was still intact. Recall that Ephesus is one of the seven churches in Revelation.

35. See Eusebius, *Hist. eccl.* 5.1.1–5.2.8. For Sanctus, see 5.1.17, 20–24, 36–39. I accept Pierre Nautin's argument (*Lettres et écrivains chrétiens des ií et iií siècles* [Paris:1961], 56–59) that Irenaeus is the author.

When Jesus attended the last day of the festival of Tabernacles, he stood up and shouted—"If anyone thirsts, let her/him come to me; and let the one believing in me drink, just as the scripture said—'rivers of living water shall flow out of his stomach'" (7:37–38). Jesus was referring to the Spirit whom believers would receive after his death (7:39).

The eschatological hope of Tabernacles focused on "living water" flowing from the temple, forming a river and giving life to fish, plants, and humans. Tabernacles was an eight-day festival in which on each of the seven days a libation of water and a libation of wine were poured into respective bowls which sat on the altar. From the perforated libation bowls, the water and wine flowed onto the altar.

The libation bowl of water signified the water which the Israelites received in the wilderness and the eschatological hope of the life-giving presence of the Divine dwelling with Israel as King. The libation bowl of wine linked the Tabernacles' ceremony of water libation with the daily sacrifice of a lamb in the Tamid service with its blood being sprinkled on the altar together with a libation of wine flowing onto the altar. In the Tamid service, the wine libation was called "the blood of the grape" (*Sirach.* 50:15).

When the Evangelist underscores the testimony of blood and water issuing from the body of the crucified Jesus (when the Roman soldier thrusts his spear into the side of Jesus, 19:34), he is expressing a correlation with the water and wine libations that flow onto the temple altar during the festival of Tabernacles (water libation) in conjunction with the offering of Tamid (wine libation). This testimony expresses the Johannine gospel: Jesus is the Passover/Tamid lamb of God whose death, as a sacrificial libation of blood—destroys the power of death, washes away sin, and bestows the life of the Divine Spirit ("living water" issuing forth from Jesus' body; cf. 7:38–39) on anyone who follows him.

When the testimony of the Evangelist (of water and blood issuing from Jesus' side when he died) is understood in the context of 7:38 (of Jesus being "living water" flowing from the temple [Jesus' body] in the eschatological age) and the context of Jesus' sacrificial death as a martyrdom that washes and purifies his disciples (see 13:1–16) so they might receive the Holy Spirit, then Jesus' claim to give water that will become in the believer "a spring of water welling up to eternal life" (4:14) takes on a martyrial connotation. In Revelation, the marytrs (who had "washed their robes and made them white in the blood of the lamb" 7:14) are led by the lamb/shepherd and receive as a reward "springs of living water" (7:17). Here again, the redemptive power of blood being shed as a sacrificial libation is linked to water that gives life.

In addition, a comparison of the Johannine (*1 John*) understanding of Jesus' death with that of the martyrs of Judaism in 4 Maccabees shows both traditions employing the same sacrificial images (purification, consecration, and propitiation through the blood shed in the martyrs' redemptive deaths in behalf of Israel). The meaning of John 19:34 is clear: Jesus' death is a sacrificial libation of blood that destroys the power of death, washes away sin, and bestows the life of the Divine Spirit ("living water") to anyone who follows him.

The indwelling of Jesus' Spirit in a disciple is linked to the image of the "living water" of Jesus given in his sacrificial act of agape, and martyrdoms of the second century—Ignatius (ca. 125 CE), Polycarp (157 CE), and Sanctus at Lugdunum, Gaul (ca. 177 CE)—confirm this conclusion.

Chapter 6

The Tomb of Polycarp: Sacrificial Libation and a Refrigerium

1. THE DEATH OF POLYCARP AND WORSHIP AT HIS TOMB

Polycarp, bishop of Smyrna (40 miles north of Ephesus), was martyred 157 CE, after he refused to recant of his Christian identity in his trial before the Pro-consul of Asia (8.1–12.1).[1] Polycarp was burned at the stake. Confident that he would be able to endure the flames, he refused to have his hands (which had been tied behind him) fastened to the stake (13.1–3). When the flames could not consume his body, the executioner stabbed him with a dagger. What came forth from the wound was a "dove" (περιστερά) and "a large amount of blood" (πλῆθος αἵματος) that put out the fire (15.1–16.1).

The similarity with *John* 19:34 is evident. Both Jesus and Polycarp in their deaths are represented figuratively as sacrificial animals: Jesus is the Passover/Tamid lamb who is sacrificed; Polycarp is "the noble ram" (κριὸς ἐπίσημος) taken "out of the great flock" (ἐκ μεγάλου ποιμνίου) and "prepared as a sacrificial whole burn offering acceptable to the Divine" (εἰς προσφορὰν ὁλοκαύτωμα δεκτὸν θεῷ ἡτοιμασμένον, 14.1). When Polycarp is stabbed, the libation of blood bursts forth and extinguishes the fire, that is, figuratively his sacrificial libation puts an end to persecution (cf. 1.1). And rather than water issuing forth from the wound (as is the case in John 19:34), a dove comes forth. But in both traditions, the symbolism signifies the Divine Spirit. Perhaps also, "living water" is implied as the reason why Polycarp could not be consumed by the fire.

---

1. Polycarp (age 86) was executed on 23 Feb. 157 CE. See Timothy D. Barnes, *Early Christian Hagiography and Roman History* (Tübingen: Mohr Siebeck, 2010), 367–78.

The flames did not burn Polycarp to death because they formed a vault-like arch, like a sail of a ship filled out "by the air" (ὑπὸ πεύματος) surrounding "the body of the martyr" (τὸ σῶμα τοῦ μάρτυρος, 15.2). Hence Polycarp was within the vaulted walls of fire, "not as burning flesh but as bread being baked" (οὐχ ὡς σὰρξ καιομένη, ἀλλ' ὡς ἄρτος ὀπτώμενος) and "we [the Smyrnaean Christians] received a fragrant scent like that of incense or other precious perfumes" (15.2).

The reference to the vaulted walls of fire surrounding Polycarp so as not to burn him to death could be veiled reference to the action of the Divine Spirit's protection since the flames are vaulted "by the air" (ὑπὸ πνεύματος) and πνεύμα can also connote Spirit (cf. *John* 3:3). "Bread being baked" appears to be a eucharistic reference to Polycarp becoming "pure bread" (cf. *Ign. ad Rom.* 4.1) in a death that imitates that of Jesus. And the reference to Polycarp's body giving off the fragrant scent of incense and perfume underscores the sanctity of Polycarp's life. Even before his martyrdom, as a revered bishop/presbyter in Smyrna, Christians desired to touch him and come in contact with him (13.2).

After Polycarp died, a Roman centurion had his body completely burned. Later, Christians took up Polycarp's bones and placed them in a suitable place. They were "more precious than expensive gems and more valuable than gold" (18.1–2). This description together with a statement of what the gathered community did each year at his tomb—"in so far as possible the Lord will grant us, assembled as a synagogue (ἡμῖν συναγομένοις) with gladness and joy, the opportunity to celebrate the birthday of his martyrdom (ἐπιτελεῖν τὴν τοῦ μαρτυρίου αὐτοῦ ἡμέραν γενέθλιον) in memory of both those martyr-athletes who have preceded him (εἴς τε τὴν τῶν προηθληκότων μνήμην) and also for the discipline and training of those who are destined [for martyrdom]" (18.3)—suggests that Polycarp's tomb was an important shrine-altar for worship and meal fellowship of Smyrnaean Christians with one another and with the spirit of Polycarp.

Polycarp's martyrdom was an "oblation" (προσφορά, 14.1) offered to the Divine in behalf of his community. The employment of liturgical images in order to depict Polycarp's martyrdom also suggests that his *Passio* probably was a "Diaspora letter"[2] *that* was read in house churches during a worship service or at the cemetery where Christians gathered at the tomb of a martyr or saint.

Given the thesis of this book—namely, that sacrificial libation was not only an important metaphor representing the redemptive power of Jesus'

---

2. This is the observation of Gerd Buschmann, *"The Martyrdom of Polycarp"* in *The Apostolic Fathers*, ed. Wilhelm Pratscher, ET Elisabeth G. Wolfe (Waco, TX: Baylor University Press, 2010), 135–57 here 144.

sacrificial death and the martyrdoms of Stephen, Paul, Antipas, his colleagues at Pergamum, and Ignatius, but also a ritual act in the eucharist/agape that Ignatius did at Antioch—the obvious question concerning the worship done at Polycarp's tomb is: was that worship a eucharist/agape service and did it contain the ritual act of pouring a libation on the altar shrine tomb? At this point, it is important to know something about the funerary pagan custom of a *refrigerium*.

For pagans, whether living in the eastern or western part of the Roman empire, the cemetery was a place where libations were offered. Funerary custom entailed friends and family visiting the grave of a loved one, five times within the first forty days following the burial and—thereafter, probably four more visits per year, including the birthday of the deceased one.[3]

Each visit was the occasion of a *refrigerium*, that is, a picnic in which food and wine were shared among family members and friends and in which the deceased person was invited to participate. Common belief was that "the dead were sentient beings and could be reached by the living." Hence, the *refrigerium* was an experience of fellowship around food/drink and rejoicing in which the deceased person could share. The singing of songs, the offering of prayers, and dancing could be components of such a *refrigerium*. The pouring of libations into a hole in the ground into a tube that went down to the tomb was a way of allowing the deceased to share in the *refrigerium*.[4] Common belief was that the deceased one was nourished and "refreshed" by the sacrificial libation. Hence, this funerary custom is referred to as a *refrigerium* (refreshment).

There is ample evidence that when a pagan became a Christian, they did not give up the practice of a *refrigerium*. A joint apostolic memorial to both St. Peter and St. Paul, located at mile three of the Appian Way and datable to at least 258 CE, contains an inscription (a graffito on the wall) that reads: *ad Paulum et Petrum refrigeravi*.[5] The inscription shows that *refrigerium* meals were celebrated at the joint apostolic shrine; and although it is not possible to give a one or two word translation to *refrigeravi,* the full meaning would be

---

3. Ramsay MacMullen, *The Second Church: Popular Christianity A.D. 200–400* (Atlanta, GA: SBL Press, 2009), 77. Thanks to Maxwell Johnson for directing me to this work.

4. *Ibid.*, 76–77.

5. Henry Chadwick, *The Church in Ancient Society* (Oxford: Univ. Press, 2001), 323. Chadwick also discusses different scholarly attempts to explain why there was a joint apostolic memorial on the Appian Way in the third century and separate shrines in the mid-second century, for St. Peter at the Vatican necropolis and for St. Paul on the road to Ostia (323–25). Although the precise burial site of the apostles at the joint memorial is not certain, excavation of the Church of the Apostles (now San Sebastiano), which Constantine built at the site, has disclosed its approximate location and the hundreds of graffiti Christians left, honoring the two apostles. Libation holes have been found in the gallery floor of the church. See MacMullen, *Second Church,* 79; Hans Lietzmann, "The Tomb of the Apostles Ad Catacumbas," *HTR* 16.2 (1923), 147–62 and George La Piana, "The Tombs of Peter and Paul Ad Catacumbas," *HTR* 14.1 (1921), 53–94.

something like—"I have held a meal here in remembrance of Paul and Peter; and by that meal of food and drink, I have given refreshment to Paul and Peter." Since a *refrigerium* was the occasion for sharing a meal with others, almost certainly the author of this inscription had brought with him family and/or friends in order to share with them the breaking of bread and drinking of wine in fellowship with the two great apostles who, in martyrdom at Rome, had offered up themselves as libations in imitation of Messiah's sacrificial death. Within this context, the pouring of a libation into the grave of the apostles was an offering (oblation) of refreshment and a form of communion with them. Moreover, since a sacrificial libation was linked with a prayer, the *refrigerium* graffito implies that a prayer was offered to St. Peter and St. Paul.

When this archaeological and epigraphic evidence is joined to Polycarp's *Passio*, it is difficult not to conclude that on those days when Polycarp's martyrdom was remembered at his shrine-altar, Smyrnaean Christians sang hymns, offered prayers, and poured libations into his tomb in order "to have fellowship" (κοινωῆσαι, 17.1) with him and with the Divine Spirit that had been revealed in his life and death. Was the sharing of food and drink—including bread and wine—a *refrigerium* in the guise of a eucharist, a synthesis of a *refrigerium* and eucharist, or a eucharist in the guise of a *refrigerium*? In celebrating his victorious death—which they understood as a sacrificial libation—did they share with him a eucharistic libation? Some Smyrnaean Christians no doubt could feel his presence as they "had fellowship" with him, singing hymns and participating in his certain hope of victory over death—being inspired and strengthened by his example while wondering whether some of them were destined "to share . . . in the cup of the Messiah" (*Mart. Poly.* 14.2; 18.3).

These are intriguing questions, but the evidence in Polycarp's *Passio* provides no way of answering them. Moreover, the difference in chronology (a hundred year gap between Polycarp's martyrdom and the Roman inscription concerning the *refrigerium* at St. Paul and St. Peter's tomb) and geography (Smyrna is in Asia Minor; Rome is in Italy) diminishes the likelihood that the funerary customs of Roman Christians can be projected back a hundred years and applied to a locality in Asia Minor. Nevertheless, there is a historical linkage that provides contact between the customs of Christians in Asia Minor and Western Christians, namely a movement that called themselves, *The New Prophecy*.

2. THE *NEW PROPHECY*

In the next six sections, I will describe the nature of the *New Prophecy* in Asia Minor and then show the likelihood of members of the *New Prophecy* at Carthage, North Africa (ca. 204 CE) practicing *refrigeria* and associating the *refrigerium* with the sacrificial libations of their martyrs. My assumption is that the practices of members of the *New Prophecy* in Carthage are derived from the *New Prophecy* in Asia Minor, a movement appearing only ten years after Polycarp's martyrdom. Hence, the funerary practice of the *New Prophecy* in Carthage is, more likely than not, similar to the funerary practice of Christians at Smyrna.

The *New Prophecy* originated in central Asia Minor (Phrygia), ca. 165–170 CE and soon spread to Rome and Carthage. The central leaders were Montanus and two women, Priscilla and Maximilla. They claimed to have received the Divine Spirit, spoke in tongues, enthusiastically witnessed to their faith, proclaimed a message of repentance and joy, and were acknowledged by their followers as a prophet and prophetesses.

The *New Prophecy* was not an insignificant movement in early Christianity. By 177 CE, it had split Christians in Asia and Phrygia and forced no less a figure than Irenaeus, presbyter of Lugdunum (Gaul), to intercede with a letter of peace from the confessor-martyrs of the churches of Lugdunum and Vienne in Gaul.[6] Around 200 CE, the bishop of Rome sent a letter of peace to the churches in Asia and Phrygia, recognizing the *New Prophecy*; but on the advice of a certain Praxeas, the bishop changed his mind and recalled the letter.[7]

Central to the message of the *New Prophecy* was the hope of the imminent end of the present age, the descent of the heavenly Jerusalem and the duty of Christians to confess the name publicly in the midst of threats of persecution, prosecution, and execution. This message was based in divine oracles spoken through Montanus, Priscilla, and Maximilla. Concerning the descent of the New Jerusalem, Priscilla had received a revelation from Jesus Christ in a dream:

> Christ came to me in a dream in the form of a woman clothed with a long, gleaming, flowing robe, and placed Wisdom (σοφία) in me and revealed to me that this place is sacred and that in this place the heavenly Jerusalem shall descend.[8]

---

6. Eusebius, *Hist. eccl.* 5.1.1–5.2.8.
7. Tertullian, *Adv. Prax.* 1.5. The identity of Praxeas is not known. Tertullian describes him as a confessor from Asia. Some scholars doubt the reliability of Tertullian's testimony about this Roman attitude. I think what Tertullian describes is historically plausible.
8. Epiphanius, *Pan.* 49.1.3. Maximilla had prophesized that the end of the age would follow after her own death (*Pan.* 48.2.4).

Concerning the duty of martyrdom, two oracles express the summons to voluntary martyrdom, that is, in times of hostile authorities seeking out Christians, a Christian should come forth publicly, witness to the faith, and voluntarily hand her/himself over to the authorities:

> Be exposed to the public (*publicaris*). . . . Why are you confused since you are acquiring and showing forth glory? Power comes when you are seen by humans. . . . Do not wish to die in bed or in miscarriages or gentle fevers, but in martyrdom in order that he who has died for you might be glorified.[9]

The reward for such action would be participation in the transcendent power and glory of Christ when he came to establish his kingdom. Wherever the *New Prophecy* appeared it was the occasion of division among Christians: its opponents thought voluntary martyrdom was suicidal and argued that in time of persecution, Christians should flee to safe and secret places. Moreover, those who opposed the *New Prophecy* believed that those who denied the faith when interrogated by a civil authority should not be excommunicated from the community but rather given a chance to repent, do penance, and be welcomed back into the fellowship of Christians. In contrast, the *New Prophecy* took a position not unlike that found in *Hebrews* 6:4–6, namely, that any Christian who commits apostasy (denies being a Christian when interrogated by a civil authority) cannot be restored to the fellowship through repentance.

By the early third century, the *New Prophecy* had reached Carthage, North Africa; and there, in the visions of the confessor-martyr Vibia Perpetua (martyred 7 March 204 CE),[10] one can see the power of martyrdom reflected in the image of "living water." Significant for my purpose is the fact that Perpetua is a member of the *New Prophecy* (at a time when that movement had not yet been rejected by the Carthaginian catholic community), and the author of *The Martyrdom of St. Perpetua and St. Felicitas* is also a member of the *New Prophecy*.[11] The document is an eloquent and moving testimony to the power and courage of those noble Carthaginian martyrs of whom Perpetua stands out as an inspiring leader. The dramatic impact of the document is enlivened and strengthened by the fact that the visions of Perpetua are a firsthand account that the anonymous author has excerpted from her prison diary.

---

9. Tertullian, *De fuga* 9.4. Tertullian does not indicate which leader of the *New Prophecy* spoke these oracles.
10. For the dating of her martyrdom, see Barnes, *Early Christian*, 67.
11. *Ibid.*, 73–74.

3. THE CHRISTIAN *REFRIGERIUM* AND THE *MARTYRDOM OF PERPETUA AND FELICITY*

The main source for the practices and beliefs of Carthaginian Christians contemporary with Perpetua and Felicitas[12] is Tertullian. He undoubtedly witnessed their martyrdoms; and although he is probably not the author of the *Passio*, he almost certainly knew the author. Three years after their martyrdoms, he became a member of *the New Prophecy*. As a source of information about Christian *refrigeria*, Tertullian makes only passing references.

In his essay *On Monogamy*, he says that a Christian widow has a duty to present an offering (*offere*) on the anniversary of her husband's death. The offering was a way of maintaining a life-long relationship to her husband. In describing that duty, Tertullain says—"And indeed, she prays for his soul and requests for him a refreshment during the interim."[13] In *On Spectacles*, Tertullian describes the pagan origin of *Ludi*, that is, Games, and also speaks of human sacrifices that were made at funerals.[14] He criticizes pagan funeral customs of his own day and the sacrifices offered to Roman Deities who are demons. The meal of such sacrifices is "a meal of demons" (*cena daemoniorum*).[15] *On Monogamy* reveals Tertullian's view that funeral oblations are a duty of Christians; *On Spectacles* reveals that Christians can not participate in any pagan refrigeria where oblations are made to pagan Deities.[16]

In following the custom of *refrigeria*, Carthaginain Christians would have been continuing a practice they had known as pagans prior to their conversion to Christianity. From Tertullian's comments, it appears that conversion did not entail relinquishing the custom of making an offering for their deceased loved ones. But with an initiation into a new community with a belief/value system shaped by baptism, eucharist, ecstatic prophecy, Christan didache, proclamation, prayer, and experience of the Paraclete, their understanding and experience in a *refrigerium* would have been distinctly different from

---

12. I am using the critical edition of Thomas J. Heffernan, *The Passion of Perpetua and Felicity* (Oxford: Oxford University Press, 2012), 104–135 and the critical edition of Rudolf Knopf, Gustav Krüger, and Gerhard Ruhbach, *Ausgewählte Märtyerakten* (Tübingen: Mohr Siebeck, 1965), 35–44. The chapter and versification is that of Heffernan. Unless indicated otherwise, the translations are mine.

13. *De Monog.* 10.4. *Enimuero et pro anima eius orat, et refrigerium interim adpostulat ei.* The interim is the period of time between death and the future resurrection. For further discussion of how a widow's offerings may assist her husband, see J. Patout Burns, Jr. and Robin Jensen, *Christianity in Roman Africa* (Grand Rapids, MI: Wm. B. Eerdmans Publishing Co., 2014), 495–96. I owe the above reference to their work.

14. *De Spec.* 5 and 12.

15. *Ibid.*, 13.4.

16. For another view, arguing for Tertullian's ambivalent attitude towards Christian *refrigeria*, see Eliezer Gonzalez, *The Fate of the Dead in Early Third Century North African Christianity: The Passion of Perpetua and Felicitas and Tertullian* (Mohr Siebeck, Tübingen: 2014), 170–71.

what they had known as pagans. In this section, I will examine the verb *refrigerare* in the *Passio* of St. Perpetua and St. Felicity, showing what a Christian *refrigerium* must connote; then in the next section, I will show how the traditional pagan understanding of a *refrigerium* (an offering at the tomb that refreshes the deceased loved one) is transformed by the Christian belief system reflected in the confessor-martyr Perpetua who makes an offering (her martyrdom conceived of as a sacrificial libation of blood) in behalf of a deceased loved one (her brother, Dinocrates).

The *Passio* reveals that "to refresh someone or to be refreshed by someone or something" is a rich concept entailing many dimensions of meaning—physical, aesthetic, emotional, social, and spiritual. Concerning the basic level of physical well-being and health, "to be refreshed" is the result of eating and drinking so that one is in good condition, even to the point of being a little overweight. Thus, for example, after being treated harshly in prison, Perpetua challenged the commanding prison official by appealing to his pride. She argued that since she and the other Christian prisoners were the "most noble (*noblissimi*) of all the criminals condemned to fight" in the amphitheater on the emperor's birthday, it would resound to his "glory" (*gloria*) if they could look their best, by being able "to refresh ourselves" (*nobis refrigerare*) so that "we might be brought forth" (*producamur*) into the amphitheater as "fat and in good condition" (*pinguiores,* 16.3).

The prison official responded by permitting other Christians to visit so that the prisoners "could be refreshed" (*refrigerandi,* 16.4). Here, *refrigerare* connotes receiving food and drink in order to restore physical well-being, and also the refreshment of fellowship with other Christians around food and drink. The very next sentence in the narrative describes an agape meal—"they were dining with an agape meal" (*agapem cenarent*) the day before the Christians were to enter the arena. The narrator calls it "the last supper" (*cena ultima,* 17.1)—which is almost certainly a eucharistic meal, suggesting that "to be refreshed with others" has a communal spiritual dimension. This meal took place on a different day than the meal implied in 16.4, but putting the agape meal right after the one of 16.4 suggests that the author sees a connection between the two. Hence, a Christian *refrigerium* where there is a meal at the grave site implies the probability of a eucharistic meal.

The social dimension of refreshment is revealed also in the episode where Pudens, the official in charge of prisoners, having observed a "great power" (*magna virtus*) among the Christians, favored them by permitting other Christians to visit "in order that we and they might refresh one another" (*ut et nos et illi invicem refrigeraremus,* 9.1). In this context, "refreshment" describes the power of Christian fellowship and probably presupposes that the visitors brought food and drink to share with the confessors.

"Refreshment" also has an emotional dimension. It connotes being free of fear or anxiety—not having to fear losing one's identity. After Perpetua and the other catechumens had been arrested, her father, because of his love for her, attempted to dissuade her from undergoing baptism and thereby avoid her death in the amphitheater. Perpetua does not delineate her father's arguments, but a later scene with him shows that his plea was that her death would produce a grief and sorrow in him and the family that would be unbearable (cf. 5.1–5). In that scene, he wept.

In the opening scene, when Perpetua tells him—"I am a Christian" (*sum Christiana*)—and could not give up that identity, "then Father was so deeply moved [with anger] by this word [Christian] that he lunged at me in an attempt to gouge out my eyes" (*tunc pater motus hoc verbo mittit se in me, ut oculos mihi erueret*, 3.3). That is a very violent emotional response of a father, given the fact that in a later scene with his daughter he wept over her imminent death. In the next three sentences, Perpetua describes her father's departure, her resulting "refreshment," and her baptism:

> But he shook violently; and he, along with his arguments of the devil, departed—having been defeated (*victus*). After a few days, because I was free of my father, I gave thanks to the Lord; and I found refreshment because of the absence of that one (*absentia illius*). Indeed, in a few days we were baptized; and the Spirit told me to ask from baptism for nothing other than endurance of the flesh.[17]

In this passage, Perpetua's "refreshment" is sandwiched between two events: By confessing that she was a Christian (*sum Christiana*) she overcame the arguments of her father; and he departed, vanquished and shaken by her determination to maintain her Christian identity. Then a few days later, she again confesses her Christian identity and with the other catechumens undergoes baptism. The violent reaction of her father to her confession (*sum Christiana*) is seen by Perpetua as the devil acting through her father. The departure of her father with his "arguments of the devil" shows that Perpetua's confession had vanquished the devil and when Perpetua speaks of the "refreshment" she obtained because of "the absence of that one" (*absentia illius*), the phrase—"of that one" (*illius*)—is Perpetua's reference to the devil. The devil had been attacking her through the arguments of her father; when her father departs, after being defeated by Perpetua and her confession (*sum Christiana*), the devil is now absent.

---

17. *Passio* 3.3–5. *Sed vexavit tantum, et profectus est victus cum argumentis diaboli. Tunc paucis diebus quod caruissem patrem, Domino gratias egi, et refrigeravi absentia illius. In ipso spatio paucorum dierum baptizati summus: et mihi Spiritus dictavit non aliud petendum ab acqua, nisi sufferentiam carnis.*

108   Chapter 6

Had Perpetua been referring to the absence of her father, one would expect the Latin to be *absentia eius* (the absence of him). The *absentia illius* could be a reference to *patrem* (*quod carvissem patrem*) or to *diaboli* (*cum argumentis diaboli*). But when two nouns are referred to, *illius* is used to refer to the one farther away ("that one" [*ille*] over there versus "this one" [*hic*] here). In Perpetua's diary, the sequence is *argumentis diaboli . . . carvissem patrem . . . absentia illius*.

Gramatically speaking, the *illius* must be a reference to the noun farther away. That noun is *diabolus*.[18] The "refreshment" Perpetua obtained was the result of vanquishing the devil.[19] In this context, her resulting state of mind and spirit could be translated as "peace." In that state she was ready to be baptized. The need for "refreshment" occurs again a few days after Perpetua's baptism:

After a few days, we were taken back to prison and I became greatly terrified because I had never experienced such darkness. O cruel day! Intense heat due to the crowd, rough shaking and pushing by the soldiers, and most of all, I was in a state of torment because of my anxiety over my infant child. (3.5–6)

Then two deacons, Tertius and Pomponius, came to the prison, paid money in order that "we, after being transferred to a better place in the prison, might obtain refreshment for a few hours" (*ut paucis horis emissi in meliorem locum carceris refrigeraremus*, 3.7).

In this context, "refreshment" is made possible by a change of location—from a dark, crowded cell of intense heat to a place where there was some

---

18. Tertullian believed that the devil (*diabolus*) was an angel (created by the good Creator) who had free will and who freely chose to be disobedient and do evil (*Adv. Marc.* 2.10).

19. On the day before the confessors entered the arena, Perpetua had a vision in which she saw herself in the arena—as a man fighting and defeating an Egyptian gladiator. When she awoke, her thought was—"I understood that I was going to fight not against wild animals, but rather against the devil. For indeed, then I knew that a victory [over the devil] would be mine (*intellexi me non ad bestias, sed contra diabolum esse pugnaturam: sed sciebam mihi esse victoriam*)" (10.14). I construe *sciebam* as an inceptive imperfect. Hence, Perpetua is underscoring that she knew right after waking from the prophetic vision that she would prevail in her battle with the devil and that knowledge remained part of her consciousness up to the point of recording it. This was the last thing she recorded. The anonymous narrator's depiction of her death shows the fulfillment of her prophetic vision. In order to pick an animal matching the gender of the women martyrs, "the devil" (*diabolus*, 20.1) prepared a "very fierce cow" who charged Perpetua, lifting her up and throwing her to the ground. Perpetua appeared to be in no pain, got up, walked over to where Felicitas had been thrown, and helped her up (20.6). Later, Perpetua was prepared to receive death by the sword of a young gladiator. He struck her once and she screamed in pain. Then he hesitated as though he could not bring the sword to her throat for the final slash. "And so she, herself, took the hesitating right hand of the young gladiator and brought it across her throat. Perhaps such a great woman, who was being feared by the unclean spirit, was not able to be put to death unless and until she, herself, voluntarily accepted it" (21.10).

light and opportunity to eat and drink with one another (since Tertius and Pomponius, as deacons appointed "to care" [3.7; *ministrare*][20] for the confessors, would have brought food and drink). The transfer to a room with light also gave the confessors the opportunity for leisure time.[21] During this time, Perpetua reunited with her mother and brother, was given her infant son to nurse, made arrangement for her mother to care for him, and gave encouragement to her brother who was a catechumen. But when they departed with her infant son, she began to grieve their loss, knowing that she would never see her son again and aware also, through their visit, of the impact upon them of her imminent death.[22]

After many days had passed, Perpetua obtained permission to have her infant son remain with her in prison and "immediately I recovered my health (*statim convalui*, 3.9) . . . and suddenly prison became for me a palace (*praetorium*) so that I preferred to be there rather than anywhere else" (3.9). What had deterred Perpetua from enjoying the refreshment that other confessors had found, in their transfer from the dark and crowded prison cell with its stifling heat, was the fact of experiencing how her family suffered over her imprisonment, the loss of hope it engendered, the grief and sorrow of their departure, and most of all—the separation of infant son from Perpetua as the family ended their visit and took her son along with them.

The verb used to describe the family's sadness and grief over this predicament and Perpetua's own emotional state as she felt profoundly the cost of her Christian identity on her child, mother, and brother is *tabescere*—to gradually melt, dissolve, decay, decline. "Languish" is an apt translation or perhaps—"to wilt." The verb, as employed in our passage, suggests a process in which both family and Perpetua are being consumed by their situation: the imminent death of a beloved daughter and sister, the anguish the family feels, and the resultant anguish of the daughter who sees the profound suffering which her choice for Christianity has brought to her family. And most significantly, there is the anguish of separation a mother feels when she must say goodbye to her infant son whom she is still nursing and her realization that he depends on her for his nourishment and well-being.

With the return of her infant son to her care, she immediately recovered her health and was transformed by the joy of being, once again, the source of nourishment and health for her infant son. "Refreshment as the recovery of

---

20. The verb, *ministro*, means to wait on someone at a table and give him/her food and drink. This was the function of the deacon in the agape meal of the eucharist and in caring for the poor in the community (cf. Acts 6:1–6).

21. "By exiting the dark room, all were free for leisure time" (*universi sibi vacabant*, 3.8).

22. In the words of her diary, Perpetua says: "I was languishing (*tabescebam*, 3.8) because I had observed how they were languishing on account of their affection for me."

health" brings us to the most vivid and moving expression of "refreshment" in the *Passio*.

4. THE POWER OF MARTYRDOM: BAPTISMAL GRACE AS REFRESHMENT

One day while praying with other confessors in prison, Perpetua realized that she should pray for her brother Dinocrates, who as a pagan had died of cancer of the face at the age of seven. She prayed for him with deep sighs before the Lord. That night, she was given a vision: she saw Dinocrates coming out of a dark place; she saw the odious cancer on his face. He was still suffering. His face was dirty and pale (*pallidus*). He was very hot and exceedingly thirsty. There was a pool (*piscina*) of water above him, but it was beyond his reach. It grieved Perpetua to see that her suffering brother could not drink from the water. She awoke, confident that she could help her brother. And so (in her own words) "I prayed for him day and night, sighing and shedding tears, that he be pardoned for me."[23]

Days later, Perpetua had another vision: there was Dinocrates, "with a clean body (*mundo corpore*), well-dressed and refreshed (*refrigerantem*)." The cancerous wound had healed; the pool of water was now waist high, easily within his reach (8.1–2). The changed appearance of Dinocrates in the second dream is dramatic. What is implied is that the water of the pool had been healing and cleansing. This accounts for Dinocrates' new status of being clean and healed of his cancerous wound in his face. Although no mention is made of the color of his skin, the term "refreshed" (*refrigerantem*) occuring in association with "clean body and well-dressed" suggests the renewal of the color of a healthy seven year old boy. Indeed, the use of *refrigerantem* alerts the reader to the appearance of a Dinocrates who has undergone a spiritually transformative experience.[24]

After Perpetua's description of Dinocrates' changed state, she draws our attention to the pool (*piscina*) besides which he is standing. In the first

---

23. *Passio* 7.1–10. The sentence in quotation marks is: *Feci pro illo orationem die et nocte gemens et lacrimans ut mihi donaretur* (7.10). The reference to Dinocrates' skin color as pale (*pallidus*), underscores that Dinocrates is dead. *Pallidus* is the color of the dead. See Heffernan (*Passion*, 217), who points out that the horse of the Apocalypse, upon whom death rides, is pale (*Rev.* 6:8); also in classical authors (Virgil and Apuleius), spirits in Hades had pale color.

24. In the previous section, I showed that "refreshment" can be the result of being delivered from suffering, anxiety, and fear. It can connote the joy of fellowship with others around food and drink; it can describe the peace and joy one experiences in preserving one's spiritual identity in the face of someone or something which had threatened to destroy it. Thanks to Maxwell Johnson for pointing out the occurrence of the word "*refrigerantem*" in this passage and directing me to Ramsay MacMullen's work on Christian *refrigeria*. Without that observation and guidance, this chapter would never have materialized.

dream, the top rim of the pool was too high to reach, for the seven year old boy. Hence, he had been unable to drink from it. Now, in the second dream, the top of the rim was as low as his "navel" (*umbilicus*). "And he was withdrawing/drinking water from it, without ceasing" (*aquam de ea trahebat sine cessatione*, 8.2).

The verb *trahere* can mean to drag, withdraw, extract. With regard to a liquid, it can mean drink; with regard to breath, it can mean inhale or breathe in. I think the most plausible sense in 8.2 is that Dinocrates is cupping his hands, reaching down to the water and then bringing a cupped hand full of water up to his mouth. He continues to do that until he sees a "golden bowl full of water" (*fiala aurea plena aqua*) sitting on the top rim of the pool. "And then Dinocrates went over and he began to drink of it." But the result was that "the [full] bowl was never in need of water (*quae fiala non deficiebat*). And after he had been satisfied, he came forth from the water, happy to play in the manner of young children" (*Et satiatus, accesit de aqua ludere more infantium gaudens*, 8.3–4).

What Perpetua notices is that as Dinocrates drinks from the golden bowl, it continues to remain full. The full golden bowl of water that can never be depleted must signify "living water." This must explain Dinocrates' miraculous healing and refreshment. When Perpetua awoke from her dream, she knew that her brother had been delivered from his "pain and anguish" (*poena*, 8.4) through her intercessory prayer on his behalf.

Her prayer had brought Dinocrates the life-restoring and healing power of the Divine Spirit—the Paraclete who had appeared after Jesus' resurrection and had bestowed the "living water" of his victory over darkness and death (cf. *John* 7:37–38). The fate of her dead brother had been changed: a child—who had been languishing with terminal cancer, in constant pain and anguish, thirsting for a cool drink of water while residing in a place of darkness and unending heat—had been healed and restored by the presence of the Divine Spirit and led to a pool where he could drink from a golden bowl of "living water."

The association of "living water" with the restoration/rebirth of a dead person sounds like an echo of what the Johannnine Jesus said to Nicodemus: "Unless one is born anew of water and the Spirit, one can not enter the kingdom of the Divine" (3:5). And Dinocrates drinking from a bowl of "living water" looks like an eschatological fulfillment of what the Johannine Jesus said to the Samaritan woman at the well of Jacob: "If you knew the gift of the Divine and who is asking you—'Give me a drink of water'—you would ask him for a drink, and he would give you living water. . . . Whoever drinks of the water I shall give will never ever thirst" (4:10, 14).

Moreover, the baptismal sequence of going into a pool of water where one can be healed and then coming out to receive the Divine Spirit fits what happened to Dinocrates. His restored health with clean body[25] and refreshed state of being, very probably presupposes a bath/washing; and his drinking from a bowl of "living water" connotes a reception of the Divine Spirit/Paraclete.[26]

At this point, it is enlightening to look at the Greek translation of *Passio* 8.2. After saying that the rim of the pool had been lowered to the level of Dinocrates' naval, it omits the next line—"*et aquam de ea trahebat sine cessatione*" ("and he [Dinocrates] was withdrawing/drinking water from it [the pool], without ceasing"). Instead, the line reads, "ἔρρεν δὲ ἐξ αὐτῆς ἀδιαλείπτως ὕδωρ" ("and water was flowing out of it [the pool] without ceasing").

This significantly changes the meaning of *Passio* 8.2; in the Greek translation, Dinocrates never "draws/drinks, without ceasing from the pool." The "without ceasing" now describes the water flowing from the pool. Now the meaning of the pool's water leaps out to the reader—it is a pool of "living water." Dinocrates had received his washing/bath in "living water"; and as in the Latin text, he then approaches the golden bowl of water which is sitting on the the rim of the pool. And when he drinks of it, it remains full. Thus, in the Greek translation, both the pool and the golden bowl of water symbolize "living water."

Heffernan notes the difference between the Latin and Greek texts. He construes *traho* as "reveling in the water, rather like splashing in it." In his translation, Dinocrates "drew water from it [the pool] without ceasing." And in 8.4, after Dinocrates' "thirst was quenched, he began to play in the water, rejoicing in the maner of children." Nevertheless, Heffernan acknowledges that "the pool of water is obviously miraculous, since it is never diminished" (found only in the Greek translation). And Perpetua's use of the word *piscina* (pool) "suggests both healing and baptism." The water of the pool and the cup

---

25. "Clean body" (*mundum corpus*) probably has a spirtual connotation in this vision since *mundum* can mean "pure, upright, free from sin." Perpetua says that because of Dinocrates' cancer of the face, "his death had been abhorred by everyone" (*mors eius odio fuerit omnibus hominibus*, 7.5). This may presuppose, as Heffernan suggests (*Passion*, 219–20), that Perpetua and others thought Dinocrates had died of leprosy. This would have made him ritually unclean and untouchable. Hence, he would have died in isolation and unable to be touched or caressed by his family. Receiving a "clean body" restores him back into community with others.

26. Tertullian (*De Baptismo* 6) describes baptism as being washed and healed in the water in preparation for receiving the Divine Spirit when one comes out of the water. For the text and a discussion, see Maxwell E. Johnson, *The Rites of Christian Initiation: Their Evolution and Interpretation* (Collegeville, MN: Liturgical Press, 2007), 86–87.

are "life-giving." Through the power of her intercessory prayer, her brother was freed from his purgatorial suffering and his life was restored.[27]

Through the intercessory prayer of his sister, the pagan Dinocrates had been healed of his cancer and restored to the happy, playful life of a child. Water is the primary symbol that communicates the redeemed state of Dinocrates. It denotes two things: a medium for bathing and washing the body and the liquid that quenches the thirst and sustains life. The contrast between Dinocrates of the first and second vision is vivid. In the first one, he is dirty, hot, sweaty, pale, thirsty, and suffering from cancer of the face; in the second scene, his body is clean, well-dressed, refreshed, and healthy. Obviously, the prayer of Perpetua had been effective in attaining a health-restoring bath for her brother. And among Carthaginian Christians, baptism was a "bath/washing."[28] Dinocrates' bath had communicated the baptismal power of the life-giving Spirit. A second container of water also was present for Dinocrates—a golden bowl of water from which he drank. He drank as much as he desired, but the bowl remained full. This detail, as well as the detail of the water "ceaselessly" flowing out of the pool *(piscina)* must denote "living water." As in the Fourth Gospel where Jesus' death is a washing for the disciples and where the Spirit is symbolized as "living water" and is drunk (cf. *John* 4:10–14; 7:37–8), so also in Perpetua's dream, water is for spiritual washing (the pool where one can bathe) and spiritual drinking (the golden bowl sitting on the rim of the baptismal pool of water). Hence, the act of Dinocrates drinking water from the golden bowl after receiving a health-restoring bath dramatically underscores the ongoing reality of the new life of the Spirit he had received in his baptismal bath.

It would be useful to stop and ponder what Perpetua's two visions reveal, concerning her relationship to the dead and what light it may shed on a Christian *refrigerium*. Dinocrates' healing, deliverance from suffering, and restoration of a life of joy and play, was a gift of the Holy Spirit in response to Perpetua's request for her brother's forgiveness. In fact, it was the Holy

---

27. Heffernan, *Passion*, 233–36. I think the Greek translation is based in a Latin manuscript that is now non-extant. Knopf, Krüger, and Ruhbach, *Ausgewählte Märtyrerakten, 39,* also accept the Greek translation as the original reading.

28. The document reveals this in two places, and both depend on the fact that in early Christianity martyrdom was seen as a second baptism. When the leopard attacked the confessor-martyr Saturus, he was so drenched in blood that the crowd yelled at him—"well washed, well washed" (*salvum lotum, salvum lotum,* 21.2). *Salvum lotum* is a way of greeting someone who has had a bath in a Roman bathhouse. Here the narrator expresses the irony of the hostile crowd's greeting which was intended to ridicule Saturus in his death but in fact, without knowing it, had borne witness to his death as a second baptism (21.2). This Carthaginian baptismal expression of martyrdom is similar to that in Revelation (7:14) where martyrs "washed their garments white in the blood of the lamb." The second reference to baptismal martyrdom is to the confessor-martyr Felicity, who—eight months pregnant when she had been put in prison—gave birth to her daughter in prison; and then two days later she died in the arena, gored to death by a wild heifer. Her martyrdom is called "a second baptism, a washing after birth" (*lotura post partum*, 18.3).

Spirit who had spoken to Perpetua's heart and who had directed her to begin praying for Dinocrates.[29] Perpetua had been invited by the Spirit to be part of the process that had redeemed her pagan brother. And when she awoke from her second vision, she knew that she had been chosen by the Spirit for that purpose.

What shines forth in the second vision is the extraordinary power of the imprisoned confessor who is awaiting martyrdom. According to Irenaeus, bishop of Lugdunum, Gaul (ca. 177 CE), while in prison awaiting martyrdom, a confessor can exercise "the power of martyrdom" (δύναμις τῆς μαρτυρίας). For Irenaeus, the greatest victory of this power was the act in which the confessors of Gaul, while in prison awaiting martyrdom, with a "mother's love" (μητρικὰ σπλάγχνα) prayed and shed tears to the Father, interceding for the return of life to those Christians who had denied the faith because of persecution. The Father heard their prayer and the "immeasurable mercy of Christ" was manifested: the confessors were giving grace (ἐχαρίζοντο) to the lapsed and there was "deep joy to the Virgin Mother who had miscarried [with the lapsed] as though they were dead but now was receiving them back again as living. . . . On account of the living [the confessors who had been praying], the dead were being made alive."[30]

The imprisoned confessors in Lugdunum were bestowing forgiveness on those Christians who had denied being Christian when on trial. Without that forgiveness, a lapsed Christian would die in a graceless state. Forgiveness restored them back to fellowship in the church. They had been delivered from that death and restored back among the living. "On account of the confessor/martyrs, the dead were being made alive."

The parallel with Perpetua is striking—her dead brother was made alive because she had prayed "day and night . . . with groans and tears that he be forgiven for me (*mihi*)" (7.10). The "for me" is important to note. She is a confessor in prison awaiting her martyrdom. She knows she has powers and has been chosen by the Holy Spirit to die as a martyr and to pray for her brother while awaiting her death. Like the confessor/martyrs of Lugdunum, she has exercised "the power of martyrdom" through her intercessory prayer of groans and tears. Is her "for me" an allusion to her faithful obedience which will result in her martyrdom and which is the basis for her plea for

---

29. *Passio* 7.1. While Perpetua had been praying with the other confessors, a voice (*vox*) from within her came forth and she cried out the name of Dinocrates. The voice surprised her because she had not thought of her brother for some time. The voice from within was the Divine Spirit.

30. The letter is in Eusebius, *Hist. eccl.* 5.1.4–5.2.7; for the above passage, see 5.1.45–46; 5.2.4; 5.2.6–7. Irenaeus was speaking to the conflict in the churches at Rome and Anatolia caused by the position taken by members of the *New Prophecy* who were maintaining that even when a confessor is released from prison, they still could exercise "the power of martyrdom." For more on this issue, see my essay, "The Role of Martyrdom and Persecution in Developing the Priestly Authority of Women in Early Christianity: A Case Study of Montanism," *CH* 49.3 (Sept., 1980), 251–61 at 254–56.

Dinocrates' life-giving restoration? Did she ask that the grace of her martyrdom (her second baptism) be given to her dead brother who was still suffering anguish and pain?

5. THE *REFRIGERIUM* AND A SACRIFICIAL LIBATION OF MARTYRDOM

What had "refreshed" Dinocrates was the grace of Christian baptism. How might this relate to *refrigeria* at Carthage? I assume that before Perpetua became a catechumen, she made regular visits with her family to the grave of Dinocrates. Their *refrigeria* (four visits/year including his birthday) would have consisted of food and drink along with prayers and oblations offered at the tomb. Presumably, sacrificial libations would have been poured on or into the tomb as a form of "refreshment" for Dinocrates.

It appears certain that among members of the *New Prophecy* at Carthage, martyrdom was conceived of as a sacrificial libation. When the anonymous author (a member of the *New Prophecy*) narrates Felicity's martyrdom, he says that while in prison she feared that she would not die with the other confessors because she was eight months pregnant; and therefore, in that state she would not be allowed "to pour forth (*fundere*) her holy and innocent blood" (15.2). *Fundere* is a libation verb; the Greek of 15.2 uses the verb ἐκχέω, which is also a libation verb.

Moreover, Felicity's response to the jailer, who compared the suffering of her birth pains to the suffering Felicity would experience when she faced the wild animals in the arena, reveals the intimate connection of the martyr's libation of blood to the suffering of Jesus: "Now," she said, "I alone suffer what I am suffering [labor pains]; but then [in my martyrdom] there will be another in me, who will suffer on account of me because I am about to suffer on account of that one."[31]

The anonymous author's account of Felicity reveals that in the *New Prophecy*, the martyr's suffering and death (sacrificial libation) was in union with Jesus Christ whose suffering and death had been a sacrificial libation; and the union of the martyr with Christ in a sacrificial death was expressed in the language of reciprocal suffering. Because Felicity bears the name of Christ/Messiah (*sum Christiana*), she will suffer and die. But in her suffering, Christ will be within her, sharing and bearing her suffering. The difference between her labor pains, when she gave birth to her daughter, and the pain she will endure in her martyrdom is simple: she was alone in her birth pain;

---

31. *Passio* 15.5–6. *Modo ego patior quod patior; illic autem alius erit in me qui patietur pro me, quia et ego pro illo passura sum.*

but in the pain of her martyrdom (due to her Christian identity), Christ—who suffered a sacrificial death for her salvation—will be present, sharing in her suffering.

The suffering of Felicity's martyrdom, in union with Christ who suffers with her, will be a manifestation of his Divine Spirit to the spectators in the amphitheater; and some will leave, desirous of becoming catechumens.[32] Felicity is a vivid example for revealing how the *New Prophecy* understood the relation between the suffering of the martyr and the indwelling Spirit of Christ.

Felicity's teacher, Saturus—the voluntary confessor/martyr—shows in his death the power of the martyr's blood to console and strengthen the faith and love of Carthaginian Christians. Especially powerful is the legacy which Saturus leaves to Pudens, a Roman soldier who had been in charge of the confessors during their imprisonment. During that time, Pudens was moved by the courage of the confessors and the way in which they were strengthened and consoled by Christian visitors. By the end of the imprisonment, he had become a believer. When the confessors entered the arena, he was there as a helper and aid.

When Saturus was bleeding to death, drenched in blood from a leopard's attack, he consoled Pudens, encouraged him to remain faithful, and bid him farewell. His parting legacy was a request that Pudens take off a ring from his finger and give it to him. Then Saturus dipped Pudens' ring in his bloody wound and returned it to him—"leaving a legacy to him as a pledge and memorial of blood" (*pignus relinquens illi et memoriam sanguinis*, 21.5).

The legacy of a ring dipped in blood as a pledge and memorial of Saturus' martyrdom is a striking parallel to *Luke* 22:20 where Jesus leaves a memorial ("Do this in remembrance of me") to the disciples in which the wine poured out from the libation cup represents Jesus' blood poured out (a sacrificial libation) which establishes the new covenant of forgiveness. In the eucharist, it is the wine poured out as a libation which is the pledge and memorial of Jesus' redeeming, sacrificial agape. In the case of Saturus, Pudens' ring dipped in Saturus' blood is Saturus' legacy given to Pudens—the pledge and memorial of the martyr's blood. The sacrificial libation of a martyr's death is redemptive; and as Heffernan says, in discussing the ring given to Pudens, "the purity and power" of the martyr's blood "derives its power from the slain Messiah" who, called by the name of "The Word of the Divine" (ὁ Λόγος Θεοῦ) and

---

32. Among the crowd who came to the prison on the night before the martyrdoms, some jeered and ridiculed the confessors; but after Saturus' defense of martyrdom and censure of them, some went away as believers. See *Passio* 9.1; 16.4; 17.3; 21.3. That the exalted, crucified Christ would be revealed to the spectators in the arena through the sacrificial agape of the martyr is a core belief. In the words of Tertullian: "The blood of Christians is the seed [of the church]" (*Apol.* 50.13).

wearing "a garment dipped in blood" (ἱμάτιον βεβαμμένον αἵματι), will appear in the last days, riding on "a white horse" (*Rev.* 19:11–13).³³

Although no libation verb is employed in the description of Perpetua's death, it was the slashing of her throat by the gladiator's sword that killed her. Although the narrator chose not to describe the blood that came forth, I agree with Heffernan's judgment that the grace which Perpetua received from the Holy Spirit entailed for her—"an obligation to offer herself as a sacrificial libation." ³⁴ The redemptive effect of Perpetua's sacrificial libation is also consistent with the sacrificial libations of blood previously discussed. Jesus' sacrificial libation brought forgivesness of sins (*Matt.* 26:28) and established a covenant of peace (*Luke* 22:20; *John* 20:19–23). Stephen's sacrificial libation brought forgiveness to Saul/Paul and transformed him from an enemy of the gospel into an apostle to the Gentiles (*Acts* 7:59–8:1; 22:20). Perpetua's sacrificial libation brought forgiveness to Dinocrates, the pagan, and a transformation by the Divine Spirit through baptism.

The sacrificial libations of Antipas and his companions called forth Divine judgment on imperial Rome (*Rev.* 6:9–10; 14:9–11; 16:1–7). Ignatius' sacrificial libation strengthened the unity and harmony of Christians at Smyrna, Ephesus, and Philadelphia. Polycarp's sacrificial libation brought an end to persecution at Smyrna.

The martyrs of Carthage also reflect the influence of Revelation. As they walk into the amphitheater to face bloody death by the attacks of wild animals (a bear, a leopard, a boar, a heifer) and by the swords of gladiators, they were communicating with the spectators by words and hand gestures. And when Saturus, Revocatus, and Saturninus caught the gaze of the imperial governor, Hilarianus (who had been judge at their trial), through gestures and nods they said to him: "You [judge] us but God [will judge] you." (18.8). Recall that in *Rev.* 6:9–10, the blood of the martyrs that had been poured on the heavenly altar (as a sacrificial libation) called out for justice in the confident hope that the Divine would pour forth a libation of blood on imperial Rome as a form of judgment.³⁵

---

33. Heffernan, *Passion*, 361.
34. *Ibid.*, 42.
35. The hand gestures and nods of the martyrs to Hilarianus were probably a nod to him, the pointing of a forefinger at him, then to themselves, then a thumbs down which would signify "You [judge] us." Then the pointing of their forefinger to the sky, then to Hilarianus, then a thumbs down which would signify "God [will judge] you." And for good measure, perhaps, they pointed their forefingers to the sky, then to themselves, and then a thumbs up, signifying that in the end they would be victorious. The martyrs surely thought they were living in the last days. The previous night when a crowd had come to the prison in order to jeer and ridicule them, Saturus gave a defense and ended with— "Note carefully our faces, in order that on that day [of final judgment] you might recognize us again" (17.2). The martyrs were confident that justice would ultimately prevail and they would share in that victory over their persecutors.

Presumably, during her life as a pagan, Perpetua would have poured libations into the tomb of Dinocrates as a form of refreshment for him. After being baptized and while awaiting her martyrdom, she is invited to pray for Dinocrates. In the first vision, she sees him and is profoundly grieved by his terrible suffering. And so with groans and tears she prays day and night for her brother, day after day, night after night. She prays for one thing: that he be forgiven. And she is confident that she can help him. How?

If she believed that her martyrdom would be a sacrificial libation that she could offer for her brother's deliverance and that martyrdom was a second baptism, then what she saw in her second vision of her brother is the Divine answer to her prayer; and what she saw was a healthy young boy, full of joy and play, standing beside a pool of "living water" and then drinking "living water" from a libation bowl. Her sacrificial libation offered for and to her brother had given him an eternal rest and refreshment by being washed and renewed by "living water" and drinking from a bowl of "living water."[36]

When Perpetua awoke from her vision, she knew that Dinocrates had been delivered from his pain, anguish, and punishment (*poena*). She knew that she would offer the sacrificial libation that gave eternal refreshment to her dear brother, Dinocrates. Presumably, what Perpetua had sought to do as a pagan by going (four times/year) with her family to the grave of her brother in order to offer him a sacrificial libation for his refreshment, she was able to accomplish as a Christian martyr by offering to/for him a sacrificial libation that refreshed him by restoring his health through a bath in "living water" and drinking from a cup of "living water."

6. "LIVING WATER," REFRESHMENT, AND *REFRIGERIUM*

Dinocrates' reception of "living water" and its "refreshment" reflects the eschatological hope of the *New Prophecy*. The close association of these two images in the mind and heart of Perpetua are understandable as a vision of a confessor-martyr living and nurtured in the Johannine tradition of martyrdom reflected in Ignatius, Polycarp, and Sanctus (for "living water" in those martys, see the previous chapter).

In Revelation, the martyrs who had "washed their robes and made them white in the blood of the Lamb" were led by the Lamb "to springs of living

---

36. Given the eschatological and prophetic consciousness of Christians in the *New Prophecy* (living in the last days), I see no contradiction of chronological time in Perpetua's waking from the second vision with the confidence that Dinocrates had been redeemed on the basis of her "power of martyrdom." She had not yet died. The power of her prayer request is based in a future event, but it is a power that can be exercised in the present.

water" in a place where there is neither "scorching heat" or unquenchable thirst (7:14-17). The previous chapter showed that "living water" is the fulfillment of the eschatological hope associated with the festival of Tabernacles; the experience of "refreshment" is surely implied in the above passage of Revelation. "Refreshment" is, also, itself an eschatological image. According to Acts, when one's sins are "wiped away" (ἐξαλείφω), "times of refreshment" (καιροὶ ἀναψύξεως) will come "from the Divine presence" in the Messianic age (3:19-21).

The centrality of "living water" and "refreshment" in Perpetua's second vision reflect her eschatological hope in regard to the fate of her young brother, Dinocrates, who died as a pagan. But her desire for her brother's "refreshment" is also grounded in her experience of participating in *refrigeria* at his tomb before she became a catechumen at the age of twenty-two. The desire to refresh him when she was a pagan reflects the hope common to almost all people in the ancient Greco-Roman world.

I am convinced by Heffernan's view that in the ancient Greco-Roman world of early Christianity, the desire to stay in contact with deceased loved ones and to aid them, was universal. Among many classical sources that reflect this desire, Heffernan cites two—Virgil's *Aeneid* and the *Acts of Paul and Thecla*—which are pertinent to Perpetua's visions of Dinocrates. Both works express the belief that souls in the underworld can be "rehabilitated." [37]

Virgil has a narrative in which Aeneas descends to Hades after his deceased father, Anchises, had made such a request in a dream. Aeneas learns that at death, good souls can be reborn "to the light of the upper world" and receive second bodies; but first they must be cleansed from their bad deeds.[38] His father tells him that "all scourges of the body" do not leave the soul at death; there is a need to be "disciplined by punishments" and to do "penance for old sins."[39]

In the *Acts of Paul and Thecla*, Falconilla, the deceased pagan daughter of Queen Tryphaena, appears to her in a dream and asks her to have Thecla, the disciple of Paul, pray for her so that she could ascend "to the place of righteousness." Thecla responds by praying to the Divine and requesting that Falconilla might "live forever." [40]

Since Perpetua was a Roman citizen and a well-educated woman of the upper class, who could write Latin and speak Greek, she certainly had studied Virgil before becoming a catechumen. And since Tertullian claimed to have

---

37. Heffernan, *Passion*, 214-15.
38. *Ibid*. 215; Virgil, *Aeneid* 6.679-751.
39. *Aeneid* 6.736-745. Trans. of Robert Fitzgerald (*The Aeneid* [New York: Randon House, 1983], 186).
40. Heffernan, *Passion*, 207; *Acts of Paul and Thecla* 1.28-29. Thecla had not yet been baptized when she offered her prayer.

known who had authored the *Acts of Paul and Thecla*,[41] Perpetua had probably read that work as well. I agree with Heffernan that "her Christianity is a graft onto a substantial pagan rootstock."[42]

7. *THE REFRIGERIUM* AND THE MARTYR'S LIFE IN PARADISE

Before returning to the issue of cultic worship at Polycarp's tomb and its possible connection to a *refrigerium*, one other issue in the *Passio* is important: does a Christian *refrigerium* at the tomb of a martyr give refreshment to that martyr? In Perpetua's first vision—in which she learns that she and her friend, Saturus (a voluntary martyr who was not present when Perpetua and the others had been apprehended; but when he found out about it, he gave himself up voluntarily to the authorities) are destined for martyrdom—she ascends a ladder, after treading on the head of a dragon at its base, (Saturus ascended first, indicating the pre-eminence of the voluntary martyr in the *New Prophecy*), and at the top, steps into a garden where she was surrounded by thousands clad in white. There in front of her was an aged man, clad as a shepherd, milking a sheep. He welcomed her as "child" [43] and gave her a morsel (*buccella*) of cheese (*caseus*). She received it in her cupped hands and while eating it, heard the chorus of figures sing "Amen." At the sound of that word, she awoke with the taste of something sweet in her mouth. She knew that she and Saturus were destined to suffer martyrdom (4.1–6).

Elizabeth Klein argues that this dream vision of Perpetua, occurring a few days after her baptism and foreshadowing her martyrdom, is depicting her initiation into a heavenly community. And since martyrdom is a second baptism, this depiction is revealed sequentially by using images or conceptions embedded in the baptismal and eucharistic liturgy. Just as baptism is a rite of initiation into the earthly Christian community, likewise, Perpetua's martyrdom (a second baptism) initiates her into a heavenly community of martyrs and saints. And just as participation in a eucharistic meal follows after water baptism (in which one has become a child of the Divine), so Perpetua—after climbing the ladder to heaven, is welcomed by the shepherd (Jesus Christ) as "child" and given a morsel of sweet cheese, which is the eucharistic food that

---

41. Tertullian says the author was a presbyter from Asia Minor (see *De Bapt.* 17.5).
42. Heffernan, *Passion*, 214.
43. The Latin word for *child* is *tegnon* which is a transliteration of the Greek word *teknon* (τέκνον). Perpetua could speak Greek (cf. 13.4).

initiates her into the heavenly community of martyrs who, gathered around her, sing the liturgical "Amen" as she is eating it.[44]

Klein is very persuasive in relating the rite of water baptism to Perpetua's ascent of the ladder. At the bottom of the ladder is a dragon of enormous size who would attack anyone who attempted to climb it. Perpetua asks for protection "in the name of Jesus Christ." The dragon appears reticent and afraid; Perpetua steps on his head and begins to climb the ladder (182–83). This incident symbolically corresponds to the beginning of baptism when the catechumen renounces the devil; and then while in the water, confesses her faith in the Christian Deity. Here one should recall that after Perpetua's baptism, the Spirit directed her to ask from it nothing except "the endurance of the flesh" (*sufferentiam carnis*, 3.5).

Moreover, the ladder Perpetua climbed was so narrow that only one person at a time could climb; attached to each side were sharp hooks, daggers, spikes, and swords. One slip and "the flesh" (*carnis*, 4.3) could be torn or mangled. Here are the trials of the flesh after baptism. When Perpetua reaches the top, she has prevailed in her trials of martyrdom (184).

The dream reaches its climax in Perpetua's encounter with the shepherd and the reception of the "morsel of cheese." Just as earthly baptism reaches a climax in the eucharistic meal, so Perpetua's second baptism (martyrdom) reaches its climax in reception of eucharistic cheese. Crucial to this argument is the symbolism of the shepherd milking a sheep and giving to Perpetua a morsel of cheese that unites baptism to its completion in the eucharistic meal (185).

At Carthage, after water baptism, the neophyte received a mixture of milk and honey (sweet milk) as a welcome to the Christian community and to the imminent eucharistic meal. Sweet milk united baptismal initiation to eucharistic fellowship. (Milk may also symbolize the status of the neophyte who as an infant child is given milk[45]). Likewise, after martyrdom (Perpetua's second baptism) she receives cheese (which is the solid form of milk) as the welcome into the heavenly community. (The cheese as a solid form of milk may symbolize solid food given to the child after it is weaned from the milk. The martyr is the adult Christian who can endure suffering and prevail in martyrdom.[46]) As Perpetua eats the cheese out of her cupped hands, she receives the "Amen" welcome of the gathered martyrs. "And at the sound of their voices, I awoke—chewing something sweet of which I am ignorant. And at once I told my brother [Saturus] and we understood that martyrdom was imminent:

---

44. Elizabeth Klein, "Perpetua, Cheese, and Martyrdom as Public Liturgy in the *Passion of Perpetua and Felicity*," *JECS* 28.2 (Summer, 2020), 175–202. Thanks to Maxwell Johnson for alerting me to this insightful essay of Elizabeth Klein.
45. *Ibid.*, 194–97.
46. *Ibid.*

and we began to have, no longer, any hope in the world" (*et ad sonum vocis experta sum, commanducans adhuc dulcis nescio quid, et retuli statim fratri meo, et intelleximus passionem esse futuram: et coepimus nullam iam spem in saeculo habere*, 4.10).

Whether the morsel of sweet cheese is a foretaste of the heavenly banquet or itself, one of the foods of a Carthaginian eucharist, can be debated;[47] but it seems certain that the vision presupposes the belief that martyrs do receive the refreshment of food in heaven. Martyrs also play in paradise and they are nourished by the fragrance of flowers. Both are components of the martyr's refreshment.

The vision of Saturus, which depicts his and Perpetua's journey to paradise after their martyrdom, reveals the belief that in death one leaves the flesh and is carried by angels to a paradisiacal enclosed garden where rose trees are as high as a cypress tree, the ground is radiant with violets, and the walls are made of light. There, angels lifted Saturus and Perpetua up to a white-haired man with a youthful face, who was sitting on a throne. They gave him the kiss of peace; and he, in turn, gently touched their faces. Then, the elders who were gathered at the throne, said to Saturus and Perpetua—"Go and play" *(Ite et ludite*, 12.6).

It is clear from this context that "playing" is a way of being refreshed. For when Saturus and Perpetua depart in response to this invitation, they run into Optatus, their bishop, and Aspasius, a Carthaginian presbyter and teacher. Optatus and Aspasius have quarreled and had a falling out; they plead with the two martyrs to grant them peace. Perpetua began to converse with them in Greek, but an angel intervened, chastised the bishop and presbyter for intruding on the two martyrs, and then commanded them: "Let them refresh themselves (*Sinite illos refrigerent*); and if you have any disagreements

---

47. Klein's argument for the gift of cheese as a welcome into the heavenly community of martyrs and saints is compelling. But her case for cheese as an actual component of the Carthaginian eucharist depends on her argument that the word *buccella* (morsel) is used in the Johannine depiction of the last supper (13:26). Hence, for her, it has a liturgical eucharistic connotation; and in receiving a "morsel of cheese" Perpetua was receiving eucharistic food. But this argument depends on showing that in early Christianity of the first two centuries, in references to the eucharist, *buccella*/ψωμίον is used. Klein fails to do this. Moreover, to posit cheese as a component of the eucharist at Carthage is to diminish the persuasive analogy that Klein has established. The mixture of milk and honey at Carthage was the gustatory symbol that joined water baptism to participation in the earthly eucharistic meal fellowship. Milk/honey was not a component of the eucharistic meal. It symbolized what awaited the child of the Divine who had just been born from the baptismal water: the sweetness of life which would be received through a participation in eucharistic fellowship. Likewise, the cheese symbolizes the sweetness of life that Saturus and Perpetua would find in the paradisiacal community (a sweetness she had been ignorant of while in the flesh). Perpetua describes the difference between these two kinds of lives, when (in Saturus' dream of their arrival in paradise) after the elders tell them to "Go and play," she says to Saturus—"Thanks be to the Divine; even as in the flesh I was joyful, so now here—I am even more joyful." (*Deo gratias, ut quomodo in carne hilaris fui, hilarior sum et hic modo*, 12.7). To argue for cheese as a component of the eucharist at Carthage (in order to account for it in her vision) diminishes the spiritual and creative power of Perpetua's imagination.

between yourselves, forgive one another" (13.5).[48] Recall also that the association of "refreshment" and playing was seen in Perpetua's second vision of Dinocrates: his body was healed and clean, he was well-dressed and refreshed; and after he drank from the bowl [of "living water"] "he came forth from the water, full of joy, in order to play (*ludere*) in the way children do" (8.1–4).

In the paradisial garden, Saturus and Perpetua recognized many Carthaginian Christians who had died and also some martyrs. "We were," he said (while standing in a garden of violets and rose trees), "all nourished by a fragrance that cannot be put in words, a fragrance which was satisfying us completely. Then, full of joy, I awoke." [49] This ending of Saturus' vision almost certainly points to the common custom of a *refrigerium* in which flowers, especially roses and violets, were left at the grave site, in the belief that the spirit of the departed is refreshed by the beauty and scent of flowers. In pagan *refrigeria*, roses were "regarded as pledges of eternal spring in the life beyond the grave." [50]

In summary, I have shown, based on a document authored by a member of the *New Prophecy* and based on the visions of Perpetua and Saturus—confessor-martyrs in that movement—that the funerary custom of *refrigerium* (refreshment of a deceased person by the offering of flowers, food, and libations) is reflected in the powers portrayed by a martyr. By drawing on "the power of martyrdom" while a confessor in prison awaiting her martyrdom, Perpetua was able to give "refreshment," that is, physical and spiritual transformation to her seven year old brother, Dinocrates, who had died as a pagan from cancer of the face and was still suffering in the afterlife. Through

---

48. The encounter with Optatus and Aspasius is enigmatic. They had not been apprehended, imprisoned, or martyred. They are still alive at Carthage. Saturus' vision depicts the journey that he and Perpetua would take after they were martyred and had left "the flesh" (*carnis*, 11.2). The martyrs and other Christians whom Saturus and Perpetua recognize are all inside the gate which is attached to the walls of light. But Optatus and Aspasius are in front of the gate when Perpetua and Saturus see them. As they are conversing, the martyrs lead them into the garden, under a rose tree. That Optatus and Aspasius can converse with the martyrs in front of the gate of paradise points to a belief that Christians on earth may approach the martyrs in paradise through prayer. Their prayer request is for reconciliation with each other through forgiveness and peace which the martyr can give. Saturus and Perpetua were willing to listen to the bishop and presbyter; Perpetua leads them into the garden, under a rose tree. But the angel intervenes, chastises Optatus and tells the bishop and Aspasius to work out the forgiveness, themselves. Optatus is told to return to his church at Carthage and "to reform" (*corrigere*, 13.6) his unruly parishioners. Saturus' dream vision must reflect some issue he is struggling with as a confessor-martyr. As a voluntary martyr, Saturus has pre-eminent status among the confessors in prison. He had voluntarily given himself over to the authorities so that he could be with the catechumens he had taught. He was Perpetua's catechist. What is the issue? Is it about whether a confessor-martyr in prison (who has no clerical status) should involve her/himself in the affairs of the church concerning the power of forgiveness and the bestowal of peace? This was an issue in the *New Prophecy* and its catholic opponents in Asia Minor. See my essay, "The Role of Martyrdom," 254–57.
49. *Passio* 13.8 *universi odore inenarribili alebamur, qui nos satiabat. Tunc gaudens expertus sum.*
50. For the prominence of roses and violets at a pagan *refrigerium*, see J.M.C. Toynbee, *Death and Burial in the Roman World* (London: Camelot Press LTD, 1971), 61–63.

her "prayer, day and night, while sighing and shedding tears for him that he be forgiven," Perpetua delivered Dinocrates from his suffering; and he was washed, made clean, refreshed and restored to health through "the living water" of the Divine Spirit.

Perpetua had applied to her brother the healing grace of her imminent martyr's death—the baptismal washing had been provided by her sacrificial libation of blood.[51] Her sacrificial libation had bestowed on him the life-giving power of the Divine Spirit. What happened to Dinocrates shows that a confessor/martyr has the power to bring about a spiritual and physical transformation of others. Martyrdom has transformed the conception of *refrigerare*.[52]

In addition, I have shown that in the *New Prophecy*, martyrs do receive post-mortem refreshment in heaven—both in the form of food/drink and the sweet fragrance of flowers. And there is sufficient evidence to say that in pagan *refrigeria*, both food and drink were poured down piping in order to reach the remains (whether ashes or bones) of a departed loved one. This practice was "not an uncommon feature of cemeteries in very diverse areas of the Roman world."[53] My analysis of *refrigerare* in the *Passio* suggests that the meal shared in a Christian *refrigerium* was probably in some instances a eucharist/agape, and that it was fellowship around the meal of eating and drinking that provided "refreshment." Moreover, the affirmation of Christian identity with others in and through the meal fellowship was an experience of "refreshment." It seems very probable that Carthaginian Christians believed that the departed could share in the meal fellowship and could be moved by the beauty and fragrance of flowers offered at the tomb. It also appears

---

51. Perpetua had been baptized during her house arrest and detention. Did she need a second baptism? Are the benefits of her second baptism (martyrdom) transferred to her brother, Dinocrates?

52. The similar pattern of Dinocrates and Perpetua is intriguing. He receives a baptism based in the ability of Perpetua to draw on the power of her martyrdom (her second baptism—a libation of blood). His health and well-being is restored. He drinks his fill from a golden bowl of "living water"; and then he "plays in the way children are accustomed to play." Perpetua undergoes a baptism of blood ("well washed"), ascends to a paradisiacal garden, is greeted by a shepherd as "child" and given a morsel of sweet cheese; and (in Saturus' vision) she and Saturus are told "to go and play"—which in this context is associated with their "refreshment." One sees a similar pattern: a baptism; drinking and eating—either the gift of drinking "living water" or eating a gift of cheese from the shepherd; then either childlike "playing" after being "refreshed" (Dinocrates) or children (Perpetua and Saturus) invited "to go and play" as an expression of refreshment. Baptism, eating and drinking, refreshment and childlike play. If eating and drinking connotes the agape meal of the eucharist, then the pattern is: baptism, meal fellowship of the agape/eucharist, refreshment, and childlike joyous play. This describes the pattern of the day when catechumens are baptized. In Revelation, the cluster of shepherd, water, blood, and refreshment are united in the depiction of the martyrs, who "have washed their garments . . . in the blood of the lamb," being led by a lamb who guides them like a shepherd to "the springs of living water" (Rev. 7:14–17). The most important traditions of the *New Prophecy* were the Fourth Gospel and Revelation. The mind, heart, consciousness, and imagination of Perpetua and Saturus appear to be immersed in those traditions.

53. Toynbee, *Death and Burial,* 51.

that in paradise, martyrs play like children. And no doubt, prayer requests would have been offered to a martyr although it seems that on this issue, the Carthaginian community was in the process of sorting out what limits should be imposed concerning the power of a martyr and what s/he could provide to the supplicants.

Although one cannot say for sure what those limits were, archeological excavation clearly demonstrates that Carthage's *Basilica Maiorum* (Basilica of Ancestors) was a church built over the graves of the martyrs of *The Passio of Perpetua and Felicity* in a cemetery that contains both pagan and Christian graves. A fragmentary inscription there reads "Here are (hic sunt) . . . " and then what follows are the names of Saturus, Saturninus, Revocatus, Secundulus, Felicitas and Perpetua.[54]

It is certain that Carthaginian Catholics did visit the graves of these martyrs and offered prayers for aid and help. It is difficult not to conclude that those prayers were joined to the offering of sacrificial libations.

My excursion to Carthage was an attempt to determine the character of the *New Prophecy* there with regard to the power of a martyr's death as a sacrificial libation, its relation to a *refrigerium,* and whether a martyr receives post-mortem nourishment in heaven. I see no evidence supporting the view that a picture of a Christian *refrigerium* derived from the *Passio* would be essentially different from a catholic Carthaginian or an Anatolian Christian *refrigerium*. What can be deduced concerning a catholic Carthaginian *refrigerium* is dependent on Tertullian and the *Passio of St. Perpetua and St. Felicitas.* So the crucial question of what in the *Passio* is due to the *New Prophecy* and what is due to the catholic Carthaginian customs that existed prior to the appearance of the *New Prophecy* cannot be answered. My assumption is that what can be deduced from the *Passio* concerning a Christian *refrigerium* reflects what members of both the New Prophecy and the catholic community believed. The *New Prophecy* had not been rejected there, yet. It needs to be repeated: how much, the *Passio* reflects a Christian conception of *refrigerium* that is not due to the *New Prophecy* but instead reflects a Christian conception of a *refrigerium* which predates the *New Prophecy* cannot be known. But what is certain is that everything in the *Passio* concerning an understanding of a *refrigerium* does reflect the customs of the *refrigerium* in the *New Prophecy*. It is their document and Perpetua and Saturus are members of that movement.

Therefore, until historical evidence is forthcoming concerning a Christian *refrigerium* in Asia Minor that predates the *New Prophecy* there, I will assume that the picture of a *refrigerium* derived from the *Passio of St. Perpetua and*

---

54. Jensen and Burns, Jr., *Christianity* 113, 116, 144.

St. Felicitas does correspond with what members of that movement in Asia Minor thought about a *refrigerium*. And since the basic difference between the catholic church (that composed and redacted the *Passio* of Polycarp) and the *New Prophecy* in Asia Minor was the issue of voluntary martyrdom, it seems reasonable to assume that the *refrigerium* customs and beliefs of both Smyrnaean catholics and Christians of the *New Prophecy* were similar.[55]

However, before I examine the passage in Polycarp's *Passio* which depicts his disciples at his tomb, ca. 158 CE, there is one other component of the historical context of the *Passio that* sheds light on the probability of Christian *refrigeria* existing prior to Polycarp's martyrdom. Although the letters of Ignatius are difficult to date precisely, they are worth examining since Ignatius knew Polycarp and was martyred a generation before Polycarp's death.[56]

8. IGNATIUS AND THE REFRESHMENT OF CONFESSOR-MARTYRS

Like the confessor-martyr, Perpetua, Ignatius employs the language of "refreshment" in order to describe the aid and comfort that Christians gave him at Smyrna where Polycarp was bishop. The ten Roman soldiers, who were taking Ignatius and some other prisoners to Rome, had stopped there for a few days, giving a chance for Christians to meet with Ignatius and provide him with support and encouragement.

Ignatius is especially grateful to two Ephesian deacons—Crocus and Burrhus—for the "refreshment" they provided him, a refreshment that surely included the provisions of food and drink. But their role in aiding Ignatius in his journey to martyrdom at Rome entailed more than ministering to his physical needs. Both provided spiritual support and also performed scribal duties for Ignatius. At Smyrna, Ignatius composed letters by the hand of Crocus to Christians at Ephesus, Magnesia, Tralles, and Rome; and in each letter Ignatius makes allusions either to his gratitude for receiving "refreshment" or the duty of Christians for providing "refreshment" to confessor-martyrs.

Ignatius thanks the Ephesians for the support Burrhus and Crocus had given him, and he describes Crocus as "an exemplary model" (ἐξεμπλάριον) of the Ephesians' "agape" (ἀγάπη) for "he refreshed me in every way" (κατὰ

---

55. In the *New Prophecy* of Asia Minor, some confessors released from prison were claiming to still possess the power of the keys. This, obviously, created problems for catholic clergy. See Klawiter, "The Role of Martyrdom," 254–56.

56. For the dating of Ignatius' martyrdom, see appendix in which I argue for ca. 125 CE.

πάντα με ἀνέπαυσεν, 2.1).⁵⁷ To the Magnesians, Ignatius sends greetings from the Ephesians who together with Polycarp—"refreshed (ἀνέπαυσαν) me in every way" (15.1). And to the Trallians, Ignatius alludes to the "assemblies of God" (ἐκκλησίαι τοῦ θεοῦ) who are with him at Smyrna and who "refreshed me in every way both physically and spiritually" (κατὰ πάντα με ἀνέπαυσαν σαρκί τε καὶ πεύματι, 12.1). The allusion to "assemblies of God" may imply that the "refreshment" provided was the physical nourishment of a eucharist/ agape meal and the sustaining support and encouragement of spiritual fellowship and worship, which would have included hymns, prayers, preaching and perhaps prophetic ecstasy.⁵⁸ The support and encouragement of a eucharist/ agape meal was, in the *Passio of St. Perpetua and St. Felicity,* also associated with "refreshment" of the imprisoned confessor-martyrs.⁵⁹

As bishop of Antioch, Ignatius was concerned also about the health and well-being of other confessor-martyrs from Syria who had preceded him in making the journey to Rome. Through Crocus, he writes to Roman Christians, asking them "to refresh" those confessor-martyrs "in every way" (κάτα πάντα ἀναπαῦσαι, 10.2).

The letter makes clear that Ignatius does not want Roman Christians to intervene on his behalf in order to seek a pardon from imperial authorities. In a sense, it appears that Ignatius was "staging" his martyrdom.⁶⁰ It was important that the letter reach the church at Rome before Ignatius arrived, and Crocus almost certainly was the messenger who carried the letter from Smyrna to Rome (*Rom.* 10.1).

Burrhus takes his place and travels to Troas, accompanying Ignatius as friend and helper. There, he was the scribe of three letters—to Polycarp, to the church at Smyrna, and to the church at Philadelphia. Writing to the Smyrnaeans, Ignatius describes Burrhus as one "who refreshed me in every way," who was worthy of being "imitated" (μιμεῖσθαι) by all, and who was "an exemplary model of the diakonate of God" (ἐξεμπλάριον θεοῦ διακονίας,

---

57. Both Crocus and Burrhus were chosen and selected by the joint action of the churches at Smyrna and Ephesus to provide aid and support to Ignatius. Cf. *Phd.* 11.2; *Smyr.* 12.1; *Rom.* 10.1.

58. At Philadelphia, Ignatius had been permitted to worship with the congregation. There, he had preached and experienced prophetic ecstasy in which the Spirit spoke through him and urged unity. See *Phd.* 7.1–2.

59. See *Passio* 16.4-17.1.

60. See William R. Schoedel, *Ignatius of Antioch* (Philadelphia: Fortress Press, 1985), 12, 213.

12.1). Burrhus was the messenger who carried these letters to Smyrna and Philadelphia.[61]

Whether Christian *refrigeria* existed at Antioch is not certain; but at a minimum, given the universal existence of pagan *refrigeria* in the Roman empire, it is certain that some members of Ignatius' church had participated in that funerary practice in their former lives. When they became Christian, they would have wondered about Ignatius' attitude towards that practice. Did he reject it outright? Did he grudgingly tolerate it as long as the prayers were directed towards the Christian Deity? Did he support or sponsor the practice, even incorporating it into the funerary practice of his church?

Which of these options did Ignatius represent? Ignatius speaks positively about the "refreshment" he received while in route to Rome and he encouraged Roman Christians to give "refreshment" to the Syrian confessor-martyrs who would arrive ahead of him and who would, like him, die in the Colosseum. The similarities of Ignatius' "refreshment" and that of Perpetua, Saturus, and their comrades are evident. The Christian response to the plight of imprisoned confessor-martyrs was to visit them, provide them with food and drink, and the solidarity and encouragement of worship and fellowship. All of this was providing "refreshment"—the recovery and renewal of one's energy and well-being—in order to help confessor-martyrs prepare both physically and spiritually to give their witness in the face of death in the arena. "Refreshment" was preparing confessor-martyrs to witness to the gospel in a courageous death of joy and peace.

What the *Passio of St. Perpetua and St. Felicity* adds to this picture is that a Christian who dies and reaches paradise continues to share in meal fellowship, is capable of enjoying the scent and beauty of flowers, and is available to hear the prayers of Christians in the earthly church. All of this is offered

---

61. *Phd.* 11.1–2; see Robert M. Grant, *Ignatius of Antioch*, vol. 4 of *The Apostolic Fathers*, ed. Robert M. Grant (New York: Thomas Nelson, 1966) 108–109. I agree with Grant that Rheus Agathopous, a Syrian deacon (who—together with Philo, a Cilician deacon—had travelled from Cilicia with news that peace had been established at the church at Antioch), probably accompanied Ignatius from Troas to Rome, providing for both his spiritual and physical needs. The distance from Troas to Rome is about 1,000 miles; and depending on the means of travel, over half of that distance could be overland. The distance from Antioch to Troas is about 600 miles; and Ignatius had walked it, in the heat of summer, while chained to other prisoners. He, no doubt, welcomed the physical and spiritual "refreshment" which Rheus would provide during the rest of the journey to Rome.

in a *refrigerium* at the grave of a martyr.⁶² This view of "refreshment" places Ignatius on a continuum which is consistent with the nature of a Christian *refrigerium*. Ignatius' conception of "refreshment" is the physical (food and drink) and spiritual (the solidarity of worship and fellowship) offering given to a confessor who is about to give her/his witness in the act of dying. A Christian *refrigerium* at the tomb of a martyr is an offering of food and drink and fellowship to the confessor who had given her/his witness in the act of dying. My point is that "refreshment" given at the martyr's tomb is a continuation of "refreshment" that had been given to the confessor: "refreshment" is a way of maintaining solidarity with the confessor-martyr; "refreshment" is an aspect of an organic two stage process of giving love and support to the confessor-martyr.

Since Ignatius knows, encourages, and is consciously participating in the first stage, he most probably knows and approves of the second stage. It is highly probable that when Ignatius was bishop at Antioch, he approved and supported the funerary practice of a *refrigerium* at the tomb of a martyr. I now turn to the examination of the passage (18.2–3) in Polycarp's *Passio,* which describes Smyrnaean Christians gathered at the tomb of Polycarp.

9. THE TOMB OF POLYCARP AND A EUCHARIST—*REFRIGERIUM*

The passage (18.2–3) in the *Passio* of Polycarp describes Smyrnaean Christians, gathered as a synagogue (συναγομένοι) at Polycarp's tomb, "in gladness and joy" celebrating "the birthday of his martyrdom both in memory of those martyr-athletes who preceded him and for the discipline and training of those destined [for martyrdom]." Presumably, this passage dates the *Passio* to 158 CE.

However, the scholarly consensus is that the *Passio* (as handed down to us), expressing a criticism of voluntary martyrdom and depicting Polycarp as a Christian who fled the authorities, contains anti-*New Prophecy* redactions; hence, the redacted *Passio* cannot be dated prior to 165–170 CE (when the

---

62. A feature prominent in Ignatius' "refreshment" is that the three individuals who stand out in supporting him while he is in route to Rome are deacons (Crocus, Burrhus, and Rheus), men responsible for giving food and drink to participants in the eucharist/agape meal and distributing food and drink to the poor and needy. Crocus and Burrhus are scribes and messengers who carry Ignatius' letters to various churches. Rheus will accompany Ignatius for 1,000 miles. Undoubtedly, Ignatius viewed these acts as expressions of agape (cf. *Smyr.* 6.2). Concerning Christian messengers, Ignatius coins his own word and calls them "a divine runner" (θεοδρόμος) and says that—"A Christian has no authority (ἐξουσία) over her/himself but devotes her/his time to the Divine (θεῷ σχολάζει)." What the messenger does is "a divine deed" (τὸ ἔργον θεοῦ). See *Ign. ad Poly.* 7.2–3.

New Prophecy appeared in Anatolia). I agree with this assessment and think the redacted *Passio* is probably not much earlier than 177 CE when Irenaeus sought to reconcile the *New Prophecy* and catholic communities in Asia and Phrygia. Perhaps, it is later than this;[63] but the object of this section is not to determine the date of the final redaction of the *Passio*. Rather, it is to discuss the plausibility of a eucharist shaped by the funerary customs of a *refrigerium*.

The use of the participle—συναγομένοι (ones being gathered)—in 18.3 is a certain indication that the gatherings at St. Polycarp's tomb were sanctioned worshipping gatherings. At Smyrna, ἐκκλησία (church/assembly) and συναγωγή (synagogue/gathering/assembly) were synonyms for a worship assembly.[64] Given this fact, one can assume that a eucharist/agape meal occurred when Smyrnaean Christians gathered at St. Polycarp's tomb. The phrase—"in gladness and joy"—suggests a vital worship with hymns, prayers, and thanksgiving for the inspiring witness of Polycarp and other martyrs. But also, the worship, which included a sharing of food and drink and the experience of Christian fellowship, would be an affirmation of Christian identity and a strengthening and training for those Smyrnaens who were destined for martyrdom.[65]

The similarity of a *refrigerium* and a eucharist is striking: a meal of food and wine shared by a group whose love for the deceased person is the reason for the communal meal; the singing and offering of prayers; a desire to remember and have fellowship with the loved one. In the *refrigerium*, communing with the loved one is often expressed with a wine libation poured into their grave. The eucharistic parallel would be a communing with St. Polycarp by pouring a libation on his shrine-altar (below which are his bones, "more precious than gems or gold" 18.2). The difference between a customary *refrigerium* and a eucharist at St. Polycarp's shrine-altar tomb would be that "libation" is also a metaphor representing his death, and communion includes a fellowship with St. Polycarp and Jesus Christ—whose victorious death was a libation and the foundation model for Polycarp's death (1.1–2; 19.1).

---

63. Hans von Campenhausen (*Bearbeitungen und Interpolationen der Polycarpmartyrium* [Heidelberg: Carl Winter, 1957], 20) placed the *Passio* in the late second or early third century; Candida R. Moss (*Ancient Christian Martyrdom* [New Haven: Yale University Press, 2012], 60–74) thinks it could be as late as the first half of the third century.

64. In his greeting to the church at Philippi, Polycarp uses ἐκκλησία (church/assembly). Ignatius, in his letter to Polycarp (4.2), calls the gatherings of Christians at Smyrna—synagogues (συναγωγαί). According to Irenaeus who, as a young man, had been a student of Polycarp, the church (ἐκκλησία) is called the "synagogue of the Divine" (συναγωγὴ θεοῦ) because it has been "gathered" (συνάγω) to the Divine through the death of the Son (*Adv. haer.* 3.6.1; 5.2.1).

65. Recall that in the case of Perpetua and her fellow confessors, an important component of their "refreshment" in prison was an agape meal with other Christians who visited and brought food and drink. Their agape meal was held the day before they entered the arena. It was called "the last supper" (*ultima cena*, 17.1). For Perpetua, it was an experience that reinforced her Christian identity (*sum Christiana*), strengthening her for facing the ordeal of death by wild animals and vanquishing the devil (*diabolus*).

If the eucharist at Smyrna was like that of Ignatius', then a libation of wine poured on the shrine-altar of Polycarp's tomb is at the same time both eucharistic (symbolizing the libation of blood of Christ and his disciple, Polycarp) and a wine libation which is believed to nourish Polycarp and be an act of fellowship with him. As a symbol of a libation of blood, the wine libation is a memorial of those martyr-athletes of the past and an act of discipline and preparation of Smyrnaean Christians present at the tomb, some of whom are destined for martyrdom.

One can see how a congregational reading of the *Martyrdom of Polycarp* at his tomb and a shared eucharistic meal of bread and wine could create a group identity and be a preparation for enduring an imminent persecution. But also, one can see how a eucharist/agape service that incorporates the wine libation of a *refrigerium* could lead a participant to think that they were worshipping both Jesus Christ and Polycarp since both suffered a redemptive death that is represented as a sacrificial libation; and—a wine libation was being offered to St. Polycarp. Perhaps this accounts for *Mart. Poly.* 17.3 where the redactor thinks it necessary to say—"For this one [the Lord] we worship as the Son who is of the Divine, but the martyrs we love as disciples and imitators of the Lord. . . . May it be that we become both their companions (κοινωνόι) and co-disciples (συμμαθητάι)."

10. CONCLUSION

I have shown that Polycarp's martyrdom was understood as a sacrificial libation of blood that bestowed the Divine Spirit and brought an end to the persecution of Christians at Smyrna. The fact that Smyrnaean Christians worshipped at the tomb of Polycarp raises the question of whether that worship incorporated the funerary customs of a *refrigerium*.

The *Martyrdom of St. Perpetua and St. Felicitas* at Carthage, North Africa (204 CE), shows that the sacrificial libation of martyrdom could give refreshment to a deceased loved one. Since Perpetua was a member of the New Prophecy (which originated in Anatolia, ca. 165–170 CE), that belief probably reflects the funerary practice of the *New Prophecy* in Asia Minor and the funerary practice of Christians at Smyrna where St. Polycarp's martyrdom was celebrated and remembered by Christians.

An analysis of Ignatius' letters shows that a generation before Polycarp's death, Smyrnaean and Ephesian Christians together with Polycarp practiced the custom of giving aid and support to Ignatius, a confessor-martyr who, in chains and the custody of ten Roman soldiers, was in route to Rome where he would die in the Colosseum. Ignatius called this his "refreshment"; and in his letter to the Roman church, he encouraged Christians there to give "refreshment" to other Syrian confessor-martyrs whom he knew were ahead of him on the road, destined also for the Roman Colosseum. "Refreshment" appears to be the process of preparing a confessor-martyr to give their witness by facing death in the arena. It appears quite probable that Ignatius knew and approved of the practice of Christian *refrigeria* at Antioch.

The *Passio of St. Perpetua and St. Felicitas* reveals the belief of the *New Prophecy*—that when a confessor gives their witness unto death and attains paradise, they continue to share in meal fellowship, are capable of enjoying the scent and beauty of flowers, and are available to hear the prayers of Christians in the earthly church. All of this is offered in a *refrigerium* at the grave of a martyr—a *refrigerium* that gives refreshment to the martyr.

In addition, Perpetua's visions of her brother, Dinocrates (age seven) reveals the belief that a confessor, while in prison awaiting martyrdom, has the power to offer her martyrdom (a second baptism) as a sacrificial libation that bestows forgiveness of sins to a deceased pagan. In her vision, she sees Dinocrates (who died as a pagan from cancer of the face) coming out of a dark place. He was still suffering from the odious cancer; he appeared shabby, filthy, feverishly hot, and exceedingly thirsty. Perpetua awoke and began praying for him through the night and day, shedding tears in the hope that he would be "forgiven on my behalf." Days later, in another vision she saw him—"with a clean body, well-dressed, and refreshed (*refrigerantem*)." He was standing beside a pool of water and water was flowing from the pool, "without ceasing." Dinocrates had been baptized in "living water."

By drawing on the power of her imminent martyrdom (a second baptism) conceived of as a sacrificial libation of blood, Perpetua had offered it as a sacrificial libation for/to her brother. The "refreshment" of Dinocrates must presuppose Perpetua's *refrigerium* belief that a wine libation offered at the grave of a deceased person does refresh that person. Both pagan and Christian believed that. But in Perpetua's case, that belief is transformed by the fact that as a confessor/martyr she offers not a sacrificial wine libation but instead, a sacrificial libation of blood (martyrdom as a second baptism). Martyrdom is a sacrificial libation that can be offered up for the redemption of others.

Since Perpetua was member of the *New Prophecy*—a movement that originated in Asia Minor, ca. 165–170 CE, it is quite probable that catholic Christians at Smyrna (who had "refreshed" Ignatius, ca. 125 CE, while he was in route to Rome) were already by the time of Polycarp's death (157 CE) holding *refrigeria* that gave "refreshment" to their martyrs.

Assuming that the eucharist at Smyrna was similar to that of Ignatius', the incorporation of *refrigerium* funerary customs into a eucharist/agape at the tomb of Polycarp would have been facilitated by the similarity of a sacrificial libation—performed in both eucharist and *refrigerium*. But there would have been a difference. A eucharist/agape wine libation poured onto the shrine-altar tomb of Polycarp would signify a remembrance of the victorious deaths of Polycarp and Jesus Christ (their libations of blood poured out in their redemptive deaths). A *refrigerium* libation poured on the tomb would have been a wine libation offered by the supplicant as a form of fellowship with and refreshment of St. Polycarp. And whether it be a eucharist/agape libation or a *refrigerium* libation—both would be expressions of gratitude and prayer requests to those (Jesus the Messiah and those disciples who followed him by drinking of his cup)—who had vanquished the devil and had overcome the power of death.

Chapter 7

Conclusion

This study breaks new ground in the understanding of the eucharist in the thought of St. Ignatius, bishop of Antioch (ca. 125 CE). Chapter 2 demonstrated that Ignatius did not (contrary to the consensus of scholarship in the twentieth century) hold to sacramental realism, that is, the belief that in the eucharist the elements of bread and wine were, per se, the reality of the flesh and blood of the risen, crucified Jesus Christ. By examining the three texts (*Eph.* 20.2; *Smyr.* 7.1; *Rom.* 7.3) that have been used by scholars to support his alleged sacramental realism, I showed that in each case, there is a more plausible interpretation than that of sacramental realism.

1. IGNATIUS: NO SACRAMENTAL REALISM

Concerning the Ephesians' text that speaks of their "breaking one loaf which is the medicine of immortality, the antidote of not dying" (20.2), I showed that "breaking one loaf" refers to the whole eucharistic service—the fellowship in the episcopal assembly in which through the meal of food and drink, choral song, prayer, ecstatic prophecy, healing and preaching, the crucified and risen Messiah is made known in the unity and harmony of all members. "The medicine of immortality" is the unity of "imperishable agape" (cf. *Rom.* 7.3) experienced in the fellowship of one episcopal body.

Concerning *Smyr.* 7.1, I showed that there the terms *eucharist* and *flesh of Jesus Christ* have ecclesial connotations so that the traditional English translation—"the eucharist is the flesh of our savior Jesus Christ" should be instead—"the eucharistic assembly is the flesh of our savior Jesus Christ." "The flesh of Jesus Christ" is a reference to the eucharistic assembly as the body of Jesus Christ.

The other important fact is that Ignatius will use a term that in the same sentence can have both an ecclesial and Christological connotation. The term "*flesh* of *Jesus Christ*" has both connotations. Ignatius is arguing that the heterodox at Smyrna refuse to attend Polycarp's eucharistic assembly "because they do not confess that the eucharistic assembly [of Polycarp] is the flesh of our savior Jesus Christ—the flesh which suffered for our sins, which the Father raised by his goodness." "The flesh of our savior Jesus Christ" refers to the eucharistic assembly [of Polycarp] as the church, the body of Christ; it refers also to the flesh of the historical Jesus that suffered and was raised by the Father. In one sentence, Ignatius refutes the two errors of the schismatic Smyrnaeans who have separated from Polycarp's church (assembly) and who claim that Jesus never suffered (the docetic heresy). The heterodox have lost contact with the crucified and risen Messiah because they have separated from Polycarp's episcopal eucharistic assembly where Messiah resides. And the heterodox, being docetic, deny that Jesus suffered in the flesh for their sins.

2. JOHN 6:51B-58: NO SACRAMENTAL REALISM

My response to the third text, *Rom.* 7.3, is given in both chapters 2 and 3, where I examine the meaning of *John* 6:53, since a number of scholars (who maintain sacramental realism in Ignatius), see *Rom.* 7.3 as an echo of *John* 6:53. When Ignatius contemplates his death in the Roman Colosseum, he says—"I receive no pleasure in perishable food or the delights of this life. I desire the bread of God which is the flesh of Jesus Christ. . . . And as drink, I desire his blood, which is, imperishable agape" (7.3).

The similarity with *John* 6:53 is striking. There, Jesus says to his disciples—"Unless you eat the flesh of the Son of Man and drink his blood, you have no life in you." In the latter half of the twentieth century, a dominant interpretation of this Johannine saying was to argue that *John* 6:51b-58 reflected the thought of a Redactor, in distinction from the rest of chapter 6, which came from the hand of the Fourth Evangelist. In this view, Ignatius knew the Gospel of John, was a sacramental realist, and used eucharistic language strikingly similar to *John* 6:53. Hence, the conclusion: the Redactor is a sacramental realist. The case for arguing that *John* 6:51b-58 represents sacramental realism is quite doubtful once one sees that Ignatius was not a sacramental realist.

In the rest of chapter 3, I show that *John* 6:51b-58 fits well into *John* 6, which is the Johannine depiction of a prophetic Messiah at a Galilean synagogue gathering, foretelling his violent death by likening it to the slaughter of a Passover lamb and employing the image of a sacrificial meal of eating and drinking as a metaphor of belief—the internalizing of Jesus' life and violent death as a revelation of Divine Wisdom. "Eating the flesh and drinking the blood of the Son of Man" is also a metaphor which, in the context of persecution and risk of death at the hands of provincial authorities, expresses the necessity of martyrdom as the cost of discipleship. In the context of martyrdom, the necessity of "eating the flesh and drinking the blood of the Son of Man" is the necessity of sealing one's witness by shedding one's blood in imitation of and sharing in the suffering and death of the Son of Man.

Chapters 2 and 3 clear the way for a fresh view of Ignatius' understanding of the eucharist—viewing him without the lens of sacramental realism. In chapter 4, I set forth the central thesis of this study: that the ritual act of a wine libation was a component of the eucharist/agape of Ignatius, bishop of Antioch, in the first half of the second century.

3. MARTYRDOM AND EUCHARIST/ AGAPE: SACRIFICIAL LIBATION

Sacrificial wine libations were a common feature of Greco-Roman culture, and they were offered when wine was drunk—whether at a family meal, the gathering of members of a club or association, a festive celebration of a birth, a rite of initiation, a marriage, or a visit to a cemetery in order to remember a loved one and offer them a sacrificial libation, or the sealing of a peace treaty between two parties.

A cup/bowl is filled with wine and the supplicant pours some of the wine into a dish on the table where members are eating or on the hearth of a home or on the altar of a temple while invoking/praying to the Deity. At a cemetery, the wine libation is poured on the tomb, down a pipe that leads to the ashes or corpse of the loved one at the bottom of the tomb.

In the ritual of animal sacrifice, a libation completes the sacrifice when wine is poured on the flames of the altar where the flesh of the animal is being burned. Thus, libation and sacrificial flesh on the altar are intimately linked in the religious imagination. In Hellenistic Judaism, a wine libation was a significant feature of the Tamid temple service: the twice daily (at sunrise and sunset) congregational worship in which there was a whole burnt offering of a lamb and a grain offering together with the blood of the lamb and a wine libation poured on the altar. The wine libation was called "the blood of the grape" (*Sirach.* 50:15).

Among some Christians in apostolic Christianity, the sacrificial wine libation was a red thread in their fabric of understanding the death of Jesus, martyrdom as an imitation of his death, and the eucharist/agape as a meal that proclaimed the redemptive power of Jesus' death. The apostle Paul understood his imminent death as a libation that would be offered in behalf of the Philippian Christians who had given him aid in his imprisonment (*Phil.* 2:17). According to Acts, Paul's change of heart and mind—from being a persecutor of the church to his summons as an apostle—was produced by the redemptive power of Stephen's sacrificial libation of blood offered as a prayer of forgiveness for his enemies (*Acts* 7:59–8:1; 22:20).

The prophet John understood the death of Jesus (the slaughtered/sacrificed lamb) in light of the Tamid service and the deaths of Antipas and his fellow martyrs as sacrificial libations (poured on the altar) that completed Jesus' sacrifice (*Rev.* 5:6; 6:9–10; 16:5–7; 17:4–6). The Apocalypse of John shows that Christian Jews depicted martyrdom as a libation poured on a heavenly altar (6:9–10). When the Jerusalem temple and altar were destroyed in 70 CE, martyr altar shrines probably evolved in the cemeteries of the seven churches of Revelation; and the practice of using an altar table probably evolved in the house churches of those communities.

All four gospels portray Jesus' passion as "his cup" (*Mark* 10:38; *Luke* 22:42; *Matt.* 26:39; *John* 18:11). In the narration of the last supper, a libation verb (ἐκχέω) is employed in all three Synoptic Gospels.[1] In Mark, it is a verbal adjective attached to "my blood of the covenant which is being poured out as a sacrificial libation in behalf of the many" (τὸ αἷμά μου τῆς διαθήκης τὸ ἐκχυννόμενον ὑπὲρ πολλῶν, 14:24); in Matthew, the verbal adjective also modifies "blood"; but Matthew adds to the formula—"for the forgiveness of sins," thus making clear the redemptive effect of Jesus' blood being poured out—"my blood of the covenant which is being poured out as a sacrificial libation in behalf of the many for the forgiveness of sins" (τὸ αἷμά μου τῆς διαθήκης τὸ περὶ πολλῶν ἐκχυννόμενον εἰς ἄφεσιν ἁμαρτιῶν, 26:28).

There is nothing in Mark or Matthew indicating that a libation has been poured from the cup. The libation participle modifies "my blood of the covenant" and, therefore, is describing Jesus' death as a sacrificial libation of blood that seals Jesus' covenant with his disciples and makes effective the forgiveness of sins. However, in Luke (22:20), the libation character of Jesus' death is explicitly tied to the eucharist/agape cup. "This cup is the new covenant in my blood—the cup being poured out as a sacrificial libation in behalf of you" (Τοῦτο τὸ ποτήριον ἡ καινὴ διαθήκη ἐν τῷ αἵματί μου, τὸ ὑπερ ὑμῶν ἐκχυννόμενον). The pouring of wine from a libation cup is the analog for expressing the shedding of Jesus' blood unto death: the sacrificial wine libation symbolizes the offering of his sacrificial love in behalf of his disciples. The wine in the cup symbolizes his blood.

---

1. Significant is the fact that although Paul can imagine his martyrdom as a blood libation (Phil. 2:17), when he narrates his version of the last supper—unlike the Synoptic versions—he does not employ the language of libation (1 Cor. 11:23–26) either with regard to the cup or the blood of Jesus; and Paul's version is earlier than the Synoptic versions. What separates Paul from the Synoptic Evangelists is the destruction of the temple and its altar in 70 CE. After 70 CE, there are no more Tamid services in which the wine of the libation cup ("the blood of the grape") flows onto the altar. I am arguing that the Synoptic versions of the last supper are a response to the loss of sacrificial worship (post 70 CE) of the Tamid service.

The pre-70 CE Tamid temple service of a sacrificial offering of a lamb and a grain offering together with the blood of the lamb and a wine libation poured on the altar has been transformed in the Christian Jewish eucharist/agape remembrance of Jesus, the slaughtered lamb of God who poured out his blood as a sacrificial libation for the forgiveness of sins. In Luke's community, the pouring of wine from a eucharist/agape cup onto a dish or bowl on the altar symbolizes the redemptive sacrificial death of Jesus the Messiah.

The best evidence for a conscious linking of martyrdom as a libation of blood with a libation poured from a eucharist/agape cup is found in Ignatius (ca. 125 CE). While in route to Rome (chained to other prisoners in the custody of ten Roman soldiers), Ignatius wrote to Roman Christians, expressing his desire to face the wild animals in the Colosseum, to be ground into "pure bread" as a "sacrifice" and "to pour out himself as a libation to the Divine while the [Roman] altar is still prepared in order that you [Roman Christians], as a choir of agape might sing to the Father in Messiah Jesus . . ." (2.2; 4.1–2).

The assumption seems to be that Ignatius hopes his own martyrdom as a sacrificial libation will coincide with the moment in which Roman Christians are enacting a sacrificial libation in their eucharist/agape. He views his martyrdom in the Colosseum as in some sense a re-enactment of the eucharist/agape. His body will be an offering of bread, his blood will be poured out as a sacrificial libation of agape, and his witness as one sharing in the passion of Jesus the Messiah will be a proclamation of "the Word of God" to the pagan spectators (*Rom.* 2.1; 6.3; 7.3).

A similar link between martyrdom as a sacrificial libation and eucharist/agape is also evident in Ignatius' letter to the Philadelphians in which he encourages unity in their "one eucharist/agape assembly—for there is one flesh of our Lord Jesus Messiah [cf. Pauline *Eph.* 5:31–32] and one cup for unity of his blood [cf. *1 Cor* 10:16], one altar. . . . My brethren, I am overflowing with agape for you, like a sacrificial libation . . ." (4.1–5.1). It seems, quite probable, that the cluster of "eucharist/agape assembly—cup—altar—sacrificial libation" are held together in Ignatius' imagination, because at Antioch the character of a eucharist/agape contained the ritual of pouring wine from a cup into a dish on an altar table as a memorial of the redemptive, sacrificial death of Jesus Messiah. This conclusion makes sense of Ignatius' desire to be poured out as a libation in the Colosseum "while a [Roman Christian] altar is still prepared," and it is consistent with the Synoptic Gospels' depiction of the last supper where Jesus' death is imagined as a drinking of his cup and understood as a sacrificial libation poured out, thus sealing his covenant with his disciples.

Ignatius is good evidence for the thesis that a sacrificial wine libation is not simply a ritual metaphor for understanding the sacrificial power of Jesus' death and viewing Christian martyrdom as an imitation of his passion; it is also a ritual act in the Christian eucharist/agape. The pouring of a wine libation into a libation bowl or cup, sitting on an altar table, was a remembrance of Jesus' sacrificial death, of the giving up of his life in service of others.

4. SACRIFICIAL LIBATION AND THE *REFRIGERIUM*

The offering of a wine libation in order to remember the life and death of a loved one would not in any way have seemed strange to a Gentile who became a Christian. Indeed, in both the western and eastern parts of the Roman Empire, a pagan would go to the cemetery, four times/year, in order to remember a deceased relative or friend and offer them—food, drink, and flowers. It was not uncommon to pour a wine libation down a pipe which carried the wine to the bottom of the tomb, where the ashes or corpse resided.

The visit to the cemetery of friends and family of the deceased loved one was the occasion of a *refrigerium,* that is, a picnic in which food and wine was shared among family and friends and in which the deceased person was believed to be present and able to participate in the gathering. The *refrigerium* was an experience of fellowship around food and drink, of sharing stories about the deceased loved one, of singing songs and the offering of prayers. The pouring of a wine libation into a hole in the ground—into a tube that went to the bottom of the tomb—was a way of allowing the deceased to share in the *refrigerium*, and to receive "refreshment."

There is ample evidence that when a pagan became a Christian, they did not give up the practice of a *refrigerium*. At Rome (at mile three of the Appian Way), there is an inscription (a wall graffito) at the joint memorial (ca. 268 CE) of St. Peter and St. Paul that reads: *"ad Paulum et Petrum refrigeravi"*— "I have refreshed Peter and Paul." The inscription shows that *refrigerium* meals were held at the joint apostolic shrine; and by those meals, refreshment was given to the apostles. Although the precise burial site of the apostles is not certain, excavation of the Church of the Apostle (now San Sebastiano), which Constantine built at the site, has disclosed its approximate location and the hundreds of graffiti left there by Christians. Libation holes have been found in the gallery floor of the church.

The similarity of a pagan *refrigerium* and a Christian *refrigerium* at the tomb of a martyr is noteworthy. In both cases, there is a gathering of people who share in a meal of fellowship and who offer the deceased loved one a wine libation as a way of sharing in the meal.

5. A *REFRIGERIUM* AT ANTIOCH IN IGNATIUS' EPISCOPATE

The evidence at the joint memorial leaves one wondering about the earliest date for such a practice that focused on honoring the memory of Christian martyrs. If one could show that Ignatius knew of and supported Christian *refrigeria* at the tomb of a martyr, then one has another instance of the ritual of wine libation that must be factored into his experience of wine libation.

Chapter 6 examines Ignatius' letters and shows that "refreshment" was the physical (food/drink) and spiritual (worship and fellowship) offering given to a confessor-martyr who is preparing to offer a sacrificial libation of blood in the arena; and although Ignatius never mentions a *refrigerium* at the tomb of a martyr, nevertheless, the similarity of Ignatius' "refreshment" given to the confessor and "refreshment" at the tomb of a martyr is striking. A *refrigerium* at the tomb of a martyr is "refreshment" of food, drink, and fellowship offered to one whose witness has been completed in a sacrificial libation of blood. The difference between Ignatius' notion of "refreshment" and a *refrigerium* offered at the tomb of a martyr is the difference between "refreshment" offered to a confessor-martyr in anticipation of their death and "refreshment" (*refrigerium*) as an offering to the confessor-martyr after they have been martyred. Refreshment given at the tomb is a continuation of refreshment that had been given to the confessor: each refreshment is a way of maintaining solidarity with the confessor-martyr; each refreshment is an aspect of an organic two stage process of giving love and support to a confessor-martyr.

Since Ignatius knew, encouraged, and was consciously participating in the first stage, he almost certainly knew and approved of the second stage. It is highly probable that when Ignatius was bishop at Antioch, he approved and supported the funerary practice of a *refrigerium* at the tomb of a martyr.

6. *REFRIGERIUM*, THE *NEW PROPHECY* AND THE *PASSIO OF PERPETUA AND FELICITY*

The best case for Christian *refrigeria* in Asia Minor, contemporary with Polycarp (who was a friend of Ignatius and martyred in 157 CE, a generation after Ignatius' death) is the existence of Christian *refrigeria* at Carthage, North Africa (ca. 204 CE). It is there that the *Passio of St. Perpetua and St. Felicitas* reveals the beliefs of the *New Prophecy*—that when a confessor gives their witness unto death and attains paradise, they continue to share in meal fellowship, is capable of enjoying the scent and beauty of flowers, and is available to hear Christian prayers rising from the earthly church. All of this is offered in a *refrigerium* at the grave of a martyr—a *refrigerium* that gives refreshment to the martyr.

Perpetua's visions of her brother, Dinocrates (age seven), reveals also the belief that a confessor-martyr, while in prison awaiting martyrdom, has the power to offer her martyrdom (a second baptism) as a sacrificial libation that effects the forgiveness of sins. In her first vision, she sees Dinocrates (who died as a pagan from cancer of the face) coming out of a dark place. He was still suffering from the odious cancer; he appeared shabby, filthy, feverishly hot, and exceedingly thirsty. Perpetua awoke and began praying for him through the night and day, shedding tears in the hope that he would be "forgiven on my behalf." Days later, in another vision she saw him—"with a clean body, well dressed, and refreshed (*refrigerantem*)." He was standing beside a pool of water and water was flowing from the pool, "without ceasing." Dinocrates had been baptized in "living water."

By drawing on the power of her imminent martyrdom (a second baptism) conceived of as a libation of blood, Perpetua had offered it as a sacrificial libation for/to her deceased brother. The "refreshment" of Dinocrates must presuppose Perpetua's *refrigerium* belief that a wine libation offered at the grave of a deceased person does refresh that person. Both pagan and Christian believed that. But in Perpetua's case, that belief is transformed by the fact that as a confessor-martyr she offers not a sacrificial wine libation but instead, a sacrificial libation of blood (martyrdom as a second baptism).[2]

Since Perpetua was a member of the *New Prophecy*—a movement that originated in Asia Minor, ca. 165–170 CE, it is quite probable that Christians at Smyrna (who had "refreshed" Ignatius, ca. 125 CE while he was in route to Rome) were already by the time of Polycarp's death (157 CE) holding *refrigeria* that gave "refreshment" to their martyrs. More likely than not, Christian *refrigeria* were practiced at Smyrna even during the generation of Ignatius.

7. SACRIFICIAL LIBATION AT POLYCARP'S TOMB

Chapter 6 showed the high probability that a eucharist-*refrigerium* was celebrated at the tomb of Polycarp. According to *The Martyrdom of Polycarp,* after Polycarp died, a Roman centurion had his body completely burned.

---

2. The belief that martyrdom as a baptism of blood can be offered to/for another person makes sense in the case of Perpetua. She had very recently been baptized, during her house arrest and detainment. Does she need another baptism? From her perspective, it would have made sense to offer it to/for Dinocrates who was in need of baptismal grace. This is a powerful example of the apostolic belief that a martyr's death (as an act of sacrificial love and obedience) is redemptive for others. The same view was held in post-70 CE Hellenistic Judaism. See 4 Maccabees 6:28–9; 17:20–2. For dating (late first century) and discussion, see Jan Willem van Henten, *The Maccabean Martyrs as Saviors of the Jewish People* (Leiden: E. J. Brill, 1997), 58–82.

Later, Christians took up Polycarp's bones and placed them in a tomb. They were "more precious than expensive gems and more valuable than gold" (18.1–2). This description together with a statement of what the gathered community did each year at the tomb—"in so far as possible the Lord will grant us, assembled as a synagogue with gladness and joy, the opportunity to celebrate the birthday of his martyrdom in memory of both those martyr-athletes who have preceded him and also for the discipline and training of those who are destined [for martyrdom]" (18.3)—suggests that Polycarp's tomb was an important shrine-altar for worship and meal fellowship of Smyrnaean Christians with one another and the spirit of Polycarp. If their eucharist was like that of Ignatius', there would have been a sharing of food and drink and a pouring of a wine libation on the altar-shrine tomb. But these also are acts done in a *refrigerium*. Smyrnaeans knew that Polycarp's death had been a libation of blood that ended the persecution at Smyrna. Were they offering him a wine libation as thanksgiving for his libation of blood?[3]

8. SACRIFICIAL LIBATION IN A EUCHARIST/ AGAPE AND IN A *REFRIGERIUM*

To those scholarly critics who would agree—that the image of a sacrificial wine libation is employed to express the redemptive power of Jesus' death and to depict the redemptive power of his disciples who in their martyrdoms imitated Jesus' sacrificial agape—but who, nevertheless, would argue that sacrificial libation remains only a metaphor and is not a ritual act in the eucharist, I offer a threefold response. One, in the Lukan narrative of the last supper, the libation participle—τὸ ἐκχυννόμενον—is not attached to the blood of Jesus (as it is in Mark and Matthew); rather, it is attached to the cup—"the cup, which is the new covenant in Jesus' blood, is poured out as a

---

3. In chapter 5, I showed that John 19:34 proclaims that the death of Jesus is an eschatological fulfillment of the hopes associated with festivals of Tabernacles, Passover, Hanukkah, and daily worship (Tamid) at the temple. When the Evangelist underscores the testimony of blood and water issuing from the body of the crucified Jesus (when the soldier thrusts his spear into the side of Jesus) he expresses a correlation with the water and wine libations that flow onto the temple altar during the festival of Tabernacles (water libation) in conjunction with the offering of Tamid (wine libation). This testimony is the Johannine gospel: in Jesus' sacrificial death (his blood poured out as a sacrificial libation), the power of death is overcome and the life of the Divine Spirit ("living water" issuing forth from Jesus' body; cf. 7:38–39) is present for his disciples. Likewise, the martyrdom of Polycarp—as a drinking of Jesus' cup, that is, an imitation of and sharing in the death of Jesus (as depicted in the Gospel of John)—is a libation of blood that releases the Divine Spirit (*Mart. Poly.* 14.2; 16.1). The other incident that reveals the Johannine view of Jesus' death (as a libation of blood that will wash the disciples) is the prophetic action of Jesus—during the last supper—assuming the role of a slave and washing the feet of his disciples (13:1–11). They will be washed by his sacrificial death. In Revelation, the martyrs, who imitated his passion, are described as those who "washed their garments and made them white in the blood of the Lamb" (7:14).

sacrificial libation in behalf of you" (22:20). A ritual of libation is explicitly mentioned and tied to the eucharist/agape cup. I assume that this is not a literary creation of Luke but instead reflects the libation practice in his community in the late first century. To argue (as some scholars have) that *Luke* 22:20 is a literary creation and does not reflect the eucharist/agape practice of the Lukan community is unsustainable. For surely that community used Luke's gospel in its catechesis. If one assumes that 22:20 is only a literary creation of a community that poured no libation from the eucharist/agape cup, how would the catechist respond to a question that would certainly arise from a catechumen who either read 22:20 or heard it read: namely, why is no libation poured from our eucharist/agape cup? If the catechist responded with—"*Luke* 22:20 does not describe our eucharist/agape practice; it is simply a literary creation"—what would that catechumen think of such a community?[4]

Moreover, catechumens would have experienced, in their former lives as pagans, participating in a *refrigerium* at the grave site of a loved one in which libations of wine had been offered in a remembrance of that loved one. The Lukan eucharist/agape of 22:19–20 contained a libation that was a memorial of Jesus' death. Would not Lukan catechumens have anticipated that their baptism would be an initiation leading to a eucharist/agape meal, containing a libation done in remembrance of the death of Jesus the Messiah?

Two, when Ignatius depicts his martyrdom in the Colosseum as a "libation poured out to the Divine" while the Roman Christian "altar is still prepared" so that they (Roman Christians) could "sing with agape to the Father in Messiah Jesus," he is expressing his hope that his death would be synchronized with Christian worship at Rome. The statement seems to presuppose Ignatius' assumption that in worship, a wine libation is poured on the altar as a memorial of Jesus' death.

Three, the (almost certain) existence of a Christian *refrigerium* at the tomb of Polycarp by 158 CE (the first anniversary of his martyrdom) shows that sacrificial libations were performed at the tomb of a martyr.[5] In addi-

---

4. I am not arguing that the Lukan community employed a eucharist/agape liturgy that contained the ritualistic words found in that gospel concerning the bread and wine. Rather, I argue that in its ritual acts, there was a libation poured from the cup.

5. Admittedly, the meaning of a wine libation in a *refrigerium* and a eucharist/agape are different. Since a Gentile catechumen would have been familiar (as a pagan) with the meaning of a wine libation poured into the tomb of a loved one in order to refresh her/him, little instruction would have been necessary in order to understand the meaning of a wine libation at the tomb of a martyr. But in order to understand that a eucharist/agape libation represents the death of Jesus as a redemptive libation of blood, a catechumen would have needed catechesis. Nevertheless, there was cause for confusion. Like the death of Jesus, Polycarp's death was also a libation of blood which released the Divine Spirit. That similarity together with the similarity of eucharist/agape and a martyr refrigerium—a meal of fellowship commemorating and giving thanks for a spiritual man whose sacrificial death released the Divine Spirit—probably accounts for the distinction made at the end of Polycarp's *Passio* (17.3)—"For this one [the Lord] we worship as the Son who is of the Divine, but the martyrs we love as disciples and imitators of the Lord. . . . May it be that we become both their companions and co-disciples."

tion, it appears highly probable that at Antioch, during Ignatius' episcopate, Christian *refrigeria* took place at the tombs of martyrs.

In light of these three points—the Lukan eucharistic practice in the late first century of pouring a libation from the cup, signifying Jesus shedding his blood as a sacrificial libation that seals the covenant of forgiveness and peace with his disciples; Ignatius' desire to synchronize his death as a libation poured out while the altar of Roman Christians was still prepared; the almost certain existence of a *refrigerium*/eucharist at the tomb of Polycarp (ca. 158 CE)—the conclusion seems unavoidable: the ritual of a sacrificial wine libation was, very probably, part of a Christian's worship life and part of a Christian way of remembering their loved ones—whether they be saints, martyrs, or dear friends and relatives. In other words, sacrificial libation had metaphoric power, eucharistic-liturgical power, and "refreshment" funerary power to inspire, encourage, and maintain a solidarity of fellowship, laughter, joy, love, affection, and admiration between the living and the dead. Sacrificial wine libation was both image and ritual act in the one hundred year period of 70–170 CE for Christians in Anatolia and Syria.[6]

9. SACRIFICIAL LIBATION AND CHRISTIAN IDENTITY

In my attempt to demonstrate the existence of a sacrificial libation in the eucharist/agape of Ignatius, what was critical was showing that Jesus' death was understood as a sacrificial libation; and that a number of martyrdoms in the late first and early second century were also understood as sacrificial libations whose model was the passion of Jesus. However, martyrdom was more than an imitation of Jesus' innocent suffering and death in behalf of others. Through the intimate communion of the martyr and the crucified, risen Jesus, the confessor's innocent suffering and death became a revelation of the continuing presence of the sacrificial agape of the crucified, risen Jesus. Hence, when Ignatius speaks of his imminent death in the Roman Colosseum as a sacrificial libation, he has confidence that that libation will be a communication of the Divine Word. He believed that the Divine had "summoned" him from the East to come to the Roman Colosseum in order to proclaim and

---

6. I assume that all the churches of Ignatius' correspondence as well as the other churches of the Apocalypse of John had a eucharistic service that included a eucharistic libation, that is, wine poured from the cup into a bowl or dish resting on a table-altar or a libation poured on the shrine-altar of a martyr's tomb. The churches are: Antioch, Ephesus, Rome, Smyrna, Philadelphia, Magnesia, Tralles, Pergamum, Sardis, Thyatira, Laodicea. The testimony of Justin Martyr at Rome, a generation after Ignatius, shows that sacramental realism evolved there by 150 CE. Similarly at Lugdunum, Gaul, the testimony of Irenaeus, ca. 180 CE, shows that sacramental realism existed there. For a discussion of the eucharist at these places, see Paul F. Bradshaw and Maxwell E. Johnson, *The Eucharistic Liturgies* (Collegeville, MN: Liturgical Press, 2012), 26–28, 44–49, 52–53.

convey through his death—the redeeming, sacrificial agape of the crucified, risen Jesus who is the Divine Word who came forth from the Divine.[7]

In Ignatius' eucharist/agape worship at Antioch, the ritual pouring of a wine libation on the altar and then the act of each Christian drinking from the cup represented in a symbolic way—the pouring out of Jesus' blood in his act of sacrificial agape in his crucifixion and then each Christian partaking of Jesus' "imperishable agape." In a time when confessing the name of Jesus entailed the risk of death by the hands of Roman provincial authorities, the sharing in the eucharist/agape meal fellowship of believers strengthened and prepared them for confessing their Christian identity in the face of such a threat.

Participation in the eucharist/agape meal fellowship of sharing food and drink gave each Christian a taste of the "imperishable agape." The cultic act of offering a sacrificial wine libation and the participation of all members in drinking from the cup was a powerful symbol communicating what was at the heart of Christian fellowship: the imperishable agape of the Divine who had become a human being, creating fellowship with sinners and through the suffering love in his crucifixion, offering his flesh and blood as a redemptive event. The death of Jesus as a sacrificial libation of blood destroyed the power of death, washed away sin, and gave the life of his Spirit of forgiveness and peace to the members of his assembly/church. Those members were aware of the possibility of being chosen to confess their identities and offer a sacrificial libation in the amphitheater.

The martyrdoms discussed in this study show that the sacrificial agape of Jesus Christ revealed in his crucifixion continued to live in society through the sanguinary witness of his disciples and their martyrdoms. Those deaths—offered in behalf of others—were understood as sacrificial libations of blood that were also redemptive. For example, Stephen's death brought forgiveness to Saul/Paul, an enemy of the gospel, and transformed him into an apostle to the Gentiles; Ignatius' death strengthened the unity of the church and was a proclamation of the Divine Word to pagan spectators in the Roman Colosseum; Perpetua's death brought baptismal grace and the new life of the Spirit to her seven year old pagan brother, Dinocrates, who had died of cancer.

The cultic act of pouring a sacrificial wine libation into a dish on an altar at a eucharist/agape service and then each member drinking from the cup of wine—was available only to baptized members gathered behind closed doors.

---

7. For the communion between martyr and the crucified, risen Jesus, see *Ign. Rom.* 6.3; for a striking parallel in the anonymous author's description of Felicity's suffering, see *Passio of Perpetua and Felicity*, 15.5–6. Recall that the anonymous author of the *Passio* was a member of the New Prophecy, a movement of confessors and martyrs originating in Asia Minor, a decade after Polycarp's martyrdom. For martyrdom as a proclamation of the Divine Word, see *Ign. Rom.* 2.1–2; *Mag.* 8.2; *Eph.* 19.1. The association of sacrificial libation with proclamation of the Divine Word probably also indicates that in Ignatius' eucharist/agape service, preaching came after the meal of food and drink.

But such a cultic act found its public expression in the acts of the martyrs who poured out their blood in an amphitheater and thus proclaimed in their deaths what was at the heart of their Christian identity: the fellowship of those who are seeking to live in unity of agape with one another and with the abiding presence of the Spirit and Wisdom of the imperishable agape of the crucified and risen Jesus Christ.[8]

---

8. Scholarship has shown the profound connection between martyrdom and the eucharist in the sacrificial offering of the eucharistic prayer. Maxwell E. Johnson ("Martyrs and the Mass: The Interpretation of the Narrative Institution into the Anaphora," *Worship* 87.1 [Collegeville, MN: Liturgical Press, 2013], 2–22) suggests that with the peace of Constantine (early fourth century) and the termination of martyrdom, only then did the institution narrative become part of the eucharistic prayer in order to retain "the inseparable connection between sacrifice and eucharist" (22). I have shown that the ritual act of sacrificial libation in the eucharist/agape of Ignatius was one of the prayerful acts that maintained "the inseparable connection between sacrifice and eucharist" for the churches in Syria and Anatolia, during the period of ca. 70–170 CE.

Appendix: The Dating of Ignatius

1. THE INSIGHT OF TIMOTHY D. BARNES

Since 1979, the dating of Ignatius' martyrdom has been vigorously debated. Timothy D. Barnes summarizes that debate and then sets forth a new view, arguing for a date early in the reign of Antoninus Pius (138–161 CE).[1] Barnes observes that in describing the incarnation, both Ignatius and Ptolemaeus, a Valentinian teacher at Rome (ca. 140 CE), use identical adjectives—"visible and touchable and passible" (ὁρατὸν καὶ ψηλαφητὸν καὶ παθητόν) in their teaching about the incarnation. But where Ignatius employs these three adjectives (*Poly.* 3.2), he warns Polycarp to beware of those "who teach strange doctrine" (3.1). Barnes concludes that "Ignatius is quoting, answering, and contradicting Ptolemaeus" because in all Greek literature from Homer to John of Damascus (early eighth century CE), the combination of the words ψηλαφητός (touchable), ὁρατός (visible) and παθητόν (passible) is found only in Ignatius and Ptolemaeus (as quoted in Irenaeus' *Adv. haer* 1.6.1, Rousseau/Doutreleau; 1.1.11, Harvey).[2] For Barnes, the "obvious inference" is that "Ignatius knew the teaching of Ptolemaeus" (125).

I am not persuaded by Barnes' reasoning. Admittedly, the uniqueness of the adjectives in only Ignatius and Ptolemaeus cannot be coincidence. One of them must be responding to the other. But it does not necessarily follow that Ignatius is refuting "the teaching of Ptolemaeus" at Smyrna where Polycarp resides. It is equally plausible that Ptolemaeus, whom Irenaeus was quoting, was refuting the teaching of Ignatius at Rome, ca. 140 CE.

If Ignatius was martyred at Rome a decade or two before 140 CE, Roman Christians already would have had the seven letters of Ignatius before

---

1. Timothy D. Barnes, "Date of Ignatius," *Expository Times*, 120.3 (2008): 119–130.
2. *Ibid.*, 124–25.

Ptolemaeus showed up in 140 CE.[3] Ignatius had been the bishop of Antioch; his thought reflects the influence of the apostle Paul and the Johannine tradition. Roman Christians would have witnessed his martyrdom in the Colosseum. Later, when they encountered the Gnostic teaching of Valentinus and his disciple, Ptolemaeus, ca. 140 CE, it is plausible that they would have used Ignatius' thought to refute that Gnostic teaching.

The church's struggle with Gnosticism was intense and passionate. Each side thought it had the truth about the nature and destiny of human life and about the nature of redemption in Jesus Christ. And each side sought to refute the other and win converts to its view of the gospel.

The unique combination of the adjectives "visible and touchable and passible" found only in Ptolemaeus and Ignatius may show that two groups of Christians at Rome—followers of Ptolemaeus and followers of Ignatius—were in a heated debate with one another over the nature of the incarnation and its redemptive meaning for human life. Thus, in that debate, Ptolemaeus may well have responded to Ignatian vocabulary but given it a different Gnostic twist. As Irenaeus says of Ptolemaeus and his disciples, "they affirm that . . . he [Christ] clothed himself in a body that had a breathing essence . . . fashioned with inexpressible skill, so that he became seeable, touchable, and passible (ὁρατὸν καὶ ψηλαφητὸν καὶ παθητόν). But they do not say that he took on a material quality, since <they believe> that matter cannot receive salvation."[4] The first part of this Ptolemaean teaching could be an echo of Ignatius' teaching. Compare *Ign. Poly.* 3.2: "Wait for the one who is above temporality—eternal, who is invisible (though for our sake visible), untouchable, impassible (though for our sake passible), who in every way endured in our behalf."

The basic question raised by the uniqueness of the three adjectives in Ignatius and Ptolemaeus is: who is responding to whom? If the three adjectives occur in traditions found in the New Testament and/or the church of Antioch, then it is highly probable that Ignatius' immersion in those traditions accounts for his vocabulary (rather than that he encountered that vocabulary in Ptolemaeus and used it in order to refute Ptolemaeus' Gnosticism). In addition, since Gnostic Christianity predates Valentinus and Ptolemaeus, one can not assume that the mere occurrence of any of these three words in Ignatius' thought presupposes that he is refuting the Gnostic Ptolemaeus.[5]

I agree that Barnes' insight of the unique occurrence of a cluster of three adjectives in *Poly.* 3.2 and a fragment of Ptolemaeus (quoted by Irenaeus)

---

3. The letters had been collected by Polycarp (cf. *Poly. ad Phil.* 13.2).
4. This is the trans. of Barnes, "The Dating," 125.
5. According to Henry Chadwick (*The Early Church* [London: Penguin, 1956], 34) "Gnosticism is a generic term . . . to refer to theosophical adaptions of Christianity propagated by a dozen or more rival sects which broke from the early church between A.D. 80 and 150."

concerning the incarnation has to be the starting point for dating Ignatius' letters. The fact that these three adjectives are together as a cluster in only Ignatius and Ptolemaeus, and nowhere elsewhere in ancient sources from Homer to John of Damascus, early eighth century CE, is startling. The probability that this fact is coincidental is infinitesimal. Which source is the basis for the other?

2. IGNATIUS AND THE THREE ADJECTIVES

Is the Ignatian vocabulary found elsewhere in his letters or in traditions found in the New Testament or the church of Antioch? Concerning "touchable," Ignatius quotes a saying of the resurrected Jesus to the disciples—"Take, touch me (ψηλαφήσατέ με) and see that I am not an incorporeal demon" (*Smyr.* 3.2). This appears to reflect the tradition of *Luke* 24:39: "Touch me (ψηλαφήσατέ με) and see; for a ghost does not have flesh and bone like you see me having." In regard to "visible" (ὁρατός), compare *Poly.* 3.2 "the invisible one (ἀόρατον) who for our sake became visible (ὁρατόν)" and *Col.* 1:15: "who is the image of the invisible God (εἰκὼν τοῦ θεοῦ τοῦ ἀοράτου) . . . in him all things were created . . . things visible and invisible" (τὰ ὁρατὰ καὶ τὰ ἀόρατα, 1:15–16). In two places, Ignatius refers to "things visible and invisible" (*Trall.* 5.2; *Rom.* 5.3). Ignatius probably knew Colossians.

Concerning "touchable and visible," their respective verbs occur in combination in *1 John* 1:1–2: "That which was from the beginning . . . which we have seen (ἑωράκαμεν) . . . which we have looked upon and our hands have touched (αἱ χεῖρες ἡμῶν ἐψηλάφησαν) concerning the word of life. . . ." Ignatius knew the Johannine tradition. It seems quite probable that the two adjectives "visible" and "touchable" in *Poly.* 3.2 reflect his appropriation of Johannine tradition.

Concerning "passible" (παθητός), compare the creedal expression in Ignatius' letter to the Ephesians (7.2)—"There is one physician, both flesh and spirit, begotten and unbegotten, God in man, true life in death, both from Mary and from God, first passible (παθητός) and then impassible (ἀπαθής), Jesus Christ our Lord." The creedal character of the expression suggests that Ignatius is reflecting the tradition of the Antioch church.

The same can be said about Ignatius' use of the noun πάθος. Writing to the Smyrneans (1.1–2), Ignatius appears to be paraphrasing an Antiochene creed—"I glorify Jesus Christ the God . . . being truly of the race of David according to the flesh, Son of God according to the will and power of God, having been born of a virgin . . . truly (under Pontius Pilate and Herod, the Tetrarch) nailed, in behalf of us, in the flesh from which we are the fruit of his divinely blessed passion . . ." (ἀφ' οὗ καρποῦ ἡμεῖς ἀπὸ τοῦ θεομακαρίστου αὐτοῦ πάθους). The noun is found in every letter except the one to Polycarp. Sometimes it occurs with "resurrection" and is a way of speaking of Jesus' death (cf. *Mag.* 11; *Smyr.* 5.3; 12.2; *Phd.* 9.2). Other times, it appears alone and represents the suffering of Christ, which Ignatius desires to imitate (cf. *Mag.* 5.2; *Rom.* 6:3). In the Smyrnaean passage, the church is the fruit of the divinely blessed passion, the working out of the divine plan—to realize in community the unity of agape between the Son and Father that was disclosed in the passion (τὸ πάθος). Compare *Smyr.* 1.1–2; *Trall.* 11.2; *Phd.* 3.3; *Eph.* 20.1. Undoubtedly, Ignatius is refuting Gnostic docetic views of the incarnation. But they may well be docetic views of Gnostics who predated Valentinus and Ptolemaeus; and the thought and vocabulary of πάθος, παθητός, and ἀπαθής appear to have their roots in the creedal statements of the church at Antioch where Ignatius had been bishop.

Hence, Ignatius' three adjectives (visible, passible, and touchable) can be understood as revealing his knowledge of Johannine tradition, Pauline Colossians, a post-resurrection saying of Jesus found in Luke, and creedal tradition of the church of Antioch. In short, there is no necessity of inferring that in his letter to Polycarp (3.2), Ignatius is responding to the vocabulary of Ptolemaeus in order to refute Gnostic docetic views.

3. SILENCE (ΣΙΓΗ) AND THE DIVINE WORD

Barnes attempts to bolster his argument by showing that Ignatius, in his letter to the Magnesians, is refuting the Valentinian/Ptolemaean teaching that Christ descended from the Divine pair of Silence (Σιγή) and Depth (βυθός). According to Ignatius, the prophets of Judaism, "inspired by grace," taught that "there is one God who manifested himself through Jesus Christ his Son Who is the [eternal] Word [not] proceeding from silence (σιγή) and Who in every respect pleased Him Who sent him" (8.2).

Barnes argues that since the bracketed words—"eternal" and "not"—are in both the Middle and the Long Greek Recensions as well as in a Latin translation, those words must be what Ignatius wrote. Scholars, like J.B. Lightfoot and Theodor Zahn, who chose to omit the words in their critical editions of Ignatius, point to an Armenian translation and a citation of the Monophysite theologian, Severus of Antioch (early sixth century), which do not have these words. Lightfoot and Zahn thought the words in the Middle and Long Recension were those of an anti-Gnostic redactor who altered Ignatius' thought in order to use his episcopal authority to refute the Gnostic teaching of Valentinus/Ptolemaeus. Barnes argues instead that *Mag.* 8.2 reveals that Ignatius must have been writing, ca. 140 CE, and that he was refuting the

Gnostic view of Christ as the Logos (Word) who came forth from the Divine pair of Silence and Depth.[6]

Undercutting Barnes' view of *Mag.* 8.2, however, is the fact that in two other letters, Ignatius speaks positively about *silence* and its association with Jesus Christ and revelation. To the Ephesians, Ignatius says—"the Lord's death . . . was accomplished in the silence of God" (ἐν ἡσυχίᾳ Θεοῦ, 19.1; cf. also 15.2). This passage makes it quite probable that the bracketed words of *Mag.* 8.2 ("eternal" and "not"), even though they occur in both the Middle and Long Greek Recensions, are redactional and express an anti-Gnostic addition to a text that originally must have spoken of Jesus Christ as "the Word proceeding from silence. . . ."

That Ignatius saw a positive correlation between *silence* and Word of God can be discerned in what he says to the Romans. Believing that Roman Christians might use their influence to gain his pardon when he reached Rome (cf. *Rom.* 1.2; 4.1; 6.2–3), Ignatius sought to persuade them that God had summoned him "to be an imitator of the suffering of my God" (6.3). For Ignatius, the best thing Roman Christians could do was to remain silent. "For if you are silent concerning me, I shall be a Word of God" (ἐὰν γὰρ σιωπήσητε ἀπ' ἐμοῦ, ἐγὼ λόγος Θεοῦ, 2.1). Then, in the next line, Ignatius expresses his desire to shed his blood in the Colosseum as a sacrificial libation to God (2.2). Hence, the self-designation of becoming a Word of God is Ignatius' belief that since the shedding of his blood in imitation of his Lord's suffering will be a fellowship with the divine Son (cf. *Smyr.* 4.2), his death will be a revelation of God—a Word of God—to the spectators in the Roman Colosseum.

Just as in *Mag.* 8.2, where Jesus Christ is "the divine Son who is the Word having come forth from silence" so also in *Rom.* 2.1, Ignatius thinks of his martyrdom as a Word of God coming forth from silence. The difference is that in *Mag.* 8.2, the silence is the silence of God; in *Rom.* 2.1 the silence is that of God's people (who remain silent, choosing not to intervene on Ignatius' behalf).[7]

The correlation of *silence* and word of God in *Rom.* 2.1 together with the correlation of *silence of God* and the death of Jesus in *Eph.* 19.1 shows that the words "eternal" and "not" are, almost certainly, not what Ignatius wrote

---

6. Barnes, "Dating Ignatius," 125.
7. This is the insight of Virginia Corwin, *St. Ignatius and Christianity in Antioch* (New Haven: Yale Univ. Press, 1960), 126.

in *Mag.* 8.2. The words appear to be the insertion of an anti-Valentinian redactor.[8]

Barnes' perceptive insight concerning the three adjectives being unique to Ignatius and Ptolemaeus in their teaching about the incarnation presents an either/or. Either, Ignatius was himself correcting the teaching of Ptolemaeus (which contained the three adjectives) while in route to his execution at Rome (in which case, Ignatius must be dated no earlier than ca. 140 CE); or, after Ignatius' martyrdom, Christians at Rome were using his letters (which employed the three adjectives) in order to teach about the incarnation and oppose the Gnostic view. In this latter option, the Gnostic Ptolemaeus responded to the Roman—Ignatian teaching with his own three adjective view of the incarnation.

My analysis of the three adjectives in Ignatius shows that all three are integral to his thought and occur in sources available to and known by him. This makes it doubtful that their appearance as a cluster in *Poly.* 3.2 is a response to a Ptolmaean teaching in which these three adjectives were employed. The only way to pursue this doubt is to examine Ptolemaeus' thought and see whether these three adjectives are integral to his system.

4. PTOLEMAEUS AND THE THREE ADJECTIVES

Ptolemaeus was a prominent Gnostic teacher at Rome, ca. 140–160 CE. Irenaeus, in his attempt to refute Gnosticism (ca. 180 CE), presents some of Ptolemaeus' theological system in *Against Heresies*, 1.1.1–1.8.5.[9] I will analyze what Irenaeus indicates as the teaching of Ptolemaeus.

There can be no doubt about the importance of the adjective "invisible" in describing Ptolemaeus' understanding of Divine transcendence—the "perfect pre-existing Aeon" Who dwells "in the invisible and unnameable heights" (ἐν ἀοράτοις καὶ ἀκατονομάστοις ὑψώμασι). That one is "incomprehensible and invisible" (ἀχώρητον καὶ ἀόρατον) and is called "Pre-beginning and Forefather and Depth" (Προαρχὴ καὶ Προπάτερ καὶ Βυθός).[10]

Co-existing with Depth was his female partner, Thought (Ἔννοια) Who is called Silence (Σιγή). Silence received the seed of Depth and gave birth

---

8. This is also the view of Robert M. Grant, *Ignatius of Antioch* (Camden, NJ: Thomas Nelson & Sons, 1966), 62. Moreover, he suggests that Ignatius' source for word of God proceeding from silence is the Wisdom of Solomon 18:14–15: "When still silence enclosed everything . . . your all-powerful word leaped from heaven. . . ." (trans. of Grant, 50).

9. I am using the Sources Chrétiennes' critical edition, Adelin Rousseau and Louis Doutreleau, eds. *Contre Les Herésies*, Livre I, Tome II (Paris: Les Editions du Cerf, 1979). For a useful translation of the Ptolemaean section in Irenaeus, as well as Ptolemaeus' letter to Flora, see Robert M. Grant, *Gnosticism* (New York: Harper and Brothers, 1961), 163–90.

10. Irenaeus, *Adv. haer.* 1.1.1.

to Mind (Νοῦς) Who is called Only-Begotten (Μονογενῆ). Only Mind could "comprehend the greatness of the Father" (χωρεῖν τὸ μέγεθος τοῦ Πατρός). Along with Mind, Truth (Ἀλήθεια) was also put forth. Hence, the two male-female pairs—Depth/Silence and Mind/Truth constitute the first four Aeons.[11]

By a series of further emanations—26 more Aeons (13 male/female pairs) appear: Only-Begotten and Truth emitted Word (Λόγος) and Life (Ζωή), who in turn emitted Man (Ἄνθρωπος) and Church (Ἐκκλησία).[12] Word and Life emitted 10 more Aeons and Man and Church emitted 12; the last pair was Willed One (Θελητός) and Wisdom (Σοφία).[13] This constitutes the Pleroma of 30 Aeons whose attributes are "invisible, spiritual, and unknowable" (ἀόρατος, πνευματικός, οἱ μὴ γινωσκόμενοι).[14] In Ptolemaeus, the attribute of being "invisible" is closely associated with the conception of a Spiritual Transcendence that is unknowable. And Ptolemaeus, like Ignatius, knew the Pauline *Colossians* 1:16—". . . in Him all things might be created, the visible and the invisible (τὰ ὁρατὰ καὶ τὰ ἀόρατα), thrones, divine ones, lordly ones."[15]

"Passion" (πάθος) is also a significant concept in Ptolemaeus' understanding of the falling away of Wisdom from the Pleroma, the creation of humans, and their redemption. In the Pleroma, none of the Aeons, except Only-Begotten, could comprehend the Forefather. For the other Aeons, the Forefather remained "invisible and incomprehensible" (ἀόρατον καὶ ἀκατάληπτον). Hence, those Aeons "had desired silently in some way to see the One who put forth their seed and to understand the root without a beginning."[16]

It was Wisdom who "felt a passion" (ἔπαθε πάθος), not from her consort's embrace, but "the passion which was the search for the Father" (τὸ δὲ πάθος εἶναι ζήτησιν τοῦ Πάτρος). "For she was, as they say, constant in her desire to comprehend His greatness" (ἤθελε γάρ, ὡς λέγουσι, τὸ μέγεθος αὐοῦ καταλαβεῖν). But because of "the inscrutability of the Father" (τὸ ἀνεξιχνίαστον τοῦ Πάτρος), she failed. By the power of Limit (Ὅρος) she saw her error and recognized that "the Father is incomprehensible (ἀκατάληπτος)."[17]

The Father through the Only-Begotten emitted Limit (Ὅρος) and Limit purified Wisdom, restoring her to the Pleroma, separating passion (πάθος)

---

11. *Ibid.*
12. *Ibid.*
13. *Ibid.*, 1.1.2.
14. *Ibid.*, 1.1.3.
15. *Ibid.*, 1.4.5.
16. *Ibid.*, 1.2.1. ἡσυχῇ πως ἐπεπόθουν τὸν προβολέα τοῦ σπέρματος αὐτῶν ἰδεῖν καὶ τὴν ἄναρχον ῥίζαν ἱστορῆσαι.
17. *Ibid.*, 1.2.2.

and desire (ἐνθύμησις) from her and crucifying them. In order to make sure that other Aeons did not fall to Wisdom's temptation, the Only-Begotten emitted the pair of Christ and Holy Spirit; and Christ taught the Aeons the "recognition" (ἐπίγνωσις) of the Father—"that He is both uncontainable (ἀχώρητος) and incomprehensible (ἀκατάληπτος) and that it is not possible to see (ἰδεῖν) or hear (ἀκοῦσαι) him except through only the Only-Begotten." [18]

"The Desire of Wisdom above" (ἡ Ἐνθύμησις τῆς ἄνω Σοφία)[19] also called Achamoth (Ἀχαμώθ), together with her "passion" (πάθος), had been banished from the Pleroma. She could comprehend nothing; but through the cross, she was given a longing to return to the Pleroma.[20] But because she was still "entwined with passion" (τὸ συμπεπλέχθαι τῷ πάθει), she suffered its consequences—grief (λύπη), because she lacked comprehension, fear (φόβος) of being abandoned by life, and perplexity (απορία). These three emotions combined to produce "ignorance" (ἀγνοία).[21]

Achamoth contained these three emotions, but she also possessed a "disposition of conversion [a return= ἐπιστροφῇ] to the one who created" (διάθεσις τὴν τῆς ἐπιστροφῆς ἐπὶ ζωοποιήσαντα). Grief, fear, and perplexity together with desire to return (ἐπιστροφῇ) became "the substance of matter" (οὐσία τῆς ὕλης) from which this world (κόσμος) existed. The Savior relieved Achamoth of her passion and enabled her through his healing to create the world.[22]

Achamoth made the world out of three kinds of things—matter (ὕλη) which came from passion (πάθος), psychic (τὸ ψυχικόν) which came from the longing to return to the Pleroma (ἐπιστροφή), and the spiritual (τὸ πνευματικόν), which she gave birth to. From the psychic she formed the Demiurge who then became the "maker of all things—both psychic and material things" (ποιητὴ πάντων ψυχικῶν τε καὶ ὑλικῶν).[23]

All psychic beings are formed from fear (φόβος) and the longing to return (ἐπιστροφή) to the Pleroma. All corporeal things (τὰ σωματικά) are formed from fear, grief, and perplexity. And ignorance (ἄγνοια) is hidden (ἐγκεκρύφθαι) in these three passions (τοῖς τρισὶ πάθεσιν). The fleshly thing (τὸ σαρκικόν) is formed from matter (ὕλη), which is incapable of receiving imperishability (ἀφθαρσία).[24]

The human being has their soul from the Demiurge, the body from liquid (χοῦς), the flesh from matter (ὕλη) and the spiritual from the mother Achamoth. In order for the Savior to redeem, he had to assume all the

---

18. *Ibid.*, 1.2.4–5.
19. The reference to "Wisdom above" is a reference to Wisdom, one of the 30 Aeons.
20. This evidently is the meaning of Limit having crucified the passion and desire of Wisdom after she had been separated from the Pleroma.
21. *Ibid.*, 1.4.1.
22. *Ibid.*, 1.4.1–2,5.
23. *Ibid.*, 1.5.1–2.
24. *Ibid.*, 1.5.4,6; 1.6.1.

elements of the human being. He took the spiritual from Achamoth, he took the psychic Christ from the Demiurge, and from "the cosmic order of things, he clothed himself with a body which possessed a psychic substance and which was crafted by a mysterious skill in order to become visible and touchable and capable of suffering. At the same time, they say [the Ptolemaeans] that he received nothing whatsoever of the material (τὸ ὑλικὸν); for matter is not capable of receiving salvation."[25]

Here is the passage in Ptolemaeus (as quoted by Irenaeus) with the same three adjectives found in Ignatius' letter to Polycarp (3.2). *Visible* and *passible* are clearly integral to Ptolemaeus' conception of Deity and salvation. The Savior who came from the Pleroma was, like the Pleroma, invisible and unchangeable; but in order to save He had to assume what he would save, namely, a body (σῶμα) and soul (ψυχή) that was visible, touchable and capable of suffering (παθητόν).

In Ptolemaeus' system, the adjective *invisible* and the noun *passion/desire* are used more than once in order to describe the Deity (*invisible*) and to describe Wisdom's fall due to the passion (πάθος) to know what was incomprehensible. One cannot argue that Ptolemaeus took these two terms from Ignatius. They are integral to his system. However the same cannot be said for the adjective *touchable* (ψηλαφητόν). The only place in the Ptolemaean system (at least the system as Irenaeus presents it) where that adjective occurs is in the above passage which appears to be a mirror image of Ignatius' use of the three adjectives in describing the incarnation. The (more likely than not) conclusion is that Ptolemaeus was responding to the teaching of Ignatius, which Roman Christians were employing in order to oppose the docetic Gnostic views at Rome, ca. 140–160 CE.

5. A PLAUSIBLE DATE FOR THE MARTYRDOM OF IGNATIUS

What needs to be determined is the time required for Polycarp's collection of Ignatius' letters to reach Rome, exerting their influence and becoming the basis of an anti-Gnostic refutation of the teaching of Ptolemaeus.[26] Polycarp's collection of Ignatius' letters probably began before Ignatius was martyred.

---

25. *Ibid.*, 1.6.1 ἀπὸ δὲ τῆς οἰκονομίας περιτεθεῖσθαι σῶμα, ψυχικὴν ἔχον οὐσίαν, κατεσκευασμένον δὲ ἀρρήτῳ τέχνῃ πρὸς τὸ καὶ ὁρατὸν καὶ ψηλαφητὸν καὶ παθητὸν γενέσθαι καὶ ὑλικὸν δὲ οὐδ' ὁτιοῦν εἰληφέναι λέγουσιν αὐτόν μὴ γὰρ εἶναι τὴν ὕλην δεκτικὴν σωτηρίας.

26. Although the provenance of the anti-Valentinian/Ptolemaean redaction of *Mag.* 8.2 is unknown, the probability of it being at Rome, ca. 140–160 CE, is not implausible. At the very least, the existence of *Mag.* 8.2—in both the Middle and Long Recension as well as in a Latin translation—is evidence of some Christian group employing Ignatius' thought in combatting a Valentinian/Ptolemaean group. It could have been a Christian group at Rome.

Roman Christians saw the bishop of Antioch die in the Colosseum. Some of them had visited him in prison and given him "refreshment."[27] They already possessed the letter he had written them from Smyrna. One can plausibly assume that they possessed Polycarp's collection within a year or two after Ignatius' death.

It is, more likely than not, that Roman Christians who opposed Ptolemaeus' teaching by employing Ignatius' teaching were of the same generation in which Ignatius was martyred. In other words, the time between his death and the Roman-Ignatian anti-Gnostic opposition to Ptolemaeus is probably not much more than twenty years. This means that some of those Roman Christians who opposed Ptolemaeus had seen Ignatius die in the Colosseum. Ignatius had sealed his teaching of the Divine Son, who was nailed in the flesh and suffered a violent death of crucifixion, by his own suffering in the flesh and violent death by the agency of wild animals. Ignatius did this in the confident hope that his flesh would be transformed and would rise from the dead.

One can imagine the debate, in which Ptolemaeus would—in response to the Roman-Ignatian description of the incarnation as the Word assuming flesh and becoming visible, touchable, and passible—agree that the body of the Savior was visible, touchable, and passible, but its material (ὑλικόν) aspect was not capable of salvation. And since flesh (σάρξ) came from the material, it could not receive immortality.

The date of this debate can only be estimated within a probable range. If the debate was ca. 140 CE, then Ignatius' martyrdom was ca. 120 CE; if the date was ca. 150 CE, then Ignatius' martyrdom was ca. 130 CE. One can reasonably assume that once Ptolemaeus began teaching at Rome, it would not have been long before he attracted the attention of Roman Christians. Hence, a date early in the residency of Ptolemaeus is quite probable. According to my hypothesis, a range of 120–130 CE for Ignatius' martyrdom corresponds to the first ten years of Ptolemaeus residency at Rome, 140–150 CE. A date of ca. 125 for Ignatius' martyrdom seems not implausible. Does this date fit other historical details associated with Ignatius?

Barnes notes that Origen says that Ignatius was the second bishop at Antioch, following Peter.[28] Eusebius also gives the name of the first bishop, Evodius.[29] Eusebius' source could be the works of Hegesippus, a Jewish-Christian of the late second century who traveled from city to city, conversing with church leaders and composing lists of episcopal successions. Eusebius mentions Corinth and Rome, but perhaps Hegesippus also had

---

27. Cf. *Ign. ad Rom.* 10.2.
28. Origen's statement is in his sixth homily on Luke where he alludes to Ignatius' letter to the Ephesians (cf. Barnes, "Date of Ignatius," 126).
29. *Hist. eccl.* 3.22.1; 3.36.2.

visited Jerusalem and Antioch.[30] Origen could have derived his information from Julius Africanus, a Christian antiquarian who composed a Chronicle in the 220's and with whom Origen corresponded.

On the other hand, Origen was one of the most learned Christians of the pre-Nicene church. He was well-read and well-traveled. He had access to the library at Jerusalem and Caesarea where he lived off and on from 215 CE to his death at Tyre in 254 CE. By 218 CE he had visited Rome and Antioch, the two cities where Ignatius was remembered. Hence, his testimony concerning Ignatius could be based on datable documents of Ignatius preserved by the church of Antioch or it may be based in the memory of Antiochene Christians.[31] Origen's testimony is helpful in balancing dates that depend on the historical connection of Evodius (the first bishop of Antioch), Ignatius and Polycarp.

Polycarp's dates are 70/1–157 CE. If one assumes that he was not a presbyter-bishop until the age of forty, then Ignatius' martyrdom can not be earlier than 110 CE; but the conclusion that it was about 125 CE must be in accord with plausible assumptions about the probable length of Antiochene episcopates and Ignatius' age when he was executed.

Assuming that Evodius became bishop about 60 CE and that Theophilus was the sixth bishop of Antioch, ca. 180 CE, the average episcopate is about 20 years.[32] Dating Ignatius to 125 CE entails two consecutive episcopates totaling 65 years. This is significantly beyond the average of 20 years/episcopate; yet, it does not seem implausible.

The unknown variables for dating Ignatius are the length of Evodius' and Ignatius' episcopates and the plausible age of a man who, in chains with other prisoners and in the custody of ten Roman soldiers, traveled across south-central Asia Minor and then north to Troas (more than 600 miles).[33] A date of 125 CE requires two long episcopates (a total of 65 years) and implies

---

30. *Ibid.*, 4.22.2–3.
31. Origen could have conversed with Antiochene Christians who were born about 140 CE. They in turn could be a source of stories their parents had handed down. In other words, it is not improbable that at Antioch, Origen may have conversed with Christians who were sons and daughters of parents who had been born around 110 CE.
32. I agree with J.B. Lightfoot (*The Apostolic Fathers*, vol. 2, sect. 1 [London: Macmillan and Co., 1885], 469) that the episcopal accessions of Evodius in 42 CE and that of Ignatius in 69 CE given in Eusebius' *Chronicon* "deserve no credit." For a careful analysis of the reliability of Eusebius' dates for Antiochene bishops, see 450–70. There were six bishops of Antioch (from Evodius to Theophilus, circa 180 CE) in a period of 120 years (if one assumes that Evodius was bishop, circa 60 CE). This gives an average of 20 years per episcopate. I assume that Peter had left Antioch by 60 CE.
33. In the judgment of W. M. Ramsay (*The Christian Church in the Roman Empire before A.D. 170* [London: Hodder and Stoughton, 1892], 318–19), the natural route to Smyrna via Philadelphia from Antioch, Syria is by way of the Syrian and Cilician Gates. After a rest at Smyrna, Ignatius was conducted north to Troas where his group boarded a ship to Neapolis, the port of Philippi. This overland route (Antioch to Troas) is more than 600 miles.

that Ignatius was somewhere between 60 and 65 years old when he traveled across south-central Asia Minor.[34]

6. DID IGNATIUS WALK FROM ANTIOCH TO SMYRNA?

I think I have established a plausible date of ca. 125 CE for Ignatius' martyrdom in the Roman Colosseum. But admittedly, it is based on some assumptions, which, although plausible, are not certain. There is one other issue I have not discussed which has a bearing on the degree of probability for the date, ca. 125 CE: did Ignatius, in chains, walk the distance from Antioch to Smyrna; or was he in a wagon pulled by donkeys? Before I answer that question, I want to alert the reader to why this question can make the date of ca. 125 CE more probable if in fact Ignatius did walk.

Let us, for a moment, assume that he did walk. The distance from Antioch to Smyrna and from there, north to Troas is about 600 miles. If one picks Barnes' date of 140 CE as the martyrdom of Ignatius, then it appears that Ignatius was probably seventy-five or more when he took that walk, in chains, in the heat of summer. That date would also presuppose two consecutive episcopates at Antioch totaling eighty years. These two assumptions seem quite improbable.[35]

On the other hand, if one thinks that 115 CE is more probable than 125 CE because Ignatius would have been somewhere between the age of 50 and 55 years old (and therefore, physically better able to walk the 600 miles than if he was 65), one is choosing a date which presupposes a time lapse of 30 years between Ignatius' death and when Roman Christians employed his anti-docetic teaching to refute Ptolemaeus.[36] This means that a generation had elapsed and most of those Christians opposing Ptolemaeus at Rome had not had direct contact with Ignatius nor had they seen him die. Hence, ca. 125 CE seems more likely than 115 CE; and 125 CE surely seems more plausible

---

34. In the next section, I will discuss the various ages Ignatius would have been, if one assumes different dates for his martyrdom. For these speculations, I will assume the base date of 100 CE as the year Ignatius became bishop at Antioch. This means that Evodius' episcopate was roughly from 60 CE to 100 CE or forty years.

35. For all of the speculations about Ignatius' age, I will assume that he became a bishop when he was somewhere between the age of 35 and 40. If one thinks that Barnes' view is correct, that is, that Ignatius died at Rome, ca. 140 CE, then Ignatius was bishop for 40 years (100–140 CE) and was somewhere between 75 and 80 when he walked from Antioch to Troas, in the summer heat while in chains. At Smyrna, Ignatius gives the date in his letter to the Romans (10.3), as August 24.

36. Recall that in arriving at ca. 125 CE for Ignatius' martyrdom (see the previous section), the assumption was that the Roman refutation of Ptolemaeus was early in his residence at Rome, ca. 145 CE.

than Barnes' 140 CE, if Ignatius walked the 600 miles of his journey from Antioch to Troas.

With these assumptions—that Ignatius became bishop, ca. 100 CE; that he became a bishop somewhere between the age of 35 and 40; that he died at Rome, ca. 125 CE—then Ignatius was somewhere between the age of 60 and 65 when he walked 600 miles in chains. What is the evidence that supports a walk?

In three of his letters, Ignatius speaks explicitly about his chains (τὰ δεσμά). To the Ephesians (11.2), he says that he "is carrying them around" (περιφέρω) as "spiritual pearls" (πνευματικοὶ μαργαρίται). They have become for him a symbol of his identity as a Christian confessor, destined to suffer and die in his encounter with wild animals in the Roman Colosseum. Indeed, his journey to Rome, in chains, is part of that passion; he refers to the ten Roman soldiers who are bringing him to Rome as "leopards" who when "treated well" (εὐεργετούμενοι) by Ignatius, "become worse" (γίνονται χείρους) in their treatment of him (*Rom.* 5.1). It is clear that his chains symbolize the suffering in his journey and, as such, a foretaste of his martyrdom at the hands of "wild animals" (θηρία, *Rom.* 5.1–2).

Thus, when he speaks of "carrying around" (περιφέρω) his chains, he is referring to the suffering that began when he became a confessor at Antioch and which will end with his death in the Colosseum at the hand of "wild animals." The figurative sense of chains depends on the literal sense and Ignatius refers three times to the chains as the chains which "I am carrying about/around" (περιφέρω).[37] He has carried them from Antioch to Smyrna, and he looks forward to carrying them all the way to Rome. When he dies and then is raised, those "spiritual pearls" will still be with him (*Eph.* 11.2) in some transformed state. The chains are an inseparable part of his identity as a confessor on a journey to martyrdom.

The letters of Ignatius show that he was very careful in his choice of words. In speaking of "carrying" his chains, he always uses the verb περιφέρω. Its basic meaning is to carry some object about/around. It presupposes that the one who is carrying the object is walking, that is, the verb conveys the notion of collateral motion. It appears almost certain that Ignatius viewed his walking in chains as part of the suffering implied in his status as a confessor: his walking in chains is an inseparable part of his identity as a confessor on a long journey ending in martyrdom. Is there any counter-evidence which calls this conclusion into question?

---

37. *Eph.* 11.2; *Mag.* 1.2; *Trall.* 12.2.

7. THE EDICT OF HADRIAN TO THE PROVINCE OF ASIA

A recently discovered edict of the emperor, Hadrian (117–138 CE) to the province of Asia, pertains to the issue of how prisoners were transported by Roman soldiers.[38] The edict, dated 129 CE, relates to Roman policy in the province of Asia about the time of Ignatius' journey there. The reader should recall that both Smyrna and Ephesus are cities in the province of Asia. Ephesus is the capital, and Smyrna is about forty miles north of Ephesus.

Hadrian was a philhellene who spent a great deal of his reign traveling in the East, speaking Greek to its inhabitants while admiring the architectural and artistic achievement of Hellenistic civilization—its amphitheaters, temples, sculptures, bas-reliefs, etc. In 129 CE he made a trip through Anatolia to Antioch, Syria. He stopped along the way to spend time listening to the complaints and grievances that residents had, concerning Roman rule. The edict reveals what he had learned from the residents in the province of Asia and how he sought to addresss those grievances.

The edict reveals that soldiers who were providing military escort for the deliverance of money to a provincial ruler/magistrate or who were transporting prisoners or wild animals through the province were abusing their authority and power. The soldiers expected or demanded free breakfast and dinner at the public inns where they stopped—probably dinner when they arrived at the end of a hard day's walk and breakfast in the morning just before departing for another day's walk. If they needed a wagon for transport, they expected the inhabitants to provide it. And they expected a free supply of fodder for the animals pulling the wagon.[39]

Hadrian's edict speaks to these abuses:

> But if someone [a soldier] is passing through while on duty or if they are bringing (κομίζοντες) the ruling power's money or transporting prisoners or wild animals (ἢ δεσμώτας ἄγοντες δὲ ἢ θηρία), public lodging shall be given only to them and provisions at the market price which was effective ten days earlier.[40]

---

38. The edict (Greek text, translation, and commentary) is found in Tor Hauken and Hasan Malay, "A New Edict of Hadrian from the Province of Asia Setting Regulations for Requisitioned Transport," in R. Haensch, ed. *Selbstdarstellung und Kommunikation: Die Veröffentlichung staatlicher Urkunden auf Stein und Bronze in der römischen Welt* (Munich: Beck, 2009), 327–48. The translation of Hauken/Malay is also given in Christopher J. Fuhrmann, *Policing the Roman Empire: Soldiers, Administration, and Public Order* (Oxford: Oxford University Press, 2012), 235–36. Thanks to Clifford Ando for directing me to Fuhrmann's work.

39. Hauken and Malay, "A New Edict," 342.

40. *Ibid.*, lines 30–35, trans. Hauken/Malay, 332.

The edict makes clear that only soldiers on duty (and not wandering soldiers on furlough) deserve lodging, meals, and fodder for animals; and the price must be determined according to market value ten days earlier. Soldiers must pay; but prices cannot suddenly escalate upon the appearance of a convoy of soldiers providing military escort for a provincial magistrate's money or transporting prisoners or wild animals, bound either for Rome or for some amphitheatre in the province of Asia.[41]

The edict mentions three kinds of transporting: bringing money to a magistrate, transporting prisoners, transporting wild animals. Bringing money to magistrates or transporting wild animals requires the use of a wagon. With regard to transporting money to a provincial magistrate, the verb κομίζω is used. Its two meanings are "to bring" or "to carry." Both meanings apply; for the money is carried in a wagon, and the military escort is bringing the wagon to the provincial magistrate.

With regard to prisoners and wild animals, the verb ἄγω is employed. The use of a double ἤ signifies "either/or." Although ἄγω refers to both prisoners and wild animals, their transportation by the soldiers are treated as separate events. Had a single καί ("and") been used, the passage would have been referring to a single convoy of prisoners and wild animals.

The Greek adjective, ἀγώγιμος, which can mean either "easily led" or "easily carried," points to the two basic ways of transporting a person or object—to lead them or to carry them. Since ἄγω has two basic meanings, what it means in a sentence depends on context.

In the transportation of wild animals, the animals would be put in cages and carried in wagons driven by soldiers. In this context, ἄγω would connote soldiers bringing animals and the animals being carried. So in a literal sense, the soldiers are not carrying the animals; they are bringing them. But surely, the bringing presupposes a carrying of the animals in wagons.

In the transporting of prisoners, the soldiers are also bringing them. But the important question is: are the prisoners being carried in a wagon? Since ἄγω has two basic meanings—to lead/bring or to carry, ἄγω could connote with regard to the prisoners—that the soldiers are leading them; or it could connote that, like the animals, they are being carried in a wagon driven by a soldier. In this case, the soldiers are bringing the prisoners who are being carried in a wagon. I do not see how one can decide which is the case. Is it

---

41. The fact that no mention is made concerning the lodging of prisoners confirms what one might assume: prisoners spent the night sleeping outdoors, exposed to the night air, and chained together. Soldiers probably took turns acting as sentries during the passing of the night. Food provisions for prisoners would have been minimal. However, in the case of Ignatius, whenever the convoy stopped in the vicinity where Christians existed, Ignatius would have been visited and ministered to with encouragment and the fellowship of food and drink. Soldiers could be bribed. This probably explains how Ignatius was able to attend a Christian assembly in Philadelphia where he preached and spoke an oracle of the Holy Spirit. See *Ign. Phd.* 7.1–2.

a leading/bringing of prisoners who are walking or a leading/bringing which presupposes that the prisoners are being carried in a wagon.[42]

There is another approach to the edict that could explain the meaning of ἄγοντες in referring to the prisoners. In an imperial edict, what the emperor sets forth is imperial law. Hence, the obvious question is whether ἄγω appears in the edict because in legal proceedings related to prisoners, it is often used.

The historical narrative of Luke/Acts may cast light on the question of whether ἄγω was an important verb used in the legal proceedings concerned with the apprehension, custody, trial and execution of individuals found guilty of a capital offense. Luke/Acts was written for a "most excellent Theophilus" (κράτιστε Θεόφιλε) and is intended to inform him about things that he had heard, concerning the Jesus movement.[43] Since the same adjective ("most excellent") is used in addressing Antonius Felix, the Roman procurator,[44] it seems quite likely that Theophilus is a provincial or Roman official; and if not, he must be at least a member of the upper class of Greco-Roman society and very probably a Roman citizen. Perhaps, he resided at Rome in the latter part of the first century.[45] Since Luke was particularly focused on communicating a picture of Christianity that showed how it evolved within the context of the Roman Empire, his use of ἄγω may in turn cast light on the question of whether ἄγω in Hadrian's edict is legal terminology describing the transporting of criminals to their death.

Indeed, in describing the legal proceedings concerning the trial and death of Jesus and Stephen and the events concerned with Paul's arrest and his transportation as one accused of a capital offense, Luke uses ἄγω repeatedly. In the narration of Jesus' arrest, Luke uses ἄγω twice. "They (the temple authorities) led (ἤγαγον) him and brought (εἰσήγαγον) him to the house of the high priest" (22:54). Concerning the two prisoners who died with Jesus at Golgotha, Luke says—"the two other criminals also were being led (ἤγοντο) with him [Jesus] in order to be put to death" (ἀναιρεθῆναι, 23:32).

In both the accounts of the trial and execution, ἄγω may be simply a way of connecting two events that involve walking. On the other hand, ἄγω may have been used because in a legal proceeding involving a death penalty or imprisonment, the judge ends the trial by commanding guard soldiers— "Take/Lead him away" (Ἀγάγετε αὐτόν). The verb is found in an aphorism

---

42. Obviously, Hadrian and the residents of the province who lived along the roads, where the convoys of animals or prisoners traveled, knew what ἄγοντες implied in each case. But living 1,900 years later, it seems unclear to me because ἄγοντες can mean either "lead" or "carry." The meaning depends on the context. Hadrian and the residents knew the context for prisoners, but I do not.
43. Luke 1:3.
44. Acts 23:26.
45. The earliest evidence for Luke/Acts is in 1 Clement whose provenance is late first century at Rome. On the evidence that the author of 1 Clement knew Luke/Acts, see Robert M. Grant and Holt H. Graham, *First and Second Clement* (New York: Thomas Nelson and Sons, 1965), 25, 71–72.

about death—"it leads to death" (ἄγει θανεῖν).⁴⁶ Jesus and the two other prisoners "were being led (ἤγοντο)" to their deaths.

In Acts, one encounters ἄγω in the narrative of Stephen's trial and the legal proceedings around Paul's alleged defilement of the temple. Those, who opposed Stephen, "seized him and led (ἤγαγον) him before the Sanhedrin" (6:12).

When Paul's defense before the Sanhedrin caused such an uproar that the Roman tribune feared for Paul's life, he "commanded (ἐκέλευσεν) the soldiers to go down and take Paul from their midst and lead (ἄγειν) him to the soldier barracks" (23:10). Since ἄγω is part of what the Roman tribune "commanded," what is implied is that in legal proceedings, soldiers are commanded—"Take/Lead him. . . ."

Later in Paul's trial before the Roman procurator, Porcius Festus, ἄγω is used to express the content of what Festus commanded—"after Festus sat down at the place of Judgment, he commanded (ἐκέλευσεν) that Paul be brought" (τὸν Παῦλον ἀχθῆναι, 25.6). Again, as in the case of what the Roman tribune had commanded of the soldiers, ἄγω is employed to describe what a Roman judge commands, namely, "Take/Bring/Lead" the prisoner.⁴⁷

The brief excursion into the use of ἄγω in Luke's narration of the legal process of arrest, custody, trial, and/or death concerning Jesus, Stephen, and Paul, leads to the conclusion that it is quite likely that ἄγω is part of the legal vocabulary employed in such proceedings. The verb, itself, does not imply that the prisoner or accused is walking or riding in a wagon or on a horse. The context is critical for drawing a conclusion concerning the mode of transportation.⁴⁸

I conclude that, quite likely, the use of ἄγοντες in Hadrian's edict is legal vocabulary. It seems plausible that in the edict, a form of ἄγω is used in describing the travel of prisoners or animals through the province of Asia, because in the understanding of Hadrian and the residents of the province who lived along the road of that travel, these two kinds of convoys were tied together: the prisoners were being led to their deaths (either in a provincial amphitheater or at the Roman Colosseum) and the wild animals would function as their executioners. A form of ἄγω may be employed in the edict

---

46. Henry G. Liddell and Robert Scott, *A Greek-English Lexicon* (abridged) (Oxford: Clarendon Press, 1966), 9 at ἄγω I.2.

47. Compare also Acts 25:17, 23, where ἄγω is used, twice, as the content of what Festus, the Roman procurator, had ordered concerning Paul. "After I took my place at the judgment seat, I ordered that the man be brought" (ἐκέλευσα ἀχθῆναι τὸν ἄνδρα, 25:17). "After Festus issued his command, Paul was brought" (ἤχθη ὁ Παῦλος, 25:23).

48. The only instance where ἄγω is used and Luke is explicit about the mode of transportation is when Paul, the accused, is transported from Jerusalem to Caesarea (a distance of sixty-five miles). Paul rode on a horse. Compare Acts 23:24, 31–32.

because that verb is the traditional way of describing the legal process of "leading/taking" a prisoner to their death.

Thus, one cannot know whether the verb is referring to prisoners being led on the road—while they are walking or while they are riding in an animal drawn wagon driven by a soldier. In either case, the prisoners are being "led/taken" to their death. If this legal approach to ἄγω is correct, then its appearance in the edict does not provide an answer to whether the prisoners walked or were carried in a wagon. In my judgment, the edict neither confirms nor calls into question what I think I previously established about Ignatius: while in chains, he walked 600 miles, on the first leg of his journey—a journey to death by the agency of wild animals in the Roman Colosseum.

Before I conclude this appendix, one more statement of Ignatius calls for clarification. When he speaks of the ill treatment he is receiving from the Roman soldiers whom he refers to as the ten leopards, he says "From Syria to Rome, I am fighting with wild animals (θηριομαχῶ) by land and sea, by night and day, while being bound (δεδέμενος δέκα λεοπάρδοις) to ten leopards" (*Rom.* 5.1). A straightforward literal interpretation of that statement implies that Ignatius was chained to the ten soldiers whose ill treatment is figuratively a foretaste of the suffering that he will encounter with the wild animals in the Roman Colosseum.

But, if Ignatius was chained to other prisoners and they were all walking, as were the Roman soldiers,[49] surely the soldiers and prisoners were not chained together. The soldiers were "leading" or "taking" the prisoners to Rome. The prisoners were chained together in the custody of ten soldiers. Probably, one should not take Ignatius' statement literally. But perhaps, also, the chains that bound the prisoners together were tied to an animal drawn wagon, driven by one of the soldiers. I think this is about all that can be deduced from Ignatius' statement.[50]

---

49. Concerning the qualifications and military training of a Roman soldier, one can conclude that the ten soldiers were Roman citizens between the ages of twenty and forty, at least five feet eight inches tall (taller than the average male citizen in the Roman empire) and capable of marching twenty miles in five hours (not counting rest breaks). See G. R. Watson, *The Roman Soldier* (Ithaca, NY: Cornell University Press, 1969), 11, 16, 39, 54.

50. Ignatius never alludes to any other prisoners in his group. When referring to ill treatment by the soldiers and the struggles with them, he uses "I" (not "we"); see *Rom.* 5.1. However, he knows of a group of Syrian confessors, on the road ahead of him, being taken to Rome (see *Rom.* 10.2). Perhaps, the other prisoners in his group are not Christians and the ones ahead of him are Antiochene confessors who had been separated from him at Antioch by the provincial governor there, in order to assure that they would be without their bishop and therefore, easier to control on the journey to Rome.

8. CONCLUSION

I have shown that Timothy Barnes' dating of Ignatius—no earlier than 140 CE—is questionable. His argument rests on two observations: one, that in Ignatius' formulation of the incarnation and that of Ptolemaeus, a Gnostic Valentinian Christian active in Rome, ca. 140–160 CE, the same three adjectives—"visible and touchable and passible" (ὁρατὸν καὶ ψηλαφητὸν καὶ παθητόν) are employed;[51] two, in *Mag.* 8.2, Ignatius criticizes the Valentinian assertion that Christ proceeded from Silence (Σιγή).

I have shown that the three adjectives in Ignatius' thought are utilized in some of his other letters and are drawn from creedal expressions of the church at Antioch and New Testament traditions that Ignatius knew. The inference that Ignatius' three adjectives in *Poly.* 3.2 is his response to Ptolemaeus' Christological formulation (where the same three adjectives were employed) is not necessary. Moreover, I showed that Ignatius expressed the view that the Word of God did proceed from silence; hence, it is quite probable that *Mag.* 8.2—as it exists in the Middle and Long Greek Recensions (with its assertion that the Word of God did not proceed from silence)—is an anti-Valentinian/Ptolemaean redaction of a passage that originally had spoken of Jesus Christ as "the Word proceeding from silence." This redaction could be accounted for if in fact, Roman Christians who had witnessed Ignatius' martyrdom in the Colosseum chose to use his letters and redacted them with an anti-Gnostic twist in order to refute Ptolemaeus sometime between 140 and 150 CE.

My analysis of the three adjectives in Ptolemaeus' system shows that although "visible/invisible" and "passible/passion" are integral to his theological system, the adjective "touchable" (ψηλαφητόν) occurs nowhere except in the Ptolemaean formulation which is the mirror image of Ignatius' three adjective formulation in *Poly.* 3.2. The conclusion seems, more likely than not, that Ptolemaeus was responding to the Ignatian formulation in *Poly.* 3.2.

This means that sometime after Ignatius' martyrdom in the Colosseum at Rome, Roman Christians utilized Polycarp's collection of Ignatius' letters in order to refute the Gnostic school of Ptolemaeus at Rome. Ptolemaeus' three adjective formulation of the incarnation must have been his response to the Ignatian teaching that Roman Christians were employing in order to oppose Ptolemaeus' docetic views.

By utilizing evidence for Ignatius' episcopate at Antioch, estimating the most plausible time for his teaching to become part of the Roman Christian refutation of Ptolemaeus, and showing that Ignatius almost certainly walked

---

51. Cf. *Poly.* 3.2 and Irenaeus, *Adv. haer.* 1.6.1.

in chains a distance of 600 miles from Antioch to Troas (where his group boarded a ship to cross the Aegean to Neapolis, the port of Philippi), I arrive at a date of ca. 125 CE for Ignatius' martyrdom in the Colosseum at Rome.

Bibliography

Anderson, Paul N. "The Sitz im Leben of the Johannine Bread of Life Discourse and Its Evolving Context." In *Critical Readings of John 6*, R.A. Culpepper (ed.), 1–59. Leiden: Brill, 1997.

Aune, David E. *Apocalypticism, Prophecy, and Magic in Early Christianity*. Grand Rapids: Baker Academic, 2008.

Barnes, Timothy D. "Date of Ignatius." *ET* 120.3 (2008): 119–30.

———. *Early Christian Hagiography and Roman History*. Tübingen: Mohr Siebeck, 2010.

Bauckham, Richard. *The Testimony of the Beloved Disciple*. Grand Rapids, MI: Baker Academic, 2007.

Bauer, Walter. *A Greek-English Lexicon of the New Testament and Other Early Christian Literature*. Trans. by Wm. F. Arndt and F. Wilbur Gingrich. Chicago: Univ. of Chicago Press, 1952.

Bernier, Jonathan. *Aposynagogos and the Historical Jesus in John*. Leiden: Brill, 2013.

Bihlmeyer, Karl and Schneemelcher, Wilhelm. *Die Apostolischen Väter*, vol. I. Tübingen: J.C.B. Mohr, 1956.

Bommes, Karin. *Weizen Gottes. Untersuchungen zur Theologie des Martyrium bei Ignatius von Antiochien*. Cologne: Peter Hanstein, 1976.

Borgen, Peter. *Bread from Heaven*. Leiden: Brill, 1965.

Bornkamm, Günther. "Die eucharistische Rede im Johannes-Evangelium." *ZNW* 47 (1956): 161–69.

Bovon, François. *Luke 3: A Commentary on the Gospel of Luke 19:28–24:53*. ET James Crouch. Minneapolis: Fortress Press, 2012.

Bowersock, G.W. *Martyrdom and Rome*. Cambridge: Univ. Press, 1995.

Bradshaw, Paul F., and Johnson, Maxwell E. *The Eucharistic Liturgies: Their Evolution and Development*. Collegeville, MN: Liturgical Press, 2012.

———. *Eucharistic Origins*. Oxford: Oxford University Press, 2004.

Brent, Allen. *Ignatius of Antioch and the Second Sophistic*. Tübingen: Mohr Siebeck, 2006.

Brown, Raymond E. *The Gospel according to John*, 2 vols. Garden City, NY: Doubleday, 1986.

Bultmann, Rudolf. *The Gospel of John.* ET G.R. Beasley-Murray. Oxford: Basil Blackwell, 1971.

Burkert, Walter. *Greek Religion.* ET John Raffan. Cambridge: Harvard Univ. Press, 1985.

Burns, J. Patout Jr., and Jensen, Robin. *Christianity in Roman Africa.* Grand Rapids, MI: Wm. B. Eerdmans Publishing Co., 2014.

Buschmann, Gerd. "The Martyrdom of Polycarp." In *The Apostolic Fathers,* Wilhelm Pratscher, ET, and Elisabeth G. Wolfe (eds.), 135–57. Waco, TX: Baylor University Press, 2010.

Campenhausen, Hans von. *Bearbeitungen und Interpolationen der Polycarpmartyrium.* Heidelberg: Carl Winter, 1957.

Castelli, Elizabeth A. *Martyrdom and Memory: Early Christian Culture Making.* New York: Columbia Univ. Press, 2004.

Chadwick, Henry. *The Church in Ancient Society.* Oxford: Univ. Press, 2001.

———. *The Early Church.* London: Penguin, 1956.

———. *Origen: Contra Celsum.* Cambridge, UK: Univ. Press, 1965.

———. "The Silence of Bishops in Ignatius." *HTR* 43 (1950): 169–72.

Collins, Adela Yarbro. "Insiders and Outsiders in the Book of Revelation and Its Social Context." In *To See Ourselves as Others See Us,* Jacob Neusner and Ernest S. Frerichs (eds.), 187–218. Chico, CA: Scholars, 1985.

Coloe, Mary L. *God Dwells with Us.* Collegeville, MN: Liturgical Press, 2001.

Corwin, Virginia. *St Ignatius and Christianity in Antioch.* New Haven: Yale Univ. Press, 1960.

Crossan, John Dominic. "It is written: Structuralist Analysis of John 6." *Semeia* 26 (1983): 3–21.

Dahl, Nils A. "Paul and the Church at Corinth According to 1 Corinthians 1:10–4:21." In *Christian History and Interpretation: Studies Presented to John Knox,* W.R. Farmer, C.F.D. Moule, R.R. Niebhur (eds.), 313–35. Cambridge: Cambridge University Press, 1967.

Danby, Herbert (trans.). *Mishnah.* London: Oxford University Press, 1933.

Darling-Young, Robin. *In Procession before the World: Martyrdom as Public Liturgy in Early Christianity.* Marquette, WI: Marquette Univ. Press, 2001.

Davis, James A. *Wisdom and Spirit: An Investigation of 1 Corinthians 1.18–3:20 Against the Background of Jewish Sapiential Traditions in the Greco-Roman Period.* London: University Press of America, 1984.

De Silva, David A. *4 Maccabees: Introduction and Commentary on the Greek Text in Codex Sinaiticus.* Leiden: E. J. Brill, 2006.

Detienne, Marcel. *Dionysos at Large.* ET Arthur Godhammer. Cambridge: Harvard Univ. Press, 1989.

Dodd, C.H. *The Interpretation of the Fourth Gospel.* Cambridge: University Press, 1958.

———. "ΙΛΑΣΚΕΣΘΑΙ, Its Cognates, Derivatives, and Synonyms in the Septuagint." *JTS* 32 (1931): 352–60.

Donahue, Paul J. "Jewish Christianity in the Letters of Ignatius." *VC* 32 (1978): 81–93.

Dunn, James D. G. "John 6: A Eucharistic Discourse?" *NTS* 17 (1971): 328–38.
Fearghail, Fearghas. "Sir 50:5–21: Yom Kippur or the Daily Whole Offering." *Biblia* 59.3 (1978): 301–16.
Ferguson, Everett. "Spiritual Sacrifice in Early Christianity and its Environment." *ANRW*, W. Haase and H. Temporini (eds.), II 232. Pgs. 1152–90. Berlin: Walter de Gruyter, 1980.
Fitzgerald, Robert (trans). *The Aeneid*. New York: Random House, 1983.
Friesen, Steven. *Imperial Cults and the Apocalypse of John*. Oxford: University Press, 2001.
Fuhrmann, Christopher J. *Policing the Roman Empire: Soldiers, Administration, and Public Order*. Oxford: University Press, 2012.
Gonzalez, Eliezer. *The Fate of the Dead in Early Third Century North African Christianity: The Passion of Perpetua and Felicitas and Tertullian*. Tübingen: Mohr Siebeck, 2014.
Grant, Robert M. *Gnosticism*. New York: Harper and Brothers, 1961.
———. *An Introduction*, vol. 1 of *The Apostolic Fathers*, ed. Robert M. Grant. New York: Thomas Nelson and Sons, 1964.
———. *Ignatius of Antioch*, vol. 4 of *The Apostolic Fathers*, ed. Robert M. Grant. New York: Thomas Nelson and Sons, 1966.
——— and Graham, Holt M. *First and Second Clement*, vol. 2 of *The Apostolic Fathers*. Robert M. Grant (ed.). New York: Thomas Nelson and Sons, 1966.
Guilding, Aileen. *The Fourth Gospel and Jewish Worship*. Oxford: Clarendon Press, 1960.
Haenchen, E. *John 1*, trans. Robert W. Funk. Philadelphia: Fortress, 1984.
Harrill, J. Albert. "Cannibalistic Language in the Fourth Gospel and Greco-Roman Polemics of Factionalism (John 6:52–66)." *JBL* 127:1 (2008): 133–58.
Harrison, Percy N. *Polycarp's Two Epistles to the Philippians*. Cambridge: Cambridge University Press, 1936.
Hartog, Paul. *Polycarp and the New Testament*. Tübingen: Mohr Siebeck, 2002.
Hauken, Tor, and Malay, Hasan. "A New Edict of Hadrian from the Province of Asia Setting Regulations for Requisitioned Transport." In *Selbstdarstellung und Kommunikation: Die Veröffentlichung staatlicher Urkunden auf Stein und Bronze in der römischen Welt*, R. Haensch (ed.), 327–48. Munich: Beck, 2009.
Heffernan, Thomas J. *The Passion of Perpetua and Felicity*. Oxford: Oxford University Press, 2012.
Heilmann, Jan. "A Meal in the Background of John 6:51–58." *JBL* 137.2 (2018): 481–500.
———. *Wein und Blut: Das End der Eucharistie im Johannesevangelium und dessen Konsequenzen*. Stuttgart: W. Kohlhammer Gmb H, 2014.
Hengel, Martin. *Crucifixion in the Ancient World and the Folly of the Message of the Cross*. Trans. John Bowden. Philadelphia: Fortress Press, 1977.
———. "Interpretation of Wine Miracle at Cana: John 2:1–11." In *The Glory of Christ in the New Testament: Studies in Christology in Memory of George Bradford Caird*, L.D. Hurst and N.T. Wright (eds.), 83–112. Oxford: Clarendon, 1987.
Holloway, Paul. *Philippians*. Minneapolis: Fortress Press, 2017.

Horsley, Richard A. "Jesus and Empire." In *In the Shadow of Empire,* Richard Horsley (ed.), 75–95. Louisville: John Knox, 2008.

Horsting, Albert G.A. "Transformation of Flesh: Literary and Theological Connections between Martyrdom Accounts and Eucharist Prayers." In *Issues in Eucharistic Praying in East and West*, E. Maxwell and E. Johnson (eds.), 307–25. Collegeville, MN: Liturgical Press, 2010.

Hoskyns, Edwyn C. *The Fourth Gospel*, ed. by Francis N. Davey. London: Faber & Faber, 1947.

Hylen, Susan. *Allusion and Meaning*. Berlin: Walter de Gruyter, 2005.

Jensen, Robin and Burns Jr., J. Patout. *Christianity in Roman Africa*. Grand Rapids, MI: Wm. B. Eerdmans Publ. Co., 2014.

Jeremias, Joachim. *The Eucharistic Words of Jesus*. ET Norman Perrin. New York: Charles Scribner's Sons, 1966.

Johnson, Maxwell E. "Martyrs and the Mass: The Interpretation of the Narrative Institution into the Anaphora." *Worship* 87.1. Collegeville, MN: Liturgical Press, 2013, 2–22.

———. *The Rites of Christian Initiation: Their Evolution and Interpretation.* Collegeville, MN: Liturgical Press, 2007.

———, ed. *Issues in Eucharistic Praying in East and West*. Collegeville, MN: Liturgical Press, 2010.

———, and Bradshaw, Paul F. *The Eucharistic Liturgies: Their Evolution and Development*. Collegeville, MN: Liturgical Press, 2012.

Keener, Craig. *The Gospel of John*, II. Peabody, MA: Hendrickson Publishers, 2003.

Klauck, Hans-Josef. *The Religious Context of Early Christianity*, trans. Brian McNeil. Minneapolis, MN: Fortress Press, 2003.

Klawiter, Frederick C. "The Eucharist and Sacramental Realism in the Thought of St. Ignatius of Antioch." *SL* 27.3 (2007): 129–63.

———. "'Living Water' and Sanguinary Witness: John 19:34 and Martyrs of the Second and Early Third Century." *JTS* 66.2 (Oct., 2015): 553–73.

———. "The Role of Martyrdom and Persecution in Developing the Priestly Authority of Women in Early Christianity: A Case Study of Montanism." *CH* 49.3 (Sept., 1980): 251–61.

Klein, Elizabeth. "Perpetua, Cheese, and Martyrdom as Public Liturgy in the Passion of Perpetua and Felicity." *JECS* 28.2 (Summer, 2020): 175–202.

Klinghardt, Matthias. "Bund und Sündenvergebung: Ritual und literarischer Kontext." In *Mahl und religiöse Identitat im fruhen Christentum,* Matthias Klinghardt and Hal Tassig (eds.), 159–80. Tübingen: Francke, 2012.

———. "Der Vergossene Becher: Ritual und Gemeinshaft in Lukanischen Mahlbericht." *EC* 3.1 (2012): 33–58.

Knopf, Rudolf; Krűger, Gustav, and Ruhbach, Gerhard. *Ausgewählte Märtyerakten*. Tűbingen: Mohr Siebeck, 1965.

Koester, Helmut. "History and Cult in the Gospel of John and in Ignatius of Antioch." Translated by Arthur Bellinzoni. *JTC* 1 (1965): 111–23.

La Piana, George. "The Tombs of Peter and Paul Ad Catacumbas." *HTR* 14.1 (1921): 53–94.

Lambrecht, Jan. "Synagogues of Satan' (Rev. 2:9 and 3:9): Anti-Judaism in the Book of Revelation." In *Anti-Judaism and the Fourth Gospel,* R. Bieringen, D. Pollefeyt, and F. Vandecasteele-Vanneuville (eds.), 279–92. Louisville: Westminster John Knox Press, 2001.

Lewis, Charlton T. and Short, Charles. *A Latin Dictionary.* Oxford: Clarendon Press, 1966.

Liddell, Henry G., and Scott, Robert. *A Greek-English Lexicon.* Oxford: Clarendon Press, 1966.

Lietzmann, Hans. "The Tomb of the Apostles Ad Catacumbas." *HTR* 16.2 (1923): 147–62.

Lightfoot, J.B. *The Apostolic Fathers.* 2 Vols. London: Macmillan, 1889.

Lindars, Barnabas. "The Persecution of Christians in John 15:18–16:4a." In *Essays on John,* C.M. Tuckett (ed.), 131–52. Leuven: Leuven University Press, 1992.

———. "The Son of Man in the Johannine Christology." In *Christ and Spirit in the New Testament,* Barnabas Lindars and Stephan S. Smalley (eds.), 43–60. Cambridge: University Press, 1973.

Loeb Classical Library. *The Apostolic Fathers,* 2 vols. Cambridge: Harvard University Press, 1959.

MacMullen, Ramsay. *The Second Church: Popular Christianity A.D. 200–400.* Atlanta, GA: SBL Press, 2009.

McGowan, Andrew B. *Ascetic Eucharists.* New York: Oxford Univ. Press, 1999.

———. "Eucharist and Sacrifice: Cultic Tradition and Transformation in Early Christian Ritual." In *Mahl und Religiöse Identitat in Fruhen Christentum/Meals and Religious Identity in Early Christianity,* Matthias Klinghardt and Hal Tassig (eds.), 191–206. Tübingen: Francke, 2012.

———. "Naming the Feast: Agape and the Diversity of Early Christian Meals." *SP* 30 (1997): 314–18.

Meeks, Wayne. *The Prophet-King.* Leiden: Brill, 1967.

Meinhold, Peter. *Studien zu Ignatius von Antiochien.* Wiebaden: Steiner, 1979.

Menken, Maarten J.J. "John 6:51c-58: Eucharist and Christology?" In *Critical Readings of John 6,* R.A. Culpepper (ed.), 183–204. Leiden: Brill, 1997.

Minear, Paul S. *John: The Martyr's Gospel.* New York: Pilgrim, 1984.

Mitchell, Nathan. *Cult and Controversy.* New York: Pueblo Publishing Co., 1982.

Moss, Candida R. *Ancient Christian Martyrdom.* New Haven: Yale University Press, 2012.

Nautin, Pierre. *Letters et écrivains chrétiens des ii͎ et iii͎ siècles.* Paris: Editions du Cerf, 1961.

Neusner, Jacob (trans.). *Tosefta. Second Division: Moed.* New York: Ktav Publishing House, Inc., 1981.

Neyrey, Jerome H. *The Gospel of John in Cultural and Rhetorical Perspective.* Grand Rapids: Wm. B. Eerdmans, Publishing Co., 2009.

Nongbri, B. "Reconsidering the Place of Papyrus Bodmer XIV-XV [Papyrus 75] in Textual Criticism of the New Testament." *JBL* 135.2 (2016): 405–37.

O'Day, Gail R. "John 6:15–21: Jesus Walking on Water as Narrative Embodiment of Johannine Christology." In *Critical Readings of John 6*, R.A. Culpepper (ed.), 149–59. Leiden: Brill, 1997.

Perler, Othmar. "Das vierte Makkabaerbuch, Ignatius von Antiochien und die altesten Märtyrerberichte." *RAC* 25 (1949): 43–72.

Price, S.R.F. *Rituals and Power: The Roman Imperial Cult in Asia Minor*. Cambridge: University Press, 1984.

Ramsay, W.M. *The Christian Church in the Roman Empire before A.D. 170*. London: Hodder and Stoughton, 1892.

Reynolds, Benjamin E. "The Johannine Son of Man and the Historical Jesus: John 9:35 as a Test Case." In *John, Jesus, and History*, 3 vols., Paul N. Anderson, Felix Just, Tom Thatcher (eds.), 3:459–68. Atlanta, GA: SBL, 2016.

Robinson, Thomas A. *Ignatius of Antioch and the Parting of the Ways*. Peabody, MA: Hendrickson Publishers, 2009.

Rousseau, Adelin and Doutreleau, Louis, eds. *Contre Les Herésies*. Livre I, Tome II. Paris: Les Editions du Cerf, 1979.

Rouwhorst, Gerard. "The Roots of Early Christian Eucharist: Jewish Blessings or Hellenistic Symposia?" In *JCLW: New Insights into its History and Interaction*, Albert Gerhards and Clemens Leonard (eds.), 295–308. Leiden: Brill, 2007.

Rubenstein, Jeffrey L. *The History of Sukkot in the Second Temple*. Atlanta: Scholars Press, 1995.

Schnackenburg, Rudolf. *The Gospel According to John*, 3 vols., trans. Cecily Hastings, Francis McDonagh, David Smith, Richard Foley. New York: Seabury Press, 1980.

Schoedel, William R. *Ignatius of Antioch*. Philadelphia: Fortress Press, 1985.

Shaver, Stephen R. "A Eucharistic Origins Story Part 1: The Breaking of the Loaf." *Worship* 92 (May 2018): 204–21.

Smallwood, E. Mary. *The Jews Under Roman Rule*. Leiden: Brill, 1976.

Smith, D. Moody. *John*. Nashville, TN: Abingdon Press, 1999.

Smith, Dennis E. *From Symposium to Eucharist*. Minneapolis: Fortress Press, 2003.

Swartley, Willard M. "The Imitatio Christi in the Ignatian Letters." *VC* 27 (1973): 81–103.

Taussig, Hal. *In the Beginning Was the Meal*. Minneapolis: Fortress Press, 2009.

Tilborg, Sjef von. *Reading John in Ephesus*. Leiden: Brill, 1996.

Ulfgard, Häkan. *The Story of Sukkot*. Tübingen: Mohr Siebeck, 1998.

Ullucci, Daniel C. *The Christian Rejection of Animal Sacrifice*. Oxford: Oxford University Press, Inc., 2012.

Van Henten, Jan Willem. *The Maccabean Martyrs as Saviors of the Jewish People*. Leiden: E. J. Brill, 1997.

Warren, Meredith J.C. *My Flesh is Meat Indeed: A Nonsacramental Reading of John 6:51–58*. Minneapolis, MN: Fortress Press, 2015.

Watson, G.R. *The Roman Soldier*. Ithaca, NY: Cornell University Press, 1969.

Wehr, Lothar. *Arznei der Unsterblichkeit: Die Eucharistie bei Ignatius von Antiochien und im Johannesevangelium*. Munster: Aschendorff, 1987.

Williams, Catrin H. *I am He*. Tübingen: Mohr Siebeck, 2000.

Yee, Gale A. *Jewish Feasts and the Gospel of John.* Wilmington: Michael Glazier, Inc., 1989.
Zañartu, Sergio. "Les concepts de vie et mort chez Ignace d'Antioche." *VC* 33 (1979): 324–341.

Index

abiding, gospel of John, 51–53
Aeneid, 119
agape, 11, 19, 25–26, 30, 60, 135. See also *eucharistia*
altar, 65–67, 74–76, 90, 100, 139; in Ignatius, 76–78, 139; martyr's tomb, 66n24
Anderson, Paul N., 55n62
Antipas, martyr, 94–95
Aune, David, 33n1, 95n30

Barnes, Timothy D., 53n61, 67, 99n1, 104n10, 149
Bauckham, Richard, 90
bishop and unity of the church, 18–19
blood of Jesus Christ and agape, 11, 61n4
blood of Jesus Christ and forgiveness, 69
blood of Jesus Christ/Son of Man, drinking, 11, 47, 52, 54–55, 58, 61
blood of a martyr as a memorial: Jesus, 68–71, 138–39; Saturus, 116
Borgen, Peter, 43n38, 44n40
Bowersock, G. W., 95n32
Braaten, Carl, 1
Bradshaw, Paul F., 9, 27–28
bread of God, 11, 16, 17n21, 18, 28, 30, 100

"bread, pure," 12, 28, 100, 139
Brent, Allen, 19, 76, 78n60
Brown, Raymond E., 35n8, 50, 88n4
Bultmann, Rudolf, 34, 88n4
Burns, J. Patout, Jr., 125

Chadwick, Henry, 18n26, 19n27, 150n5
Corwin, Virginia, 79n62, 153n7
credal beliefs, church of Antioch, 22, 24, 151–52
Cyprian, bishop of Carthage, 75

Darling-Young, Robin, 79n63
death of Ignatius, sacrifice, 12–14
death of Jesus, gospel of John, wine/blood washing, 91–92
Didache, 12
Dinocrates and baptismal refreshment, 110–14, 142
Dodd, C. H., 52n59
Dunn, James D. G., 53n60

eucharistia, 11, 23–25, 30, 61n14, 139
Evodius, bishop of Antioch, 159, 160n34

flesh of Jesus Christ, 23–24, 135–36
flesh of the Son of Man, eating, 47, 52, 54–55, 137

Forde, Gerhard, 1

gnosticism: definition, 150; Ptolemaeus, 154
Grant, Robert M., 2, 18n23, 30n36, 76n56, 128n61, 154n8

Hadrian, edict of, 162–64
Hanukkah, 89–90
Harrill, J. Albert, 36n12
Hasvold, Paul, 2
Heffernan, Thomas, 112, 116–17, 119
Heilmann, Jan, 2, 47n48, 57n2, 60n10, 71n42
Hengel, Martin, 91n20
Holy One of Israel, 50n55
Hylen, Susan, 43n38, 44

"I Am," 41–43
"I Am the bread," 43–45
Ignatius: and footsteps of Paul, 51n57; and *refrigerium*, 126–29, 141
Ignatius' chains, 161
Iliad, 71–72
Irenaeus, bishop of Lugdunum, 13, 33–34, 103, 114, 154

Jensen, Robin, 125
Jeremias, Joachim, 72–73
Jesus Christ and the martyr, shared suffering: Felicity, 115; Ignatius, 10
John 6:51b–58, 3, 27, 34, 136
Johnson, Maxwell, 2, 10n4, 11n8, 110n24, 147n8
Justin Martyr, 30n36, 145n6

Keener, Craig S., 45n42, 89n11
Klauck, Hans-Josef, 47n48
Klein, Elizabeth, 120–23
Klinghardt, Matthew, 69–70
Knutson, Kent, 1
Koester, Helmut, 27
Kraabel, Tom, 1

lamb of God, 90, 97

last supper: Carthaginian confessors, 106; Paul, 73; synoptic gospels, 68–71, 73
"last supper" as "agape meal," 106
Lightfoot, J. B., 77n58, 159n32
Lindars, Barnabas, 48n51, 52n58
"living bread," 46–47
"living water," 87, 95–96, 111–13, 118–19; and refreshment, 118–19
"living water" and martyrs: Ignatius, 96; Perpetua, 111–13; Polycarp, 96, 99; Sanctus, 96

maccabean martyrs, 61n12, 92–94
MacMullen, Ramsay, 66n24, 101
martyr, definition, 95n33
martyrdom: voluntary, 103–4; washing in the blood of Jesus, 92, 97
martyrdom of Ignatius: Divine Word, 14, 16–17, 79, 139, 146, 153; sacrificial libation, 14–15, 58–61, 139; unity of the church, 14, 16, 61, 139
Martyrdom of Polycarp, 7, 99–100, 129
Martyrdom of St. Perpetua and St. Felicitas, 6–7, 104–25, 132, 141–42
martyrdom and power of forgiveness: confessors of Lugdunum, 114; Jesus, 69–70, 93; maccabean martyrs, 92–93; Perpetua, 110, 142; Stephen, 64–65
martyrdom and second baptism: Carthaginian Christians, 113; Ignatius, 10–11
martyrs of Carthage and Revelation, 117
McGowan, Andrew, 11, 62–63
meal of the 5000, 38–41
"medicine of immortality": imperishable agape, 11, 17–19, 79n64, 135; unity, 17–19
Meinhold, Peter, 62n15
Menken, Maarten, 35–36, 46n46
Minear, Paul S., 55n62
Minucius Felix, 75

New Prophecy, 6, 102–4, 125–26, 132, 142

O'Day, Gail R., 42
one cup, 20–21, 29–30, 59
one flesh of Jesus Christ, 20–24
one loaf, 12–13, 17, 28, 58
Origen, 74, 158–59

Paraclete, 51–53, 94–95, 111
Passover, 47n47, 90n16, 97
Perpetua, 6, 106–14, 117–18, 120–25
Perpetua and Dinocrates, 110–14, 142
persecution of Jewish Christians, 40, 51–52, 94
Peter, martyrdom of, 53n61
Polycarp, bishop of Smyrna, 6–7, 34, 99–100, 142–43
Polycrates, bishop of Ephesus, 33
prayer to Christ, 12
prayers to the martyr, 122–23
Priscilla, prophetess, 103
Ptolemaeus, 149

Ramsay, W. M., 159n33
refreshment: baptism, 110–15; of confessors, 126–29; of Ignatius, 126–29; of the martyr in heaven, 121–24; and meal fellowship, 106; peace, 109; and victory over the devil, 107–8
refrigeria, tombs of Carthaginian martyrs, 125
refrigerium, 5–6, 59–60, 84, 101–2, 105–6, 140–42; eucharist, 106; Paul and Peter, 101–2, 140; tomb of Polycarp, 6, 101, 129–33, 143; wine libation and blood of a martyr, 117–18
refrigerium, offerings to the deceased: *Acts of Paul and Thecla,* 119; *Aeneid* of Virgil, 119
Robinson, Thomas A., 14n16
Roman soldier, qualifications, 166n49

sacramental realism, 2, 9, 17n21, 27, 83, 135–37, 145n6
sacrificial libation, blood of martyr, redemptive: Ignatius, 14–16, 58–61; Johannine Jesus, 93–94, 97, 143n3; maccabean martyrs, 92–93, 97–98; martyrs of Revelation, 65–67; Perpetua, 116–117, 119, 147; Polycarp, 99–100; Stephen, 64–65, 147; Synoptic Jesus, 4–5, 68–71, 73, 138
sacrificial libation of Ignatius, baptismal symbol, 14, 15n19, 16
sacrificial libation and martyrdom, cultic act and public witness, 16–17, 68, 74, 76–80, 82, 116, 139, 144–47
sacrificial libation, ritual in eucharist, 3–5, 76, 80, 139–40, 143–45
sacrificial wine libation, 3–5, 15, 17, 60, 64–72, 80–82, 84, 137–40
sacrificial wine libation, peace covenant/treaty: Jesus and disciples, 70, 72; Trojans and Achaeans, 71–72
Saturus, voluntary martyr, 116
scandalize, 32, 54–55
Schoedel, William R., 9, 25–28, 17n21, 18n25, 62n15, 76n56, 127n60
Son of Man, 48n51, 54–55
Swartley, Willard M., 14n16
synagogue of the Son of Man, 38–41, 54–55

Tabernacle festival and "living water," 87n2, 88–89, 97
Tamid, 60, 89, 97
Tertullian, 72–73, 74, 103, 105
Theophilus, bishop of Antioch, 159
tomb/shrine-altar of Polycarp, 100, 129–30; *refrigerium* vs. eucharist, 130–33
Toynbee, J. M. C., 123n50

Ullucci, Daniel C., 69n33, 79n61
unity of the church, 18–19, 24–25

Warren, Meredith J. C., 36–37

water baptism, martyrdom as
  baptism, 120–21
Wehr, Lothar, 11, 27, 35

Williams, Catrin H., 42
Wisdom: Divine, 44–46, 48–51, 54–55, 103, 136; gnostic, 156–57

About the Author

Frederick C. Klawiter, Ph.D., (University of Chicago) was an ordained minister of the Evangelical Lutheran Church in America and a member of the Dept. of Religion, Philosophy, and Classics at Augustana University (Sioux Falls, SD). His previous article publications range from the Gospel of John to the early second century (Ignatius of Antioch) and late second/early third century (the New Prophecy in Anatolia and Carthage, North Africa). Those works established a foundation upon which this study rests, and this work provides further material for developing the paradigm of the ritual of sacrificial libation as central to understanding the redemptive power of martyrdom and the eucharist as a way of remembering and participating in the redemptive power of Jesus' sacrificial agape.

www.ingramcontent.com/pod-product-compliance
Lightning Source LLC
Chambersburg PA
CBHW020122010526
44115CB00008B/933